Cambridge Elements

Elements in Philosophy and Logic
edited by
Bradley Armour-Garb
SUNY Albany
Frederick Kroon
The University of Auckland

NONMONOTONIC LOGIC

Logics for Defeasible Reasoning

Christian Straßer
Ruhr University Bochum

CAMBRIDGE
UNIVERSITY PRESS

Shaftesbury Road, Cambridge CB2 8EA, United Kingdom

One Liberty Plaza, 20th Floor, New York, NY 10006, USA

477 Williamstown Road, Port Melbourne, VIC 3207, Australia

314–321, 3rd Floor, Plot 3, Splendor Forum, Jasola District Centre,
New Delhi – 110025, India

103 Penang Road, #05–06/07, Visioncrest Commercial, Singapore 238467

Cambridge University Press is part of Cambridge University Press & Assessment,
a department of the University of Cambridge.

We share the University's mission to contribute to society through the pursuit of
education, learning and research at the highest international levels of excellence.

www.cambridge.org
Information on this title: www.cambridge.org/9781009598460

DOI: 10.1017/9781108981699

When citing this work, please include a reference to the DOI 10.1017/9781108981699

First published 2025

A catalogue record for this publication is available from the British Library

ISBN 978-1-009-59846-0 Hardback
ISBN 978-1-108-98686-1 Paperback
ISSN 2516-418X (online)
ISSN 2516-4171 (print)

Nonmonotonic Logic

Logics for Defeasible Reasoning

Elements in Philosophy and Logic

DOI: 10.1017/9781108981699
First published online: October 2025

Christian Straßer
Ruhr University Bochum

Author for correspondence: Christian Straßer, christian.strasser@rub.de

Abstract: Nonmonotonic logics serve as formal models of defeasible reasoning, a type of reasoning where conclusions are drawn absent absolute certainty. Defeasible reasoning takes place when scientists interpret experiments, in medical diagnosis, and in practical everyday situations. Given its wide range of applications, nonmonotonic logic is of interest to philosophy, psychology, and artificial intelligence. This Element provides a systematic introduction to the multifaceted world of nonmonotonic logics. Part I familiarizes the reader with basic concepts and three central methodologies: formal argumentation, consistent accumulation, and semantic methods. Parts II–IV provide a deeper understanding of each of these methods by introducing prominent logics within each paradigm. Despite the apparent lack of unification in the domain of nonmonotonic logics, this Element reveals connections between the three paradigms by demonstrating translations among them. Whether you're a novice or an experienced traveler, this Element provides a reliable map for navigating the landscape of nonmonotonic logic.

This Element also has a video abstract:
www.cambridge.org/EPL_Strasser_abstract

Keywords: nonmonotonic logic, philosophical logic, defeasible reasoning, symbolic artificial intelligence, formal argumentation

ISBNs: 9781009598460 (HB), 9781108986861 (PB), 9781108981699 (OC)
ISSNs: 2516-418X (online), 2516-4171 (print)

Contents

PART IV SEMANTIC METHODS

Introduction

Nonmonotonic logic (abbreviated as NML) and its domain, defeasible reasoning, are multifaceted areas. In crafting an Element that serves as both an introduction and an overview, we must adopt a specific perspective to ensure coherence and systematic coverage. It is, however, in the nature of illuminating a scenario with a spotlight that certain aspects emerge prominently, while others recede into shadow. The focus of this Element is on unveiling the core ideas and concepts underlying NML. Rather than exhaustively presenting concrete logics from existing literature, we emphasize three fundamental methods: (i) formal argumentation, (ii) consistent accumulation, and (iii) semantic approaches.

An *argumentative approach* for understanding human reasoning has been proposed both in a philosophical context by Toulmin's forceful attack on formal logic in 1958, and more recently in cognitive science by Mercier and Sperber (2011). Pioneers such as Pollock (1991) and Dung (1995) have provided the foundation for a rich family of systems of formal argumentation.

Consistent accumulation methods are based on the idea that an agent facing possibly conflicting and not fully reliable information is well advised to reason on the basis of only a consistent part of that information. The agent could start with certain information and then stepwise add merely plausible information. In this way they stepwise accumulate a consistent foundation to reason with. Accumulation methods cover, for instance, Reiter's influential default logic (Reiter, 1980) or methods based on maximal consistent sets, such as early logics by Rescher and Manor (1970) and (constrained) input–output logic (Makinson & Van Der Torre, 2001).

While the previous two methods are largely based on syntactic or proof-theoretic considerations, interpretation plays the essential role in *semantic approaches*. The core idea is to order interpretations with respect to normality considerations and then to select sufficiently normal ones. These are used to determine the consequences of a reasoning process or to give meaning to nonmonotonic conditionals. The idea surfaces in the history of NML in many places, among others in Batens (1986), Gelfond and Lifschitz (1988), Kraus et al. (1990), McCarthy (1980), and Shoham (1987).

A central aspect of this Element is its unifying perspective (inspired by works such as Bochman (2005) and Makinson (2005)). Defeasible reasoning gives rise to a variety of formal models based on different assumptions and approaches. Comparing these approaches can be difficult. The Element presents several translations between NMLs, illustrating that in many cases the same inferences can be validated in terms of diverse formal methods. These translations offer numerous benefits. They enrich our understanding by offering different perspectives: the same underlying inference mechanism may be considered as a form of (formal) argumentation, a way of reasoning with interpretations that are ordered with respect to their plausibility, or as a way of accumulating and reasoning with consistent subsets of a possibly inconsistent knowledge base. They demonstrate the robustness of the underlying inference mechanism, since several intuitive methods give rise to the same result. While the different methodological strands of NML have often been developed with little cross-fertilization, it is remarkable that the resulting systems can often be related with relative ease. Finally, the translations may convince the reader that, despite the fact that the field of NML seems a bit of a rag rug at first sight, there is quite some coherence when taking a deeper dive. In particular, by showcasing formal argumentation's exceptional ability to represent other NMLs, this Element adds further evidence to the fruitfulness of Dung's program of utilizing formal argumentation as a unifying perspective on defeasible reasoning (Dung, 1995).

The Element is organized in four parts. Part I provides a general introduction to the topic of defeasible reasoning and NML. The three core methods are each introduced in a nutshell. It provides a condensed and self-contained overview of the fundamentals of NML for readers with limited time. Part II to IV deepen on each of the respective methods by providing metatheoretic insights and presenting concrete systems from the literature.

While some short metaproofs that contribute to an improved understanding are left in the body of the Element, two technical appendices are provided for others. In particular, results marked with '$\star$' are proven in the appendices.

Many important aspects and systems of NML didn't get the spotlight and fell victim to the trade-off between systematicity and scope from which an introductory Element of this length will necessarily suffer. Nevertheless, with this Element a reader will grow the wings necessary to maneuver in the lands of nonflying birds, that is, they will be well equipped to understand, say, first-order versions of logics that are discussed here on the propositional level, or systems such as autoepistemic logic.

PART I LOGICS FOR DEFEASIBlE REASONING

1 Defeasible Reasoning

1.1 What is Defeasible Reasoning?

> We certainly want more than we
> can get by deduction from our
> evidence. … So *real inference*,
> the inference we need for the
> conduct of life, must be
> nonmonotonic.
>
> Henry Kyburg, 2001.

This Element introduces logical models of defeasible reasoning, so-called *Non-Monotonic Logics* (in short, NMLs). When we reason, we make inferences, that is, we draw conclusions from some given information or basic assumptions. Whenever we reserve the possibility to retract some inferences upon acquiring more information, we reason defeasibly.[1] Two paradigmatic examples of defeasible inferences are:

Assumption	*Defeasible conclusion*	*Reason for retraction*
The streets are wet.	It rained.	The streets have been cleaned.
Tweety is a bird.	Tweety can fly.	Tweety is a penguin.

As the examples highlight, we often reason defeasibly if our available information is incomplete: we lack knowledge of what happened before we observed the wet streets, or we lack knowledge of what kind of bird Tweety is. Defeasible inferences often add new information to our assumptions: while being explanatory of the streets being wet, the fact that it rained is not contained in the fact that the streets are wet, and while being able to fly is a typical property of birds, being a bird does not necessitate being able to fly. In this sense defeasible inferences are ampliative.

Logics that may lose conclusions once more information is acquired are called *nonmonotonic*. The vast majority of logics the reader will typically

---

[1] The term "defeasibility" entered philosophy with Hart's discussion of legal contract as a defeasible concept (Hart, 1948). Applied to duties, the idea occurs even earlier in Ross (1930), albeit under a different name, when elaborating on the prima facie character of duties. The defeasibility of arguments has been central to argumentation theory, starting from the writings of its pioneers such as Aristotle in his *Topics* (Aristotle, 1984) to modern classics such as Toulmin (1958) and Perelman and Olbrechts-Tyteca (1969) (for more on the history of the concept see Loui (1995)). In recent years, the notion of defeat has also gained significant attention in epistemology; see e.g., Moretti and Piazza (2017), Sudduth (2017), and Brown and Simion (2021).

encounter in logic textbooks are monotonic, with classical logic (in short, CL) being the celebrity. Whenever the given assumptions are true, an inference sanctioned by CL will securely pass the torch from the assumptions to the conclusion, warranting with absolute certainty the truth of the conclusion. Truth is preserved in inferences sanctioned by CL. No matter how much information we add, how many inferences we chain between our premises and our final conclusion, or how often the torch is passed, truth endures: the flames reach their final destination. Thus, inferences are never retracted in CL, and conclusions accumulate the more assumptions we add. This property, called monotonicity, is highly desirable for certain domains of reasoning such as mathematics, a domain where CL reigns.

However, a key motivation behind the development of NML is that out in the wild of commonsense, expert, or scientific reasoning, good inferences need not be truth preservational: we often change our minds and retract inferences when watching a crime show and wondering who the most likely murderer is; medical doctors may change their diagnosis with the arrival of more evidence, and so do scientists, sometimes resulting in scientific revolutions. In less idealized circumstances than those of purely formal sciences (such as mathematics), we usually need to reason with incomplete, sometimes even conflicting information. As a consequence, our inferences allow for exceptions and/or criticism. They are adaptable: learning or inferring more information may cause retraction, previous inferences may get defeated. Outside the ivory tower of mathematics, in the stormy domain of commonsense reasoning, the torch's fire may get extinguished.

It is therefore not surprising that examples of defeasible reasoning are abundant. In what follows, we will list some paradigmatic examples.

Example 1. We first imagine a scenario at a student party.[2]

1. *Peter*:   "I haven't seen Ruth!"
2. *Mary*:   "Me neither. If there's an exam the next day, Ruth studies late in the library."
3. *Peter*:   "Yes, that's it. The logic exam tomorrow!"
4. *Anne*:   "But today is Sunday. Isn't the library closed?"
5. *Peter*:   "True, and indeed, there she is!"
              [pointing to Ruth entering the room]

In her reply to Peter's observation concerning Ruth's absence (1), Mary states a regularity in form of a conditional (2): If there's an exam the next day, Ruth

---

2 The example is inspired by Byrne (1989).

studies late in the library. She offers an explanation as to why Ruth is not around. The explanation is hypothetical, since she doesn't offer any insights as to whether there is an exam. Peter supplements the information that, indeed, (3) there is an exam. Were our students to treat information (2) and (3) in the manner of CL as a material implication, they would be able to apply modus ponens to infer that Ruth is currently studying late in the library.[3] And, indeed, after utterance (3) it is quite reasonable for Mary and Peter to conclude that

($\star$) Ruth is not at the party since she's studying late at the library.

Anne's statement (4) casts doubt on the argument ($\star$), since the library might be closed today. This does not undermine the regularity stated by Mary, but it points to a possible exception. Anne's statement may lead to the retraction of ($\star$), which is further confirmed when Peter finally sees Ruth (5): this is defeasible reasoning in action!

Defaults.   Statements such as "Birds fly." allow for exceptions. It is therefore not surprising that one of the most frequent characters in papers on NML is Tweety. While the reader may sensibly infer that Tweety can fly when they are told that Tweety is a bird, they might be skeptical when being informed that Tweety lives at the South Pole, and most definitely will retract the inference as soon as they hear that Tweety is a penguin.[4] As we have also seen in our example, we often express regularities in the form of conditionals – so-called default rules, or simply defaults – that hold typically, mostly, plausibly, and so on, but not necessarily.

Closed-World Assumption.   Often, defeasible reasoning is rooted in the fact that communication practices are based on an economic use of information. When making lists such as menus at restaurants or timetables at railway stations, we typically only state positive information. We interpret (and compile) such lists under the assumption that what is not listed is not the case. For instance, if a meal or connection is not listed, we consider it not to be available. This practice is called the *closed-world assumption* (Reiter, 1981).

Rules with Explicit Exceptions.   Before presenting more examples of defeasible reasoning, let us halt for a moment to address a possible objection.

---

[3] Modus ponens is the classically valid inference that sanctions the conclusion B in view of the information that A, and that A implies B.

[4] We find a funny twist on defeasible reasoning with generics and a bird named Tweety in the cartoon world of *Birdy and the Beast* (Warner Bros., 1944). In the heat of hunting the canary Tweety, the cat Sylvester begins to fly and just after being reminded by Tweety that cats don't fly, he loses this ability – mid air – and crashes. Much to the amusement of Tweety, this shows that defeasible argumentation can save lives.

Is CL really inadequate as a model of this kind of reasoning? Can't we simply express all possible exceptions as additional premises? For instance,

> (†) If there's an exam the next day *and* the library is open late *and* Ruth is not ill *and* on her way didn't get into a traffic jam *and* ..., then Ruth studies late in the library.

There are several problems with this proposal. The first concerns the open-ended nature of the list of exceptions which characterizes most rules that express what typically/usually/plausibly/and so on holds. Even in the (rare) cases in which it is – in principle – possible to compile a complete list of exceptions, the resulting conditional will not adequately represent a reasoning scenario in which our agent may not be aware of all possible exceptions. They may merely be aware of the possibility of exceptions and be able, if asked for it, to list some (such as penguins as nonflying birds). Others may escape them (such as kiwis), but they would readily retract their inference that Tweety flies after learning that Tweety is a kiwi. In other words, the complexities involved in generating explicit lists of exceptions are typically far beyond the capacities of real-life and artificial agents. What is more, in order to apply modus ponens to conditionals such as (†), our reasoner would have to first check for whether each possible exception holds. This may be impossible for some, for others unfeasible, and altogether it would render out of reach the pace of reasoning that is needed to cope with their real-life situation.

In contrast to reasoning from fixed sets of axioms in mathematics, commonsense reasoning needs to cope with incomplete (and possibly conflicting) information. In order to get off the ground, it (a) jumps to conclusions based on regularities that allow for exceptions and (b) adapts to potential problems in the form of exceptional circumstances on the fly, by means of the retraction of previous inferences.

Abductive Inferences.   Another type of defeasible reasoning concerns cases in which we infer explanations of a given state of affairs (also called abductive inferences). For instance, upon seeing the wet street in front of her apartment, Susie may infer that it rained, since this explains the wetness of the streets. However, when Mike informs her that the streets have been cleaned a few minutes ago, she will retract her inference. We see this kind of inference often in diagnosis and investigative reasoning (think of Sherlock Holmes or a scientist wondering how to interpret the outcome of an experiment). As both the exciting histories of the sciences and the twisted narratives of Sir Arthur Conan Doyle reveal, abductive inference is defeasible.

Inductive Generalizations.   In both scientific and everyday reasoning, we frequently rely on inductive generalizations. Having seen only white swans, a child may infer that all swans are white, only to retract the inference during a walk in the park when a black swan crosses their path.

These are some central, but far from the only types of defeasible inferences. A more exhaustive and systematic overview can be found, for instance, in Walton et al. (2008), where they are informally analyzed in terms of argument schemes.[5]

1.2 Challenges to Models of Defeasible Reasoning

Formal models of defeasible reasoning face various challenges. Let us highlight some.

1.2.1 Human Reasoning and the Richness of Natural Language

As we have seen, defeasible reasoning is prevalent in contexts in which agents are equipped with incomplete and uncertain information. By providing models of defeasible reasoning, NMLs are of interest to both philosophers investigating the rationality underlying human reasoning and computer scientists interested in the understanding and construction of artificially intelligent agents. Human reasoning has a peculiar status in both investigations in that selected instances of it serve as role models of rational and successful artificial reasoning. After all, humans are equipped with a highly sophisticated cognitive system that has evolutionarily adapted to an environment of which it only has incomplete and uncertain information. Therefore, it seems quite reasonable to assume that we can learn a good deal about defeasible reasoning, including the question of what is good defeasible inference, by observing human inference practices.

There are, however, several complications that come with the paradigmatic status of human defeasible reasoning. First, human reasoning is error-prone, which means we have to rely on selected instances of good reasoning. But what are exemplars of good reasoning? In view of this problem, very often nonmonotonic logicians simply rely on their own intuitions. There are good reasons why one should not let expert intuition be the last word on the issue. We may be worried, for instance, about the danger of myside bias (also known as confirmation bias; see Mercier and Sperber (2011)): intuitions may be biased toward satisfying properties of the formal system that is proposed by the respective scholar.

---

5 Since the main aim of this Element is to introduce the central methods driving NMLs, we will not discuss specific applications such as abductive inferences or inductive generalizations in any further detail. For an introduction to inductive logic we refer to the Element by Eagle (2024).

Then, there is the possibility of "déformation professionnelle," given that the expert's intuitions have been fostered in the context of a set of paradigmatic examples about penguins with the name Tweety, ex-US presidents (see Examples 2 and 3), and the like.[6]

Another complication is the multifaceted character of defeasible reasoning in human reasoning. First, there is the variety of ways we can express in natural language regularities that allow for exceptions. We have "Birds fly," "Birds typically fly," "Birds stereotypically fly," "Most birds fly," and so on, none of which are synonymous: for example, while tigers stereotypically live in the wild, most tigers live in captivity. What is more important, the different formulations may give rise to different permissible inferences. Consider the generic "Lions have manes." While having a mane implies being a male lion, "Lions are males" is not acceptable (Pelletier & Elio, 1997). The inference pattern blocked is known as right weakening: if A by default implies B, and C follows classically from B, then C follows by default from A as well. It is valid in most NMLs, and it seems adequate for the "typical," "stereotypical," and "most" reading of default rules, but not for some generics.[7] For NMLs this poses the challenge to keep in mind the intended interpretation of defaults and differences in the underlying logical properties that various interpretations give rise to.

Despite these problems, it seems clear that "reasoning in the wild" should play a role in the validation and formation of NMLs.[8] This pushes NML in proximity to psychology. In practice, nonmonotonic logicians try to strike a good balance by obtaining metatheoretically well-behaved formal systems that are to some degree intuitively and descriptively adequate relative to (selected) human reasoning practices.

1.2.2 Conflicts and Consequences

Defeasible arguments frequently conflict. This poses a challenge for normative theories of defeasible reasoning, which must specify the conditions under which inferences remain permissible in such scenarios.

For this discussion, some terminology and notation will be useful. An *argument* (in our technical sense) is obtained by either stating basic assumptions

---

[6] For a list of benchmark examples, see Lifschitz (1989).

[7] Developing semantics for generics is notoriously difficult. There are many approaches, from normality-based (e.g., Asher and Pelletier (2012)), to prototype-based (e.g., Heyer (1990)), to Bayesian accounts (e.g., Tessler and Goodman (2019)). See Leslie and Lerner (2022) for an overview.

[8] Elio and Pelletier forcefully argue for a closer orientation on human reasoning practices (Elio & Pelletier, 1994; Pelletier & Elio, 1997). Empirical studies on the acceptance of central principles of NML can be found, e.g., in Benferhat et al. (2005), Pfeifer and Kleiter (2005), Saldanha (2018), and Schurz (2005).

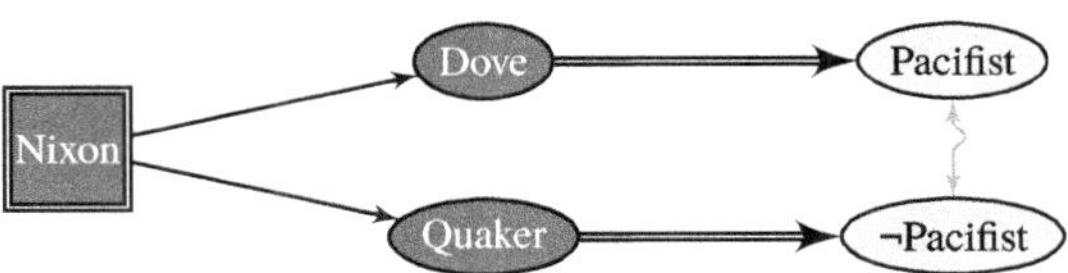

Figure 1 The Nixon Diamond from Example 2. Double arrows symbolize defeasible rules, single arrows strict rules, and wavy arrows conflicts. Black nodes represent unproblematic conclusions, while light nodes represent problematic conclusions. Rectangular nodes represent the starting point of the reasoning process. We use the same symbolism in the following figures.

or by applying inference rules to the conclusions of other arguments. An argument is defeasible if it contains a defeasible rule (such as a default), symbolized by $\Rightarrow$. Such an argument may include also truth-preservational strict inference rules (such as the ones from CL), symbolized by $\rightarrow$. A conflict between two arguments arises if they lead to contradictory conclusions A and $\neg A$ (where $\neg$ denotes negation).

Let us now take a look at two paradigmatic examples.

Example 2 (*Nixon*; Reiter and Criscuolo (1981)). One of the most well-known examples in NML is the Nixon Diamond (see Fig. 1):[9]

1. *Nixon is a Dove.* $\qquad\qquad$ Nixon $\rightarrow$ Dove
2. *Nixon is a Quaker.* $\qquad\qquad$ Nixon $\rightarrow$ Quaker
3. *By default, Doves are Pacifists.* $\qquad$ Dove $\Rightarrow$ Pacifist
4. *By default, Quakers are not Pacifists.* $\quad$ Quaker $\Rightarrow$ ¬Pacifist

Given the conflict between the arguments Nixon $\rightarrow$ Dove $\Rightarrow$ Pacifist and Nixon $\rightarrow$ Quaker $\Rightarrow$ ¬Pacifist, should we conclude that Nixon is (not) a pacifist? It seems an agnostic stance is recommended in this example.

Example 3 (*Tweety*; Doyle and McDermott (1980)). Another well-known example is Tweety the penguin (see Fig. 2) based on the following information:

1. *Tweety is a penguin.* $\qquad\qquad$ Tweety $\rightarrow$ penguin
2. *Penguins are birds.* $\qquad\qquad$ penguin $\rightarrow$ bird
3. *By default, birds fly.* $\qquad\qquad$ bird $\Rightarrow$ fly
4. *By default, penguins don't fly.* $\qquad$ penguin $\Rightarrow$ ¬fly

---

[9] In order to simplify the technical depth in this Element, we will use the language of propositional/sentential logic, rather than that of predicate logic. This will sometimes lead to less elegant translations of natural language sentences than would be possible in predicate logic (e.g., Nixon $\rightarrow$ Dove instead of Dove(Nixon)).

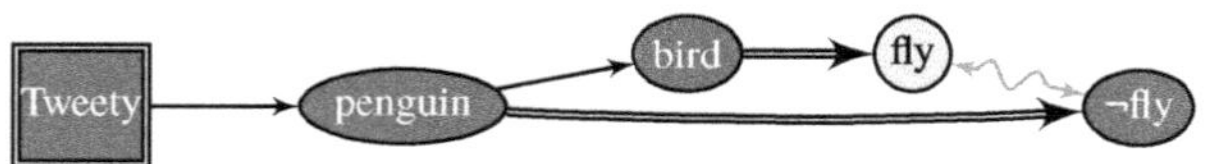

Figure 2 Tweety and specificity, Example 3.

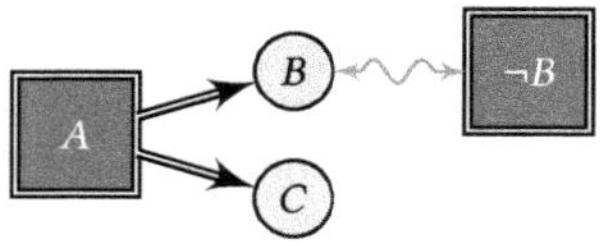

Figure 3 A drowning scenario.

We use the example to demonstrate a way to resolve conflicts among defeasible arguments, here between (a) Tweety → penguin → bird ⇒ fly and (b) Tweety → penguin ⇒ ¬fly. According to the *specificity principle* more specific defaults such as penguin ⇒ ¬fly are prioritized over less specific ones, such as bird ⇒ fly. The reason is that more specific defaults may express exceptions to the more general ones. So, in this example the preferred outcome ¬fly will be obtained since the less specific defeasible argument (a) should be retracted in favor of (b).

Our examples indicate that, first, conflicts between defeasible arguments can occur, and second, the context may determine whether and, if so, how a conflict can be resolved. We now take a look at two further challenges that come with conflicts in defeasible reasoning.

Figure 3 encodes the following information: $A \Rightarrow B$, $A \Rightarrow C$, A, and $\neg B$. Should we infer C? Nonmonotonic logics that block this inference have been said to suffer from the *drowning problem* (Benferhat et al., 1993). Examples like the following seem to suggest that we should accept C.

Example 4. We consider the scenario:

1. *Micky is a dog.*   Micky → A
2. *Dogs normally (have the ability to) to tag along with a jogger.* $A \Rightarrow B$
3. *Dogs normally (have the ability to) bark.* $A \Rightarrow C$
4. *Micky lost a leg and can't tag along with a jogger.*   Micky → ¬B

In this example it seems reasonable to infer, C, *Micky has the ability to bark*, despite the presence of $\neg B$. In other contexts one may be more cautious when jumping to a conclusion.

Example 5. Take the following scenario.

1. *It is night.* A
2. *During the night, the light in the living room is usually off.* $A \Rightarrow B$

3. *During the night, the heating in the living room is usually off.* $A \Rightarrow C$
4. *The light in the living room is on.* $\neg B$

In this scenario it seems less intuitive to infer, C, *The heating in the living room is off.* The fact that we have in (4) an exception to default (2) may have an explanation in the light of which also default (3) is excepted. For example, the inhabitant forgot to check the living room before going to sleep, she is not at home and left the light and heating on before leaving, she is still in the living room, and so on.

These examples show that concrete reasoning scenarios often contain a variety of relevant factors that influence what real-life reasoners take to be intuitive conclusions. Specific NMLs typically only model a few of these factors and omit others. For instance, although Elio and Pelletier (1994) and Koons (2017) argue that it is useful to track causal and explanatory relations in the context of drowning problems, systematic research in this direction is lacking.

Another class of difficult scenarios has to do with so-called *floating conclusions.*[10] These are conclusions that follow from two opposing arguments. For example, formally the scenario may be as depicted in Fig. 4.

Example 6. Suppose two generally reliable weather reports:

1. Station 1: *The hurricane will hit Louisiana and spare Alabama.* $A_1 \Rightarrow B_1$
2. Station 2: *The hurricane will hit Alabama and spare Louisiana.* $A_2 \Rightarrow B_2$
3. *If the hurricane hits Louisiana, it hits the South coast.* $B_1 \rightarrow C$
4. *If the hurricane hits Alabama, it hits the South coast.* $B_2 \rightarrow C$

The floating conclusion, (5), *The storm will probably hit the South coast*, may seem acceptable to a cautious reasoner. The rationale being that both reports agree on the upcoming storm and even roughly where it will hit. The disagreement may be due to different weighing of diverse factors in their respective

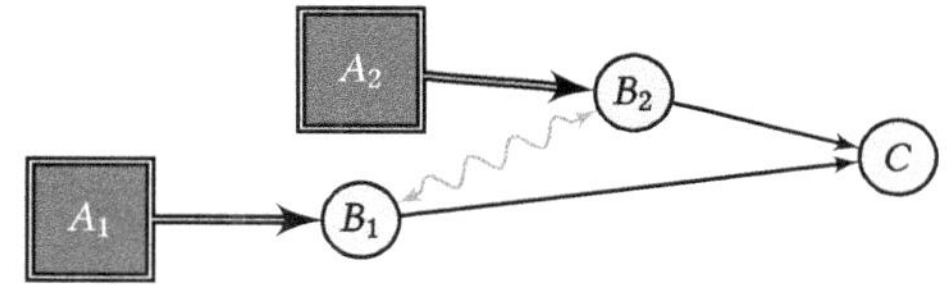

Figure 4 A scenario with the floating conclusion C.

---

[10] An overview on discussions surrounding floating conclusions can be found in Horty (2002).

underlying scientific weather models. But the combined evidence of both stations seems to rather confirm conclusion (5) than dis-confirm it. This is not always the case with partially conflicting expert statements, as the next example shows.

Example 7. Assume two expert reviewers, Reviewer 1 and Reviewer 2, evaluating Anne for a professorship. She sent in two manuscripts, A and B.

1. *Reviewer 1:* Manuscript A is highly original, while manuscript B repeats arguments already known in the literature. $\qquad A_1 \Rightarrow B_1$
2. According to Reviewer 1, one manuscript is highly original. $\quad B_1 \rightarrow C$
3. *Reviewer 2:* Manuscript B is highly original, while manuscript A repeats arguments already known in the literature. $\qquad A_2 \Rightarrow B_2$
   (We assume the inconsistency of B_1 with B_2.)
4. According to Reviewer 2, one manuscript is highly original. $\quad B_2 \rightarrow C$

Should we conclude that one manuscript is highly original, since it follows from both reviewers' evaluations? It seems a more cautious stance is advisable. The disagreement may well be an indication of the sub-optimality of each of the two reviews. Indeed, a possible explanation of their conflicting assessments could be that (a) Reviewer 1 is aware of an earlier article B' (by another author than Anne) that already makes the arguments presented in B and which is not known to Reviewer 2, and vice versa, that (b) Reviewer 2 is aware of an earlier article A' in which similar arguments to those in A are presented. In view of this possibility, it would seem overly optimistic to infer that Anne has a highly original article in her repertoire.

2 Central Concepts

Nonmonotonic logics are designed to answer the question what are (defeasible) consequences of some available set of information. This gives rise to the notion of a nonmonotonic consequence relation. In this section we explain this central concept and some of its properties from an abstract perspective (Section 2.2). Nonmonotonic consequences are obtained by means of defeasible inferences, which are themselves obtained by applying inference rules. We discuss two ways of formalizing such rules in Section 2.3. Before doing so, we discuss some basic notation in Section 2.1.

2.1 Notation and Basic Formal Concepts

Let us get more formal. We assume that sentences are expressed in a (formal) language $\mathcal{L}$. We denote the standard connectives in the usual way: $\neg$

(negation), $\wedge$ (conjunction), $\vee$ (disjunction), $\supset$ (implication), and $\equiv$ (equivalence). We use lowercase letters $p, q, s, t, \ldots$ as propositional atoms, collected in the set Atoms, and uppercase letters $A, B, C, D, \ldots$ as metavariables for sentences such as $p, p \wedge q$ or $(p \vee q) \supset r$. We denote the set of sentences underlying $\mathcal{L}$ by $\mathrm{sent}_{\mathcal{L}}$. In the context of classical propositional logic and typically in the context of a Tarski logic (see later), this will simply be the closure of the atoms under the standard connectives.[11] We denote sets of sentences by the uppercase calligraphic letters $\mathcal{A}$, $\mathcal{S}$, and $\mathcal{T}$. Where $\mathcal{S}$ is a finite nonempty set of sentences, we write $\bigwedge \mathcal{S}$ and $\bigvee \mathcal{S}$ for the conjunction resp. the disjunction over the elements of $\mathcal{S}$.[12]

A consequence relation, denoted by $\vdash$, is a relation $\vdash$ between sets of sentences and sentences: $\mathcal{S} \vdash A$ denotes that A is a $\vdash$-*consequence* of the *assumption set* $\mathcal{S}$. So, the right side of $\vdash$ encodes the given information resp. the assumptions on which the reasoning process is based, while the left side encodes the consequences which are sanctioned by $\vdash$ given $\mathcal{S}$.

We will often work in the context of *Tarski logics* L, whose consequence relations $\vdash_L$ are reflexive ($\mathcal{S} \cup \{A\} \vdash_L A$), transitive ($\mathcal{S} \vdash_L A$ and $\mathcal{S} \cup \{A\} \vdash_L B$ implies $\mathcal{S} \vdash_L B$) and monotonic (Definition 2.1). We will also assume compactness (if $\mathcal{S} \vdash_L A$ then there is a finite $\mathcal{S}' \subseteq \mathcal{S}$ for which $\mathcal{S}' \vdash_L A$). The most well-known Tarski logic is, of course, classical logic CL.

2.2 An Abstract View on Nonmonotonic Consequence

The following definition introduces one of our key concepts: nonmonotonic consequence relations.

Definition 2.1. A consequence relation $\vdash$ is *monotonic* iff ("if and only if") for all sets of sentences $\mathcal{S}$ and $\mathcal{T}$ and every sentence A it holds that $\mathcal{S} \cup \mathcal{T} \vdash A$ if $\mathcal{S} \vdash A$. It is *nonmonotonic* iff it is not monotonic.

We use $\mathrel{\vdash\mkern-7mu\sim}$ as a placeholder for nonmonotonic consequence relations. Our definition expresses that for nonmonotonic consequence relations $\mathrel{\vdash\mkern-7mu\sim}$ there are sets of sentences $\mathcal{S} \cup \{A\}$ and $\mathcal{T}$ for which $\mathcal{S} \mathrel{\vdash\mkern-7mu\sim} A$ while $\mathcal{S} \cup \mathcal{T} \mathrel{\not\vdash\mkern-7mu\sim} A$ (i.e., A is not a $\mathrel{\vdash\mkern-7mu\sim}$-consequence of $\mathcal{S} \cup \mathcal{T}$).

In the following we will introduce some properties that are often discussed as desiderata for nonmonotonic consequence relations.[13] A positive account

---

[11] Formal languages underlying specific NMLs are often richer. For instance, they may contain predicate symbols, quantifiers, modal operators or (nonmonotonic) conditionals. Nevertheless, for the introduction in this Element, a purely propositional language will suffice.

[12] We suppose that $\wedge$ and $\vee$ are commutative, associative, and idempotent.

[13] Seminal studies of these properties can be found in Gabbay (1985) and Kraus et al. (1990).

of what kind of logical behavior to expect from these relations is particularly important given the fact that 'nonmonotonicity' only expresses a negative property. This immediately raises the question whether there are restricted forms of monotonicity that one would expect to hold even in the context of defeasible reasoning? One proposal is

Cautious Monotonicity (CM). $\mathcal{S} \cup \{B\} \mathrel{\vdash\mkern-9mu\sim} A$, if $\mathcal{S} \mathrel{\vdash\mkern-9mu\sim} A$ and $\mathcal{S} \mathrel{\vdash\mkern-9mu\sim} B$.[14]

Whereas nonmonotonicity expresses that adding new information to one's assumptions may lead to the retraction resp. the defeat of previously inferred conclusions, CM states that some type of information is safe to add: namely, adding a previously inferred conclusion does not lead to the loss of conclusions.

We sketch the underlying rationale. Suppose $\mathcal{S} \mathrel{\vdash\mkern-9mu\sim} A$ and $\mathcal{S} \mathrel{\vdash\mkern-9mu\sim} B$. In view of $\mathcal{S} \mathrel{\vdash\mkern-9mu\sim} A$, the defeasible consequence A of $\mathcal{S}$ is sanctioned. So, $\mathcal{S}$ does not contain defeating information for concluding A. Now, the only reason for $\mathcal{S} \cup \{B\} \mathrel{\not\vdash\mkern-9mu\sim} A$ would be that the addition of B to $\mathcal{S}$ generates defeating information for concluding A. However, B already followed from $\mathcal{S}$, since $\mathcal{S} \mathrel{\vdash\mkern-9mu\sim} B$. Thus, this defeating information should have already been contained in $\mathcal{S}$, before adding B. But then $\mathcal{S} \mathrel{\not\vdash\mkern-9mu\sim} A$, a contradiction.

One may also demand that adding $\mathrel{\vdash\mkern-9mu\sim}$-consequences to an assumption set should not lead to more consequences.

Cautious Transitivity (CT). $\mathcal{S} \mathrel{\vdash\mkern-9mu\sim} A$, if $\mathcal{S} \cup \{B\} \mathrel{\vdash\mkern-9mu\sim} A$ and $\mathcal{S} \mathrel{\vdash\mkern-9mu\sim} B$.

Combining CM and CT comes down to requiring that $\mathrel{\vdash\mkern-9mu\sim}$ is robust under adding its own conclusions to the set of assumptions.

Cumulativity (C). If $\mathcal{S} \mathrel{\vdash\mkern-9mu\sim} B$, then $\mathcal{S} \mathrel{\vdash\mkern-9mu\sim} A$ iff $\mathcal{S} \cup \{B\} \mathrel{\vdash\mkern-9mu\sim} A$.

Instead of considering the dynamics of consequence under additions of new assumptions, one may wonder what happens when assumptions are manipulated. For instance, it seems desirable that a consequence relation is robust under substituting assumptions for equivalent ones.

Left Logical Equivalence (LLE). Where $\mathcal{S}$ and $\mathcal{T}$ are classically equivalent sets,[15] $\mathcal{S} \mathrel{\vdash\mkern-9mu\sim} A$ iff $\mathcal{T} \mathrel{\vdash\mkern-9mu\sim} A$.

Note that in the context of nonmonotonic consequence it would be too strong to require

---

14 We silently interpret this and the following properties under universal quantification over sets of sentences $\mathcal{S}$, sentences A, B, etc.

15 $\mathcal{S}$ and $\mathcal{T}$ are classically equivalent, iff, for all $A \in \mathcal{T}$, $\mathcal{S} \vdash_{CL} A$ iff $\mathcal{T} \vdash_{CL} A$.

Left Logical Strengthening (LLS). Where $A \vdash_{CL} B$, $\mathcal{S} \cup \{B\} \vdash C$ implies $\mathcal{S} \cup \{A\} \vdash C$.

In order to see why LLS is undesirable, consider an example featuring Tweety. If it is only known that Tweety is a bird, it nonmonotonically follows that it can fly, $\{b\} \vdash f$. The situation changes when it is also known that Tweety is a penguin, $\{b \wedge p\} \nvdash f$.

For the right-hand side of $\vdash$ one may also expect a property similar to LLE: if A is a consequence, so is each equivalent formula B. The following principle is stronger. It is motivated by the truth-preservational nature of CL-inferences (but recall from Section 1.2 that in the context of generics it may be problematic):

Right Weakening (RW). Where $A \vdash_{CL} B$, $\mathcal{S} \vdash A$ implies $\mathcal{S} \vdash B$.

Finally, if we take our assumptions to express certain information (rather than defeasible assumptions, see Section 4), then one may expect

Reflexivity (Ref). $\mathcal{S} \cup \{A\} \vdash A$.

Consequence relations that satisfy RW, LLE, Ref, CT, and CM are called *cumulative consequence relations* (Kraus et al., 1990).[16] The authors consider them "the rockbottom properties without which a system should not be considered a logical system." (p. 176), a point mirroring Gabbay (1985). Some other intuitive principles hold for a cumulative $\vdash$.

Proposition 2.1. *Every cumulative consequence relation $\vdash$ also satisfies:*

1. ***Equivalence.*** *If $\mathcal{S} \cup \{A\} \vdash B$ and $\mathcal{S} \cup \{B\} \vdash A$ then: $\mathcal{S} \cup \{A\} \vdash C$ iff $\mathcal{S} \cup \{B\} \vdash C$.*
2. ***AND.*** *If $\mathcal{S} \vdash A$ and $\mathcal{S} \vdash B$ then $\mathcal{S} \vdash A \wedge B$.*

Proof. Item 1 follows by CT and CM. To see this suppose (a) $\mathcal{S} \cup \{A\} \vdash B$, (b) $\mathcal{S} \cup \{B\} \vdash A$, and (c) $\mathcal{S} \cup \{A\} \vdash C$. We show $\mathcal{S} \cup \{B\} \vdash C$ (the inverse direction is analogous). By CM, (a) and (c), $\mathcal{S} \cup \{A, B\} \vdash C$. Thus, by CT and (b), $\mathcal{S} \cup \{B\} \vdash C$.

Ad 2. Suppose (a) $\mathcal{S} \vdash A$ and (b) $\mathcal{S} \vdash B$. By Ref, $\mathcal{S} \cup \{A \wedge B\} \vdash A \wedge B$ and by LLE, (c), $\mathcal{S} \cup \{A, B\} \vdash A \wedge B$. By CM, (a) and (b), $\mathcal{S} \cup \{A\} \vdash B$. By CT and (c), $\mathcal{S} \cup \{A\} \vdash A \wedge B$. By (a) and CT, $\mathcal{S} \vdash A \wedge B$. $\square$

---

[16] The original discussion in Kraus et al. (1990) concerns the case in which the left-hand side of $\vdash$ is a single sentence.

Another property of some NMLs is *constructive dilemma*: given a fixed context represented by $\mathcal{S}$, if C is both a consequence of A and of B, it should also be a consequence of $A \vee B$.

Constructive Dilemma (OR) If $\mathcal{S} \cup \{A\} \vdash C$ and $\mathcal{S} \cup \{B\} \vdash C$ then $\mathcal{S} \cup \{A \vee B\} \vdash C$.

Cumulative consequence relations that also satisfy OR are called *preferential* (Kraus et al., 1990). We show some derived principles for preferential consequence relations.

Proposition 2.2. *Every preferential consequence relation $\vdash$ also satisfies:*

1. ***Reasoning by Cases (RbC).*** *If $\mathcal{S} \cup \{A\} \vdash B$ and $\mathcal{S} \cup \{\neg A\} \vdash B$ then $\mathcal{S} \vdash B$.*
2. ***Resolution.*** *If $\mathcal{S} \cup \{A\} \vdash B$ then $\mathcal{S} \vdash A \supset B$.*

Proof. (RbC). Suppose $\mathcal{S} \cup \{A\} \vdash B$ and $\mathcal{S} \cup \{\neg A\} \vdash B$. By OR, $\mathcal{S} \cup \{A \vee \neg A\} \vdash B$ and by LLE, $\mathcal{S} \vdash B$. (Resolution). Suppose now that $\mathcal{S} \cup \{A\} \vdash B$. By RW, (a), $\mathcal{S} \cup \{A\} \vdash A \supset B$. By Ref, $\mathcal{S} \cup \{\neg A\} \vdash \neg A$ and by RW, (b), $\mathcal{S} \cup \{\neg A\} \vdash A \supset B$. By RbC, (a) and (b), $\mathcal{S} \vdash A \supset B$. $\qquad\square$

A more controversial property than CM is *rational monotonicity (RM)*.[17] The basic intuition is similar to CM: given an assumption set $\mathcal{S}$, we are interested in securing a safe set of sentences under the addition of which $\vdash$ is monotonic. While for CM this was the set of the $\vdash$-consequences of $\mathcal{S}$, RM considers the set of all sentences that are consistent with the consequences of $\mathcal{S}$ (consistent in the sense that their negation is not a $\vdash$-consequence of $\mathcal{S}$).

Rational Monotonicity (RM) $\mathcal{S} \cup \{B\} \vdash A$, if $\mathcal{S} \vdash A$ and $\mathcal{S} \nvdash \neg B$.

One way to think about RM is as follows. Let us (i) say that *B is defeating information for $\mathcal{S}$* if there is an A for which $\mathcal{S} \vdash A$, while $\mathcal{S} \cup \{B\} \nvdash A$, and (ii) *B is rebutted by $\mathcal{S}$* in case $\mathcal{S} \vdash \neg B$.[18] Then, when putting CM and RM in contrapositive form,

- CM expresses that no defeating information for $\mathcal{S}$ is derivable from any $\mathcal{S}$: formally, if $\mathcal{S} \vdash A$ and $\mathcal{S} \cup \{B\} \nvdash A$ then $\mathcal{S} \nvdash B$;
- RM expresses the stronger demand that every defeating information for $\mathcal{S}$ is rebutted by $\mathcal{S}$: formally, if $\mathcal{S} \vdash A$ and $\mathcal{S} \cup \{B\} \nvdash A$ then $\mathcal{S} \vdash \neg B$.

---

[17] See, for instance, Kelly and Lin (2021) and R. Stalnaker (1994) for critical views on RM.

[18] The notions of defeat and rebuttal will be discussed in more detail in the context of formal argumentation (Part II).

So, RM requires that reasoners take into account potentially defeating information by having rebutting counterarguments at hand. This is quite demanding, since, as we have discussed in Section 1, (a) the reasoner may not be aware of all possibly rebutting information to her previous inferences and (b) it may be counterintuitive to conclude that each and every possible defeater is false.

Poole (1991) points out another problem. Consider the statement that Tweety is a bird. Now, all bird species are exceptional to some defaults about birds: penguins don't fly, hummingbirds have an unusual size, sandpipers nest on the ground, and so on. But, then RM requires us to infer that Tweety is not a penguin, not a hummingbird, not a sandpiper, and so on, and therefore does not belong to any bird species.

In this section we have seen various properties of nonmonotonic consequence relations, many of which are considered desiderata by nonmonotonic logicians. Their study is therefore of central interest in NML and we will come back to them in the context of many of the methods presented in this Element.

2.3 Plausible and Defeasible Reasoning

A fundamental question underlying the design of NMLs is whether to model defeasible reasoning

1. by means of classical inferences based on defeasible assumptions, or
2. by means of (genuinely) defeasible inference rules.

The former is sometimes called PLAUSIBLE REASONING, the latter DEFEASIBLE REASONING.[19] Table 1 provides an overview on which of the two reasoning styles is modeled by various NMLs discussed in this Element. We illustrate with an abstract example. Suppose we want to model that

- p defeasibly implies q, and that
- q defeasibly implies $\neg r$.

In the first approach we encode these two defeasible regularities in terms of classical implications. It can be realized in two ways.

PLAUSIBLE REASONING via abnormality assumptions. One way is by formalizing the defeasible rules by

$$p \wedge \neg \mathrm{ab}_1 \supset q \quad \text{and} \quad q \wedge \neg \mathrm{ab}_2 \supset \neg r,$$

---

[19] See Prakken (2012), Rescher (1976), and Vreeswijk (1993). We capitalize these technical terms to distinguish them from their more general informal usage, i.e., "defeasible reasoning" refers to the general phenomenon as described in Section 1, while DEFEASIBLE REASONING is the technical term described in this section.

Table 1 Reasoning styles modelled by various logics discussed in this Element. ($\star$) A NML with genuine defaults, such as Reiter's default logic can "simulate" PLAUSIBLE REASONING by encoding defeasible assumptions A by defaults with empty bodies $\Rightarrow A$.

NML	DEFEASIBLE REASONING	PLAUSIBLE REASONING	
ASPIC$^+$	$\checkmark$	$\checkmark$	Section 8
Logic-based argumentation		$\checkmark$	Section 9
Rescher & Manor		$\checkmark$	Section 11.3.1
Default Assumptions		$\checkmark$	Section 11.3.1
Adaptive Logic		$\checkmark$	Section 11.3.1
Input–Output Logic	$\checkmark$	$\checkmark^\star$	Section 11.3.2
Reiter Default Logic	$\checkmark$	$\checkmark^\star$	Section 12
Logic Programming		$\checkmark$	Section 16

where ab_1 and ab_2 are atomic sentences that encode exceptional circumstances, that is, abnormalities, for the respective rules. These abnormalities are assumed to be false, by default. Suppose that p is true. Then, by also assuming the falsity of ab_1 and ab_2 we can apply modus ponens to both material implications and conclude $\neg r$.

Let us see how retraction works in this approach by supposing r. In this case we can classically derive $ab_1 \lor ab_2$, but neither ab_1 nor ab_2. Note that contraposition of defeasible rules is available in this approach. For instance, $q \land \neg ab_2 \supset \neg r$ is CL-equivalent to $q \land r \supset ab_2$.[20] So, we know (at least) one of the assumptions must be false, but we don't know which. Absent any other reason to prefer one over the other, we can't rely on $\neg ab_1$ to derive q. In view of this, q should not be considered a nonmonotonic consequence of the given information.

PLAUSIBLE REASONING via naming of defaults. Another way to proceed is by naming defaults (see, e.g., Poole (1988)). Here, we make use of defeasible assumptions r_1 and r_2, which name defeasible inference rules and which are assumed to be true, by default. In our example, we add

$$r_1 \supset (p \supset q) \quad \text{and} \quad r_2 \supset (q \supset \neg r)$$

to the (nondefeasible) assumptions. Note that $r_1 \supset (p \supset q)$ (resp. $r_2 \supset (q \supset \neg r)$) is classically equivalent to $r_1 \land p \supset q$ (resp. $r_2 \land q \supset \neg r$). So, when substituting

---

[20] A conditional $\to$ is *contrapositable* in case $\neg B \to \neg A$ follows from $A \to B$, or more general, if $C \land \neg B \to \neg A$ follows from $C \land A \to B$.

r_1 for $\neg ab_1$ and r_2 for $\neg ab_2$ the approach based on naming defaults and the approach based on abnormality assumptions boil down to the same.

DEFEASIBLE REASONING. In this approach, regularities are expressed as genuinely defeasible rules (written with $\Rightarrow$), that is, without additional and explicit defeasible assumptions that are part of the antecedent of the rule. We encode our preceding example by

$$p \Rightarrow q \quad \text{and} \quad q \Rightarrow \neg r.$$

Note that $\Rightarrow$ is not classical implication, in particular $A \wedge B \Rightarrow C$ does, in general, not follow from $A \Rightarrow C$ in this approach. In the first scenario, where only p is given, we apply a defeasible modus ponens rule to obtain q and then again to obtain $\neg r$. Many NMLs implement a *greedy* style of reasoning, according to which defeasible modus ponens is applied as much as possible. Now, if r is also part of the assumptions, we derive q from p and $p \Rightarrow q$, but then stop, since inferring $\neg r$ from $q \Rightarrow \neg r$ and q would result in inconsistency.

Example 8. For a more general context, we consider an example with defaults $p_1 \Rightarrow p_2, \ldots, p_{n-1} \Rightarrow p_n$ and the (certain) information p_1 and $\neg p_n$ depicted in Figure 5. In the greedy style of reasoning underlying DEFEASIBLE REASONING we will be able to apply defeasible modus ponens to derive $p_2, p_3, \ldots, p_{n-1}$. Only the last application resulting in p_n is blocked by the defeating information $\neg p_n$. The situation is different for PLAUSIBLE REASONING. Since contraposition is available, for each argument $p_1 \Rightarrow p_2 \Rightarrow \ldots \Rightarrow p_i$ (where each $p_j \Rightarrow p_{j+1}$ is modeled by $p_j \wedge \neg ab_j \supset p_{j+1}$) there is a defeating argument $\neg p_n \Rightarrow \neg p_{n-1} \Rightarrow \ldots \Rightarrow \neg p_i$. Altogether, we obtain

$$\{p_i \wedge ab_i \supset p_{i+1} \mid 1 \leq i < n\} \cup \{p_1, \neg p_{n-1}\} \vdash ab_1 \vee \ldots \vee ab_{n-1}.$$

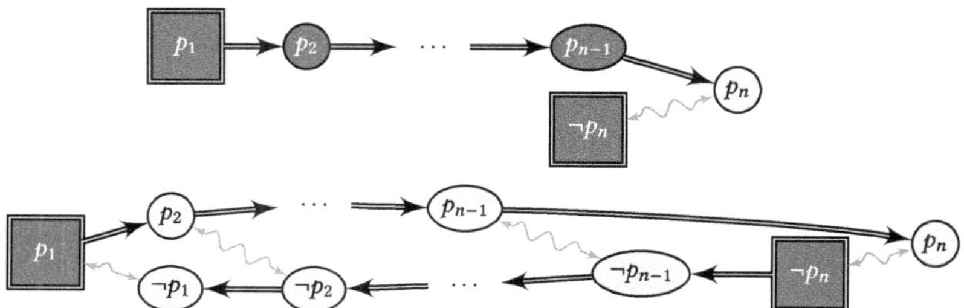

Figure 5 Top: DEFEASIBLE REASONING giving rise to a greedy reasoning style. Bottom: PLAUSIBLE REASONING giving rise to contrapositions of defeasible rules.

This means that at least one ab_i cannot be assumed to be false, but we don't know which one. Thus, no p_i (for $i \in \{2, \ldots, n\}$) is derivable according to PLAUSIBLE REASONING.

3 From Knowledge Bases to Consequences and NMLs

Nonmonotonic logics represent the information relevant for the reasoning process (*knowledge representation*) and determine what follows defeasibly from the given information (*nonmonotonic consequence*, see Fig. 6).

The task of knowledge representation concerns, for instance, the structuring of the starting point of defeasible reasoning processes in terms of *knowledge bases* (Section 4) in which different types of information are distinguished, such as different types of assumptions and inference rules. Another task is to organize the given information in a way that is conducive of determining its defeasible consequences. As we have seen, this is challenging since the given information may give rise to conflicts and inconsistencies. NMLs provide methods for generating *coherent chunks* of information. We will highlight several ways of doing so, most roughly distinguished into *syntactic* and *semantic* approaches. The following three concepts play essential roles in the ways knowledge is represented in these approaches:[21]

Extensions In syntactic approaches, coherent units of information are typically called *extensions*. What exactly extensions are differs in various NMLs. They may, for example, be sets of defeasible information from the knowledge base, sets of arguments (given a underlying notion of argument), or sets of sentences. In Sections 5.1 and 5.2 we will introduce two major families of syntactic

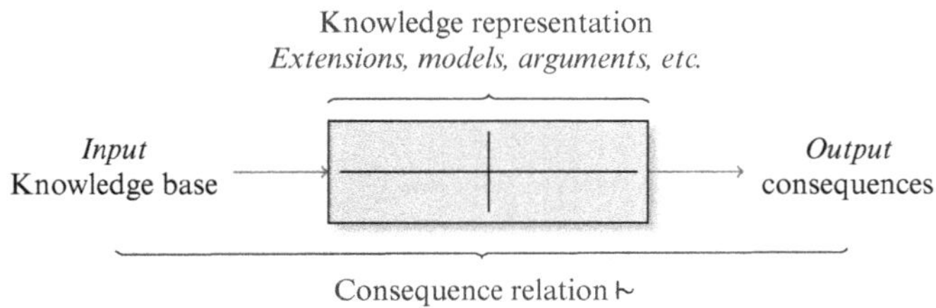

Figure 6 The workings of NMLs.

---

[21] One should not put too much philosophical emphasis on the term *knowledge* in the context of knowledge representation (e.g., knowledge bases may contain defeasible assumptions which do not have the status of true and justified beliefs). From a Brandomian perspective one may think of knowledge bases as representing base commitments of a reasoner, where the defeasible inference rules open an argumentative space of prima facie entitlements (Brandom, 2009).

approaches: *argumentation* and *consistent accumulation*. In Parts II and III they will be studied in more detail.

Arguments In syntactic approaches, arguments (or proofs) play a central role when building extensions. Arguments are obtained by applications of the given inference rules to the assumptions provided in the knowledge base.

Models In semantic approaches the focus is on classes of *models* provided by a given base logic. In Section 5.3 we will introduce semantic approaches and study some of them in more detail in Part IV.

The attentive reader will have noticed that we did not yet define what exactly NMLs are. In the *narrow sense*, one may consider them as *nonmonotonic consequence relations* (see Section 2.2), so a theory of what sentences follow defeasibly in the context of some knowledge base. In the *wider sense* they are *methods* for both knowledge representation and for providing nonmonotonic consequence relation(s).

In this Element we minimally assume that every NML nmL comes with a formal language $\mathcal{L}$ including a notion of what counts as a formula or sentence (written $\mathrm{sent}_{\mathcal{L}}$), an associated class of knowledge bases $\mathbf{K}_{\mathrm{nmL}}$ (see Section 4 for details), at least one consequence relation and one of the following two:

- in syntactic approaches: a notion of (in)consistent sets of sentences, of argument or proof, and a method to generate extensions (see Sections 5.1 and 5.2 and Parts II and III);
- in semantic approaches: a notion of model and a method to select models (see Section 5.3 and Part IV).

4 Defeasible Knowledge Bases

Reasoning never starts in a void but it is initiated in a given context. For instance, some information will be factually given and some assumptions may hold by default. Moreover, when we reason we make use of inference rules. Some of these may be truth-preservational (such as the rules provided by CL), others defeasible, allowing for exceptional circumstances. *Defeasible knowledge bases* structure reasoning contexts into different types of constituents, such as different types of assumptions and inference rules. Most broadly conceived they are tuples of the form:

$$\mathcal{K} = \langle \; \overbrace{\mathcal{A}_s, \quad \mathcal{A}_d}^{\substack{\text{strict and} \\ \text{defeasible} \\ \text{Assumptions}}} , \; \overbrace{\mathcal{R}_s, \quad \mathcal{R}_d, \quad \mathcal{R}_m,}^{\substack{\text{strict,} \\ \text{defeasible,} \\ \text{and meta Rules}}} \quad \overbrace{\leq}^{\substack{\text{preferences} \\ \text{among defeasible} \\ \text{elements}}} \; \rangle \qquad (4.0.1)$$

Table 2 The class of associated knowledge bases for specific NMLs. In gray the nonfixed parts. For example, for specific input–output logics the set of metarules $\mathcal{R}_m$ is fixed, while the strict assumptions and defeasible rules vary in their applications. $\mathcal{R}_L$ is the class of strict rules induced by a logic L, where CL is classical logic.

NML	$\mathcal{A}_s$	$\mathcal{A}_d$	$\mathcal{R}_s$	$\mathcal{R}_d$	$\mathcal{R}_m$	
ASPIC$^+$	✓	✓	✓	✓		Section 8
Logic-based argumentation	✓	✓	✓($\mathcal{R}_L$)			Section 9
Rescher & Manor		✓	✓($\mathcal{R}_{CL}$)			Section 11.3.1
Default Assumptions	✓	✓	✓($\mathcal{R}_{CL}$)			Section 11.3.1
Input–Output Logics	✓		✓($\mathcal{R}_L$)	✓	✓	Section 11.3.2
Reiter Default Logic	✓		✓($\mathcal{R}_{CL}$)	✓		Section 12
Logic Programming			✓			Section 16

We let $\mathrm{Def}(\mathcal{K}) =_{\mathrm{df}} \mathcal{A}_d \cup \mathcal{R}_d$ be the *defeasible part of* $\mathcal{K}$ consisting of its defeasible assumptions and rules.

A concrete nmL has an associated fixed class of knowledge bases $\mathbf{K}_{\mathrm{nmL}}$. Its underlying consequence relation(s) $\vdash$ are relations between $\mathbf{K}_{\mathrm{nmL}}$ and sent$_{\mathcal{L}}$.[22]

In concrete NMLs, usually not all components of (4.0.1) are utilized or explicitly listed. For example, some NMLs do not consider defeasible rules, some come without defeasible assumptions, some without priorities, many without metarules. Take, for instance, NMLs that model PLAUSIBLE REASONING. Here, we omit $\mathcal{R}_d$ since such NMLs do not work with defeasible rules. Moreover, specific components of the knowledge base are fixed for many NMLs, or they are constrained. For instance, only specific preferences relations $\leq$ may be allowed for, such as transitive ones. Or, often the strict rules are induced by classical logic. (In such cases, the strict rules are often omitted from $\mathbf{K}_{\mathrm{nmL}}$.) In some NMLs the strict rules vary over different applications (e.g., in logic programming where strict rules usually represent domain-specific knowledge such as "penguins are birds"). In Table 2 we provide an overview for NMLs presented in this Element.

We now explain in more detail the components of $\mathcal{K}$.

Strict assumptions $\mathcal{A}_s$ is a set of sentences expressing information that is taken as indisputable or certain.

---

[22] In Section 2.2 we considered properties for consequence relations of the type $\vdash \subseteq \wp(\mathrm{sent}_{\mathcal{L}}) \times \mathrm{sent}_{\mathcal{L}}$. A generalized study for $\vdash \subseteq \mathbf{K}_{\mathrm{nmL}} \times \mathrm{sent}_{\mathcal{L}}$ is presented in Section 10.3.

Defeasible assumptions $\mathcal{A}_d$ is a set of sentences that are assumed to hold normally/typically/and so on but which may be retracted in case of conflicts.
Strict rules $\mathcal{R}_s$ is a set of truth-preservational inference rules or relations, written $A_1,\ldots,A_n \to B$.[23] There are two types of such rules. On the one hand, we have material inferences, such as "If it is a penguin, it is a bird" which may be encoded by $p \to b$. On the other hand, we have inferences that are valid with respect to an underlying logic L, such as classical logic. If such inferences are considered, we let $A_1,\ldots,A_n \to B \in \mathcal{R}_s$ if $\{A_1,\ldots,A_n\} \vdash_L B$. If $\mathcal{R}_s$ consist exclusively of such rules, we say that it is *induced by the logic* L and write $\mathcal{R}_L$ for the set containing them. All logics L considered in this Element will be Tarski logics. If $\mathcal{R}_s$ is induced by a logic (with an implication $\supset$) one may model the former class of material inferences simply by means of $\supset$. For example, in our example one may add $p \supset b$ to the strict assumptions $\mathcal{A}_s$. Sometimes we find strict assumptions A being modeled as strict rules with empty bodies $\to A$.

Given a set of strict rules $\mathcal{R}_s$ and a set of sentences $\mathcal{S} \cup \{A\}$, we write $A \in \mathsf{Cn}_{\mathcal{R}_s}(\mathcal{S})$ to indicate that there is a *deduction of A* based on $\mathcal{R}_s$ and $\mathcal{S}$. This means that there is a sequence $\langle A_1,\ldots,A_n \rangle$ where $A = A_n$ and for each A_{i+1} (with $0 \leq i < n$), either $A_{i+1} \in \mathcal{S}$ or there are $j_1,\ldots,j_m \leq i$ for which $A_{j_1},\ldots,A_{j_m} \to A_{i+1} \in \mathcal{R}_s$.

Defeasible rules $\mathcal{R}_d$ is a set of defeasible inference rules written $A_1,\ldots,A_n \Rightarrow B$, often just called *defaults*. As discussed in Section 2.3, defeasible rules are sometimes "indirectly" modeled as strict rules with defeasible assumptions. In NMLs that adopt this method of PLAUSIBLE REASONING, $\mathcal{R}_d$ may be empty. In such cases we are typically dealing with a logic-induced set of strict rules $\mathcal{R}_L$ and defaults are sentences of the type $A_1 \wedge \ldots \wedge A_n \wedge \neg\mathsf{ab} \supset B$ in $\mathcal{A}_s$ where $\neg\mathsf{ab} \in \mathcal{A}_d$. Defeasible assumptions $A \in \mathcal{A}_d$ may be also considered as defaults $\Rightarrow A$ with empty bodies.

For reasons of simplicity and following the tradition of many central NMLs, we do not consider $\Rightarrow$ as a defeasible conditional operator in the object language $\mathcal{L}$, that is, an operator that can be nested within Boolean connectives. Rather, we model $A \Rightarrow B$ as representing a defeasible rule that prima facie justifies detaching B, given A. However, it should be noted that this does impose a limitation on our expressive capabilities. For instance, we cannot "directly"

---

[23] In many NMLs the deductive base system is not modeled as part of a knowledge base, but simply presupposed and provided by classical logic. Other systems, such as logic programming (see Section 16.4) or some systems of structured argumentation theory (see Section 8) explicitly model the strict rule base as part of the knowledge base. In any case, most well-known NMLs come with a deductive base system and a defeasible rule base. For reasons of generality, we model both as part of the knowledge base.

express canceling in the context of specificity, such as $\texttt{penguin} \Rightarrow \neg(\texttt{bird} \Rightarrow \texttt{fly})$. Many systems have been developed to overcome this limitation, such as Delgrande (1987) or conditional logics of normality (Boutilier, 1994a).[24]

Example 9. In Section 2.3 we presented two ways to model a scenario in which p defeasibly implies q and q defeasibly imply $\neg r$. Suppose now additionally that r and $\neg r$ both strictly imply s and that p defeasibly implies r.

In DEFEASIBLE REASONING we may work with the knowledge base $\mathcal{K} = \langle \mathcal{A}_s, \mathcal{A}_d, \mathcal{R}_s, \mathcal{R}_d \rangle$ consisting of $\mathcal{A}_s = \{p\}$, $\mathcal{A}_d = \emptyset$, $\mathcal{R}_d = \{p \Rightarrow q, p \Rightarrow r, q \Rightarrow \neg r\}$, and $\mathcal{R}_s = \{r \to s, \neg r \to s\}$. Alternatively, one may use the strict assumptions $r \supset s$ and $\neg r \supset s$ and $\mathcal{R}_{\mathsf{CL}}$ as strict rules.

In PLAUSIBLE REASONING we may utilize $\mathcal{K}' = \langle \mathcal{A}'_s, \mathcal{A}'_d, \mathcal{R}_{\mathsf{CL}} \rangle$, where $\mathcal{A}'_s = \{p,\ p \wedge \neg\mathsf{ab}_1 \supset q,\ p \wedge \neg\mathsf{ab}_2 \supset r,\ q \wedge \neg\mathsf{ab}_3 \supset \neg r,\ r \supset s,\ \neg r \supset s\}$ and $\mathcal{A}'_d = \{\neg\mathsf{ab}_1, \neg\mathsf{ab}_2, \neg\mathsf{ab}_3\}$.

Metarules $\mathcal{R}_m$ is a set of metarules, written $R_1, \ldots, R_n \mapsto R$ (where $R_1, \ldots, R_n$ are strict and defeasible rules and R is a defeasible rule) that allow one to infer new defeasible rules from those in $\mathcal{R}_d$ and $\mathcal{R}_s$. For example, metarules implementing reasoning-by-cases and right weakening are:

OR $(A \Rightarrow B),\ (C \Rightarrow B)\ \mapsto\ ((A \vee C) \Rightarrow B)$
RW $(B \to C),\ (A \Rightarrow B)\ \mapsto\ (A \Rightarrow C)$

Given a set $\mathcal{R} \subseteq \mathcal{R}_d$, we write $\mathsf{Cn}_{\mathcal{R}_m}(\mathcal{R})$ for the set of defeasible rules that are $\mathcal{R}_m$-deducible from $\mathcal{R} \cup \mathcal{R}_s$ by the metarules in $\mathcal{R}_m$ (where deductions are defined as in the context of the strict rules $\mathcal{R}_s$).[25]

Preferences $\leq$ is an order on the defeasible elements $\mathsf{Def}(\mathcal{K})$ of $\mathcal{K}$. It encodes that some sources of defeasible information may be more reliable or have more authority than others. This information can be utilized for the purpose of resolving conflicts between defeasible arguments of different strengths. Typically $\leq$ is reflexive and transitive, but it may allow for incomparabilities and for equally strong but different defeasible elements. We write $<$ for the strict version of $\leq$, that is, $X < X'$ iff $X \leq X'$ and $X' \not\leq X$.

---

[24] Pioneering research on deontic logic and subjunctive conditionals gave rise to many systems that incorporate nonmonotonic conditionals in the object language, for example, Van Fraassen (1972) and Hansson (1969) in deontic logic, logics by Lewis for deontic reasoning (Lewis, 1974) and counterfactuals (Lewis, 1973), R. F. Stalnaker (1968) on counterfactuals, etc.

[25] In this Element we will mostly consider knowledge bases for which there are no metarules, i.e., $\mathcal{R}_m = \emptyset$ (with the exception of temperate accumulation in Section 11, in particular input–output logics in Section 11.3.2).

Example 10. Consider $\mathcal{K} = \langle \mathcal{A}_s, \mathcal{R}_d \rangle$ with $\mathcal{A}_s = \{p\}$ and $\mathcal{R}_d = \{p \Rightarrow q, p \Rightarrow \neg q\}$. There is a conflict between the arguments $p \Rightarrow q$ and $p \Rightarrow \neg q$. Absent priorities, there is no way to resolve the conflict on the basis of $\mathcal{K}$. If we enhance $\mathcal{K}$ to $\mathcal{K}' = \langle \mathcal{A}_s, \mathcal{R}_d, \leq \rangle$ where $(p \Rightarrow q) < (p \Rightarrow \neg q)$ it seems reasonable to resolve the conflict in favor of $p \Rightarrow \neg q$.

The situation can get more involved, as the following example shows.

Example 11 (Example 9 cont.). We may extend our knowledge base to $\mathcal{K}_\leq = \langle \mathcal{A}_s, \mathcal{A}_d, \mathcal{R}_d, \mathcal{R}_s, \leq \rangle$ by adding the preference order: $(p \Rightarrow q) < (p \Rightarrow r) < (q \Rightarrow \neg r)$ (assuming transitivity).[26] In this case we have two conflicting arguments, $p \Rightarrow q \Rightarrow \neg r$ and $p \Rightarrow r$. Comparing their strengths is no longer straightforward, since the former involves both a stronger and a weaker default than the latter. In Part III (Examples 28 and 29) we will see that different methods give rise to different conclusions for $\mathcal{K}_\leq$ (see also Liao et al. (2016)).

5 Methodologies for Nonmonotonic Logics

We now introduce three central methodologies to obtain nonmonotonic consequence relations and to represent defeasible knowledge, namely: formal argumentation (Section 5.1), consistent accumulation (Section 5.2), and semantic methods (Section 5.3). In this part we explain basic ideas underlying each method based on simplified settings (e.g., without metarules and preferences). More details are presented in the dedicated Parts II to IV.

5.1 The Argumentation Method

The possibility of inconsistency complicates the question as to what follows from a knowledge base $\mathcal{K}$. As described earlier, the idea is to generate coherent sets of information from $\mathcal{K}$ and to reason on the basis of these. For this, arguments and attacks between them play a key role. Arguments are obtained from $\mathcal{K}$ by chaining strict and defeasible inference rules. We can define the set of arguments $\mathrm{Arg}_\mathcal{K}$ induced by $\mathcal{K}$, their conclusions, subarguments, and defeasible elements (written $\mathrm{Con}(a)$, $\mathrm{Sub}(a)$, resp. $\mathrm{Def}(a)$ for some $a \in \mathrm{Arg}_\mathcal{K}$) in a bottom-up way.[27]

Definition 5.1 (Arguments). Where $\mathcal{K} = \langle \mathcal{A}_s, \mathcal{A}_d, \mathcal{R}_s, \mathcal{R}_d \rangle$ is a knowledge base we let $a \in \mathrm{Arg}_\mathcal{K}$ iff

---

[26] Under the following interpretation, this example is known as the order puzzle in deontic logic (Horty, 2012): it is winter (p), open the window (q), turn on the heating (r).

[27] In Sections 9 and 11.3.2 we also discuss a different take on arguments, not as proof trees but as premise-conclusion pairs.

- $a = \langle A \rangle$, where $A \in \mathcal{A}_s \cup \mathcal{A}_d$.
  We let $\mathrm{Con}(a) = A$, $\mathrm{Sub}(a) = \{a\}$, $\mathcal{R}_d(a) = \emptyset$, $\mathcal{A}_d(a) = \{A\} \cap \mathcal{A}_d$.
- $a = a_1, \ldots, a_n \rightsquigarrow A$ where $\rightsquigarrow \in \{\to, \Rightarrow\}$, $a_1, \ldots, a_n \in \mathrm{Arg}_{\mathcal{K}}$ and $r = \mathrm{Con}(a_1), \ldots, \mathrm{Con}(a_n) \rightsquigarrow A$ is a rule in $\mathcal{R}_s \cup \mathcal{R}_d$.
  We let $\mathrm{Con}(a) = A$, $\mathrm{Sub}(a) = \{a\} \cup \bigcup_{i=1}^{n} \mathrm{Sub}(a_i)$, $\mathcal{A}_d(a) = \bigcup_{i=1}^{n} \mathcal{A}_d(a_i)$, $\mathcal{R}_d(a) = \bigcup_{i=1}^{n} \mathcal{R}_d(a_i) \cup (\{r\} \cap \mathcal{R}_d)$.

Where $a \in \mathrm{Arg}_{\mathcal{K}}$ we let $\mathrm{Def}(a) = \mathcal{A}_d(a) \cup \mathcal{R}_d(a)$. Where $\mathcal{D} \subseteq \mathrm{Def}(\mathcal{K})$, we let $\mathrm{Arg}_{\mathcal{K}}(\mathcal{D})$ be the set of all $a \in \mathrm{Arg}_{\mathcal{K}}$ for which $\mathrm{Def}(a) \subseteq \mathcal{D}$.

Example 12 (Example 9 cont.). Given our knowledge base $\mathcal{K}$ in Example 9 we obtain the arguments depicted in Fig. 7 (left). We have, for instance, $\mathcal{A}_d(a_5) = \emptyset$, $\mathcal{R}_d(a_5) = \mathrm{Def}(a_5) = \{p \Rightarrow q, q \Rightarrow \neg r\}$, and $\mathrm{Sub}(a_5) = \{a_1, a_2, a_3, a_5\}$.

There are many ways to define argumentative attacks and subtlety is required to avoid problems with consistency in the context of selecting arguments. We will go into more details in Part II. For now we simply suppose there to be a relation att $\subseteq \mathrm{Arg}_{\mathcal{K}} \times \mathrm{Arg}_{\mathcal{K}}$ that determines when two arguments attack each other. We end up with a directed graph $\langle \mathrm{Arg}_{\mathcal{K}}, \mathrm{att} \rangle$, a so-called *argumentation framework* (Dung, 1995).

Example 13 (Example 12 cont.). One way to define attacks in our example is to let $a \in \mathrm{Arg}_{\mathcal{K}}$ attack $b \in \mathrm{Arg}_{\mathcal{K}}$ if for some $c \in \mathrm{Sub}(b)$ of the form $c = a_1, \ldots, a_n \Rightarrow C$, $\mathrm{Con}(a) = \neg C$ or $\neg \mathrm{Con}(a) = C$. For instance, a_3 and a_4 attack each other. In Fig. 7 (right) we find the underlying argumentation framework.

Argumentation frameworks allow us to select coherent sets of arguments $\mathcal{X}$, which we will call *A-extensions* (for argumentative extensions). The latter represent argumentative stances of rational reasoners equipped with the knowledge base $\mathcal{K}$. For this we utilize a number of constraints which represent rational desiderata on these stances. Two such desiderata on sets of arguments $\mathcal{X}$ are, for instance (we refer to Part II for a more comprehensive overview):

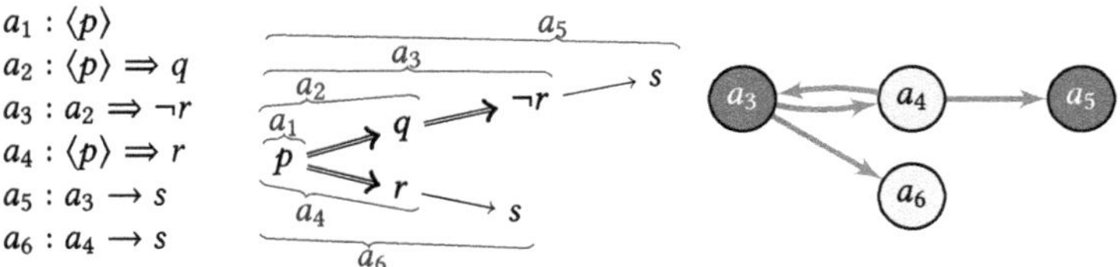

Figure 7 The arguments and the argumentation framework for Example 13 (omitting the nonattacked and nonattacking a_1 and a_2). We explain the shading in Example 14.

Conflict-freeness: avoid argumentative conflicts, that is, for all $a, b \in \mathcal{X}$, $(a, b) \notin$ att; and

Stability: additionally, be able to attack arguments that you don't commit to, that is, for all $c \in \text{Arg}_\mathcal{K} \setminus \mathcal{X}$ there is an $a \in \mathcal{X}$ for which $(a, c) \in$ att.

Such sets of constraints give rise to so-called *argumentation semantics* which determine A-extensions of a given argumentation framework (Dung, 1995). For instance, according to the *stable semantics* the set of A-extensions is the set of all sets of arguments that satisfy stability. Once we have settled for an argumentation semantics s (such as the stable semantics) we denote the set of A-extensions of $\mathcal{K}$ relative to s by $\text{AExt}_s(\mathcal{K})$.

Example 14 (Example 13 cont.). We have two stable A-extensions, that is, sets of arguments that satisfy the stability requirement (see the shaded sets in the argumentation framework of Fig. 7):

$$\mathcal{X}_1 = \{a_1, a_2, a_3, a_5\} \quad \text{and} \quad \mathcal{X}_2 = \{a_1, a_2, a_4, a_6\}.$$

Suppose we select an A-extension $\mathcal{X}$. We then commit to all of the conclusions of the arguments in $\mathcal{X}$, that is, to $\text{Con}[\mathcal{X}]$, where $\text{Con}[\mathcal{X}] = \{\text{Con}(a) \mid a \in \mathcal{X}\}$. This induces another notion of extension, which we dub *P-extensions* (propositional extensions) which are sets of conclusions associated with A-extensions. We write $\text{PExt}_s(\mathcal{K})$ for the set of P-extensions of $\mathcal{K}$ (relative to a given argumentation semantics s).

Example 15 (Example 14 cont.). The following P-extensions are associated with our A-extensions:

$$\mathcal{E}_1 = \{p, q, \neg r, s\} \quad \text{and} \quad \mathcal{E}_2 = \{p, q, r, s\}.$$

Once an argumentation semantics is fixed and the A- and corresponding P-extensions are generated, we can define three different consequence relations for two underlying reasoning styles (see Fig. 8): *skeptical* and *credulous* reasoning.

Definition 5.2. Where $\mathcal{K}$ is a knowledge base, A a sentence, and s is an argumentation semantics, we define the consequence relations in Table 3.

To avoid clutter in notation, we will omit the super- and subscripts whenever the context disambiguates or the strategy is not essential to a given claim. Note that the definition of the three consequence relations imposes a hierarchy in terms of strength, namely:

$$\mathcal{K} \vdash_{\cap\text{AExt}} A \text{ implies } \mathcal{K} \vdash_{\cap\text{PExt}} A \text{ implies } \mathcal{K} \vdash_{\cup\text{Ext}} A.$$

Table 3 Three types of nonmonotonic consequence relations.

Skeptical 1	$\mathcal{K} \vdash^{s}_{\cap PExt} A$ iff $A \in \bigcap PExt_s(\mathcal{K})$ *A is a member of every extension in* $PExt_s(\mathcal{K})$.
Skeptical 2	$\mathcal{K} \vdash^{s}_{\cap AExt} A$ iff there is an $a \in \bigcap AExt_s(\mathcal{K})$ s. t. $Con(a) = A$ *There is an argument a with* $Con(a) = A$ *that is contained in every A-extension of* $\mathcal{K}$.
Credulous	$\mathcal{K} \vdash^{s}_{\cup Ext} A$ iff $A \in \bigcup PExt_s(\mathcal{K})$ *A is a member of some extension in* $PExt_s(\mathcal{K})$.

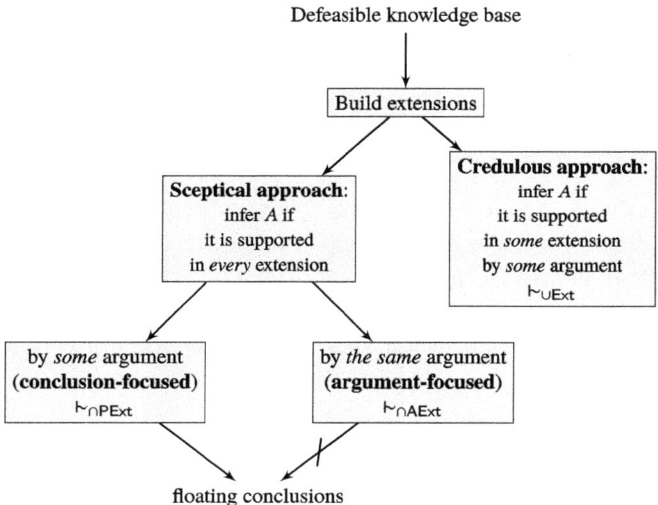

Figure 8 The skeptical and the credulous reasoning style.

Example 16 (Example 15 cont.). Based on our extensions, we have the following consequences:

	p	q	$\neg r$	r	s
$\vdash_{\cap PExt}$	✓	✓			✓
$\vdash_{\cap AExt}$	✓	✓			
$\vdash_{\cup Ext}$	✓	✓	✓	✓	✓

The example illustrates that a floating conclusion such as s follows by $\vdash_{\cap PExt}$ but not by the more cautious $\vdash_{\cap AExt}$.

5.2 Methods based on Consistent Accumulation

Given a knowledge base $\mathcal{K}$, the basic idea behind the accumulation methods is to iteratively build coherent sets of defeasible elements from $\text{Def}(\mathcal{K})$.[28] We will call such sets *D-extensions* (extensions consisting of defeasible elements). Below we identify two central methods of building D-extensions: the *greedy* and the *temperate* method. Once D-extensions have been generated by one of these methods, we can associate each D-extension $\mathcal{D}$ with an A-extension $\text{Arg}_{\mathcal{K}}(\mathcal{D})$ consisting of all the arguments based on elements in $\mathcal{D}$. Moreover, each A-extension $\mathcal{X}$ has the corresponding P-extension $\text{Con}[\mathcal{X}]$ as discussed in Section 5.1. Once A- and P-extensions are obtained, we define consequence relations just like in Definition 5.2 (see the overview in Fig. 9). We now discuss the two types of accumulation methods.

5.2.1 The Greedy Method

Given a knowledge base $\mathcal{K} = \langle \mathcal{A}_s, \mathcal{A}_d, \mathcal{R}_s, \mathcal{R}_d \rangle$, methods based on consistent accumulation build iteratively sets of defeasible elements from $\text{Def}(\mathcal{K})$. One may think of a rational agent that extends her *commitment store* $\text{Def}^\star$ consisting of elements in $\text{Def}(\mathcal{K})$ in a stepwise manner. She starts off with the empty set and in each step she adds an element of $\text{Def}(\mathcal{K}) \setminus \text{Def}^\star$ to $\text{Def}^\star$ or she stops the procedure. She stops when adding any new element d would lead to inconsistency, that is, in case she would be able to construct conflicting arguments on the basis of $\text{Def}^\star \cup \{d\}$.

According to the greedy method, she will only consider adding elements in $\text{Def}(\mathcal{K}) \setminus \text{Def}^\star$ to her commitment store that (a) give rise to new arguments (that is the greedy part) and (b) do not give rise to conflicting arguments. We will make this formally precise with the algorithm GREEDYACC in what follows, but

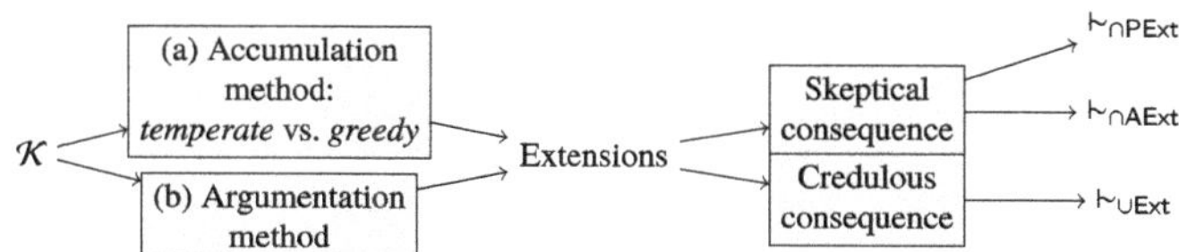

Figure 9 Types of nonmonotonic consequence based on syntactic approaches.

---

[28] Recall that (a) $\text{Def}(\mathcal{K})$ consists of the defeasible assumptions $\mathcal{A}_d$ and rules $\mathcal{R}_d$ in $\mathcal{K}$, and that (b) some NMLs come with associated knowledge bases that only contain one of the two types of defeasible elements. We use d as a metavariable for members of $\text{Def}(\mathcal{K})$.

we first need to introduce some concepts. Where $\mathrm{Def}^\star \subseteq \mathrm{Def}(\mathcal{K})$, we say that a default $r = A_1, \ldots, A_n \Rightarrow B$

- is *triggered by* $\mathrm{Def}^\star$, if $A_1, \ldots, A_n \in \mathrm{Con}[\mathrm{Arg}_\mathcal{K}(\mathrm{Def}^\star)]$,[29]
- is *consistent* with $\mathrm{Def}^\star$, if $\neg B \notin \mathrm{Con}[\mathrm{Arg}_\mathcal{K}(\mathrm{Def}^\star \cup \{r\})]$.

If r is triggered by $\mathrm{Def}^\star$, adding r to $\mathrm{Def}^\star$ gives rise to new arguments in $\mathrm{Arg}_\mathcal{K}(\mathrm{Def}^\star \cup \{r\})$. The reason for this is that for each A_i (with $i = 1, \ldots, n$) there is an argument $a_i \in \mathrm{Arg}_\mathcal{K}(\mathrm{Def}^\star)$ with conclusion A_i, and $a_1, \ldots, a_n \Rightarrow B \in \mathrm{Arg}_\mathcal{K}(\mathrm{Det}^\star \cup \{r\}) \setminus \mathrm{Arg}_\mathcal{K}(\mathrm{Det}^\star)$. We treat defeasible assumptions $B \in \mathcal{A}_d$ like defaults with empty left-hand sides: they are always triggered, and consistent with $\mathrm{Def}^\star$ only if $\neg B \notin \mathrm{Con}[\mathrm{Arg}_\mathcal{K}(\mathrm{Def}^\star \cup \{B\})]$.

The algorithm GREEDYACC implements the greedy accumulation method. We note that the element $d \in \mathrm{Def}(\mathcal{K}) \setminus \mathrm{Def}^\star$ in lines 3 and 4 is chosen nondeterministically.

Algorithm 1 Greedy accumulation

1: **procedure** GREEDYACC($\mathcal{K}$)　　　　　　　　　　▷ $\mathcal{K} = \langle \mathcal{A}_s, \mathcal{A}_d, \mathcal{R}_s, \mathcal{R}_d \rangle$
2:　　　$\mathrm{Def}^\star \leftarrow \emptyset$　　　　　　　　　　　　　　　　　▷ init scenario
3:　　　**while** $\exists d \in \mathrm{Def}(\mathcal{K}) \setminus \mathrm{Def}^\star$ triggered by and consistent with $\mathrm{Def}^\star$ **do**
4:　　　　　$\mathrm{Def}^\star \leftarrow \mathrm{Def}^\star \cup \{d\}$　　　　　　　　　▷ update scenario
5:　　　**end while**　　　　　▷ no more triggered and consistent defaults
6:　　　**return** $\mathrm{Def}^\star$　　　　　　　　　　　▷ return D-extension
7: **end procedure**

GREEDYACC takes as input a knowledge base $\mathcal{K}$ and outputs a D-extension $\mathcal{D}$. Its associated A-extension is given by $\mathcal{X} = \mathrm{Arg}_\mathcal{K}(\mathcal{D})$ and its associated P-extension by $\mathrm{Con}[\mathcal{X}]$. The latter can be used to determine our three consequence relations from Definition 5.2. We write $\mathrm{DExt}_\mathrm{gr}(\mathcal{K})$ [resp. $\mathrm{AExt}_\mathrm{gr}(\mathcal{K})$, $\mathrm{PExt}_\mathrm{gr}(\mathcal{K})$] for the set of D-[resp. A-, P-]extensions of $\mathcal{K}$ (gr for greedy accumulation). We are now in a position to define three consequence relations analogous to Definition 5.2 (see Table 3), for example, by:

$$\mathcal{K} \vdash^\mathrm{gr}_{\cap \mathrm{PExt}} A \text{ iff } A \in \bigcap \mathrm{PExt}_\mathrm{gr}(\mathcal{K}).$$

Example 17 (Example 12 cont.). We apply GREEDYACC to the given knowledge base $\mathcal{K}$. There are three different runs (due to the nondeterministic nature of the algorithm):

---

[29] Recall that $\mathrm{Con}[\mathrm{Arg}_\mathcal{K}(\mathrm{Def}^\star)] = \{\mathrm{Con}(a) \mid a \in \mathrm{Arg}_\mathcal{K}(\mathrm{Def}^\star)\}$.

	Run 1	Run 2	Run 3
Round 1	$p \Rightarrow r$	$p \Rightarrow q$	$p \Rightarrow q$
Round 2	$p \Rightarrow q$	$p \Rightarrow r$	$q \Rightarrow \neg r$
P-extension	$\{p,r,q,s\}$	$\{p,r,q,s\}$	$\{p,\neg r,q,s\}$
A-extension	$\{a_1,a_2,a_4,a_6\}$	$\{a_1,a_2,a_4,a_6\}$	$\{a_1,a_2,a_3,a_5\}$

Next we list consequences according to the three different consequence relations:

	p	q	$\neg r$	r	s
$\vdash_{\cap\text{PExt}}$	✓	✓			✓
$\vdash_{\cap\text{AExt}}$	✓	✓			
$\vdash_{\cup\text{Ext}}$	✓	✓	✓	✓	✓

Note that for $\vdash_{\cap\text{PExt}}$ we have to consider the intersection of all P-extensions $\{p,q,s\}$ and so we get the floating conclusion s (just like in Example 16). For $\vdash_{\cap\text{AExt}}$ we consider the intersection of the A-extensions $\{a_1,a_2\}$: while $p,q \in \text{Con}[\{a_1,a_2\}]$ the floating conclusion s is not in $\text{Con}[\{a_1,a_2\}]$. Finally, for $\vdash_{\cup\text{Ext}}$ we consider the union of all P-extensions $\{p,q,r,\neg r,s\}$.

5.2.2 Temperate Accumulation

Our second accumulation method is nongreedy (or, temperate) in that the defeasible elements from $\text{Def}(\mathcal{K})$ that may be added to the commitment store $\text{Def}^\star$ in each step of the algorithm can be such that they don't give rise to new arguments. In more technical terms, our agent may also add defeasible rules which are not triggered by $\text{Def}^\star$. This is described in Algorithm 2, TEMACC. We use the same notation as before: $\text{DExt}_{\text{tem}}(\mathcal{K})$ is the set of D-extensions generated by TEMACC$(\mathcal{K})$ and $\text{AExt}_{\text{tem}}(\mathcal{K}) =_{df} \{\text{Arg}_{\mathcal{K}}(\mathcal{D}) \mid \mathcal{D} \in \text{DExt}_{\text{tem}}(\mathcal{K})\}$ resp. $\text{PExt}_{\text{tem}}(\mathcal{K}) =_{df} \{\text{Con}[\mathcal{A}] \mid \mathcal{A} \in \text{AExt}_{\text{tem}}(\mathcal{K})\}$ is the corresponding set of A- resp. P-extensions. The three types of consequence relations $\vdash_{\cap\text{PExt}}^{\text{tem}}$, $\vdash_{\cap\text{AExt}}^{\text{tem}}$, and $\vdash_{\cup\text{Ext}}^{\text{tem}}$ are defined analogously to the greedy versions (see Table 3).

Remark 1. Let us make two immediate observations to better understand how the greedy approach relates to the temperate approach. First, since defeasible assumptions are always triggered, the greedy and the temperate accumlation methods coincide for knowledge bases without defeasible rules (where $\mathcal{R}_d = \emptyset$). Second, every run via GREEDYACC corresponds to the initial segment of some runs via TEMACC.

Algorithm 2 Temperate accumulation

1: **procedure** TEMACC($\mathcal{K}$)
2:      Def$^\star \leftarrow \emptyset$ ▷ init scenario
3:      **while** $\exists d \in \text{Def}(\mathcal{K}) \setminus \text{Def}^\star$ consistent with Def* **do**
4:          Def$^\star \leftarrow$ Def$^\star \cup \{d\}$ ▷ update scenario
5:      **end while**   ▷ no more consistent defaults
6:      **return** Def* ▷ return D-extension
7: **end procedure**

Example 18 (Example 17 cont.). We apply TEMACC to our knowledge base. There are six possible runs, omitting runs 1–3 which are analogous to Example 17:

	...	Run 4	Run 5	Run 6
Round 1	...	$q \Rightarrow \neg r$	$q \Rightarrow \neg r$	$p \Rightarrow r$
Round 2	...	$p \Rightarrow q$	$p \Rightarrow r$	$q \Rightarrow \neg r$
P-extension	...	$\{p, \neg r, q, s\}$	$\{p, r, s\}$	$\{p, r, s\}$
A-extension	...	$\{a_1, a_2, a_3, a_5\}$	$\{a_1, a_4, a_6\}$	$\{a_1, a_4, a_6\}$

In comparison with GREEDYACC we get three additional runs, namely 4–6. While run 4 is just a permutation of run 3, runs 5 and 6 give rise to new D-extensions. They show the nongreedy character of TEMACC. Consider, for instance, run 6: although in round 2 the default $p \Rightarrow q$ is both triggered and consistent with $\{p \Rightarrow r\}$, the algorithm chooses the nontriggered $q \Rightarrow \neg r$.

We list consequences according to the different notions of consequence, marking differences to GREEDYACC with [!]:

	p	q	$\neg r$	r	s
$\vdash_{\cap\text{PExt}}$	✓	[!]			✓
$\vdash_{\cap\text{AExt}}$	✓	[!]			
$\vdash_{\cup\text{Ext}}$	✓	✓	✓	✓	✓

We see that q does not follow anymore by $\vdash_{\cap\text{PExt}}$ and $\vdash_{\cap\text{AExt}}$.

While in our example every D-extension based on greedy accumulation is also one based on temperate accumulation, the example demonstrates this typically doesn't hold vice versa. As a consequence, temperate accumulation gives rise to a more cautious style of reasoning than the greedy approach, at least in

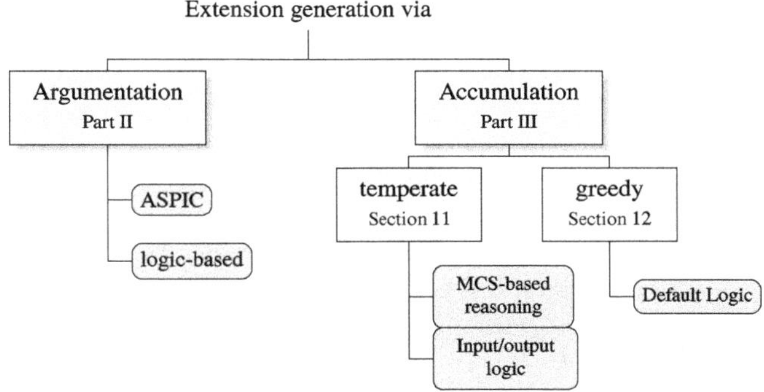

Figure 10 The syntactic approach and NMLs discussed in this Element.

terms of the skeptical consequence relations and when there are no preferences involved (see Example 29 for a counterexample with preferences).

Figure 10 gives an overview on NMLs discussed in this Element and where they fall in terms of our classification.

5.2.3 Temperate Accumulation and Maxicon Sets

Alternative to the iterative procedure TEMACC, the D-extensions of temperate accumulation can also be characterized in terms of *maxicon sets* (for *maxi*mally *con*sistent *sets*).

Definition 5.3. Given a knowledge base $\mathcal{K}$, a set $\mathcal{D} \subseteq \mathsf{Def}(\mathcal{K})$ is a *maxicon set* of $\mathcal{K}$ (in signs, $\mathcal{D} \in \mathsf{maxcon}(\mathcal{K})$) iff (i) $\mathcal{D}$ is consistent in $\mathcal{K}$ (i.e., $\mathsf{Con}[\mathsf{Arg}_{\mathcal{K}}(\mathcal{D})]$ is consistent) and (ii) for all $\mathcal{D}' \subseteq \mathsf{Def}(\mathcal{K})$, if $\mathcal{D} \subsetneq \mathcal{D}'$ then $\mathcal{D}'$ is inconsistent.

Proposition 5.1. *Let $\mathcal{K}$ be a knowledge base and $\mathcal{D} \subseteq \mathsf{Def}(\mathcal{K})$. $\mathcal{D}$ is a D-extension generated by* TEMACC *iff* $\mathcal{D} \in \mathsf{maxcon}(\mathcal{K})$.

Proof. Suppose $\mathcal{D} = \{d_1, \ldots, d_n\} \in \mathsf{maxcon}(\mathcal{K})$. We consider a run of TEMACC in which in the ith round of the loop d_i is added to $\mathcal{D}^\star$. We note that since $\mathcal{D}$ is consistent in $\mathcal{K}$, so is every of its subsets. Thus, the while loop is not exited before the nth round. When the condition of the loop is checked the $n+1$th time, $\mathcal{D}^\star = \mathcal{D}$. By the maximal consistency of $\mathcal{D}$ in $\mathcal{K}$, there is no $d \in \mathsf{Def}(\mathcal{K}) \setminus \mathcal{D}^\star$ left for which $\mathcal{D}^\star \cup \{d\}$ is consistent in $\mathcal{K}$. So, TEMACC terminates and returns $\mathcal{D}$. The other direction is similar. $\qquad\square$

Example 19 (Example 18 cont.). Our knowledge base $\mathcal{K}$ has the maxicon sets $\mathcal{D}_1 = \{p \Rightarrow q, q \Rightarrow \neg r\}$, $\mathcal{D}_2 = \{p \Rightarrow q, p \Rightarrow r\}$, and $\mathcal{D}_3 = \{q \Rightarrow \neg r, p \Rightarrow r\}$. These exactly correspond to the D-extensions of temperate accumulation.

As a consequence of Proposition 5.1 we obtain an alternative characterizations of the nonmonotonic consequence relations $\vdash^{tem}_{\cap PExt}$, $\vdash^{tem}_{\cap AExt}$, and $\vdash^{tem}_{UExt}$.

Corollary 5.1. *Let $\mathcal{K}$ be a knowledge base and $\mathcal{S} \cup \{A\}$ a set of sentences.*

1. $\mathcal{S} \vdash^{tem}_{\cap PExt} A$ *iff for every $\mathcal{D} \in \mathrm{maxcon}(\mathcal{K})$, $A \in \mathrm{Con}[\mathrm{Arg}_{\mathcal{K}}(\mathcal{D})]$.*
2. $\mathcal{S} \vdash^{tem}_{\cap AExt} A$ *iff there is an $A \in \mathrm{Con}[\cap \{\mathrm{Arg}_{\mathcal{K}}(\mathcal{D}) \mid \mathcal{D} \in \mathrm{maxcon}(\mathcal{K})\}]$.*
3. $\mathcal{S} \vdash^{tem}_{UExt} A$ *iff for some $\mathcal{D} \in \mathrm{maxcon}(\mathcal{K})$, $A \in \mathrm{Con}[\mathrm{Arg}_{\mathcal{K}}(\mathcal{D})]$.*

The consequence relation $\vdash^{tem}_{\cap AExt}$ can be equivalently characterized by means of minimal conflict sets:

Definition 5.4. $\mathcal{D} \subseteq \mathrm{Def}(\mathcal{K})$ is a *minimal conflict set* for $\mathcal{K}$ iff $\mathcal{D}$ is inconsistent in $\mathcal{K}$ but every $\mathcal{D}' \subsetneq \mathcal{D}$ is consistent in $\mathcal{K}$. The set of *innocent bystanders in $\mathcal{K}$*, $\mathrm{IB}(\mathcal{K})$, consists of all members of $\mathrm{Def}(\mathcal{K})$ that are not members of minimal conflict sets for $\mathcal{K}$.

Example 20 (Example 9 cont.). For our knowledge base $\mathcal{K}$ we have $\mathrm{IB}(\mathcal{K}) = \emptyset$ since every defeasible element is part of a minimal conflict. Were we to add, for instance, $p \Rightarrow u$ to $\mathcal{R}_d$, resulting in $\mathcal{K}'$, we would have $\mathrm{IB}(\mathcal{K}') = \{p \Rightarrow u\}$.

Proposition 5.2. *Let $\mathcal{K}$ be a knowledge base. Then, (i) $\mathrm{IB}(\mathcal{K}) = \cap \, \mathrm{maxcon}(\mathcal{K})$ and (ii) $\mathcal{K} \vdash^{tem}_{\cap AExt} A$ iff $A \in \mathrm{Con}[\mathrm{Arg}_{\mathcal{K}}(\mathrm{IB}(\mathcal{K}))]$.*

Proof. We show (i). (ii) follows then immediately by Corollary 5.1. Suppose $d \notin \mathrm{IB}(\mathcal{K})$. Thus, there is a minimal conflict set $\mathcal{D}$ in $\mathcal{K}$ with $d \in \mathcal{D}$. So, $\mathcal{D} \setminus \{d\}$ is consistent and there is a $\mathcal{D}' \in \mathrm{maxcon}(\mathcal{K})$ with $\mathcal{D} \setminus \{d\} \subseteq \mathcal{D}'$ and $d \notin \mathcal{D}'$. So $d \notin \cap \, \mathrm{maxcon}(\mathcal{K})$. The other direction is similar and left to the reader. $\square$

5.3 Semantic Methods

Let us suppose a knowledge base of the form $\mathcal{K} = \langle \mathcal{A}_s, \mathcal{A}_d, \mathcal{R}_L \rangle$ for a Tarski logic L (such as CL, see Section 4). A natural interpretation of $\mathcal{K} \vdash A$ is that A holds in the most *normal* situations that are consistent with the strict assumptions $\mathcal{A}_s$ in $\mathcal{K}$, where the standard of *normality* is contributed by the defeasible elements $\mathcal{A}_d$ of $\mathcal{K}$.

In many NMLs this idea is realized in terms of semantic selections.[30] Supposing that L provides a model semantics to interpret formulas in $\mathcal{A}_s \cup \mathcal{A}_d$,

---

[30] The idea has been proposed by various scholars (Kraus et al., 1990; Shoham, 1987). In circumscription (McCarthy, 1980) (for propositional versions see also Gelfond et al. (1989) and

we consider the models of $\mathcal{A}_s$, written $\mathcal{M}(\mathcal{A}_s)$. We write $M \models A$ if A is interpreted as true in M. On these models an order $\leq$ is imposed where $M \leq M'$ in case M is at least as normal as M'. What it means to be *more normal* is determined by the defeasible information in $\mathcal{K}$ (a concrete example is given in the next paragraph). The entailment relation is then defined by:

$$\mathcal{K} \vdash_{\leq} A \text{ iff for all } M \in \min_{\leq}(\mathcal{M}(\mathcal{A}_s)), M \models A,$$

that is, the most normal models of $\mathcal{A}_s$ validate A.

To make this idea more concrete we return to the system of PLAUSIBLE REASONING in Section 2.3. There we modeled defeasible inferences $A_1, \ldots, A_n \Rightarrow B$ in terms of implications $A_1 \wedge \ldots \wedge A_n \wedge \neg\text{ab} \supset B$ supplemented with normality assumptions $\neg\text{ab} \in \mathcal{A}_d$. The strict rules $\mathcal{R}_{\text{CL}}$ were contributed by classical logic. So, the knowledge base has the form $\langle \mathcal{A}_s, \mathcal{A}_d, \mathcal{R}_{\text{CL}} \rangle$, or in short $\langle \mathcal{A}_s, \mathcal{A}_d \rangle$. We additionally assume that $\mathcal{A}_s$ is classically satisfiable (so it has a model). According to the rationale stated earlier, $\langle \mathcal{A}_s, \mathcal{A}_d \rangle \vdash A$ means that A holds in all situations in which the assumptions of $\mathcal{A}_s$ are true and which are most normal relative to the defeasible assumptions in $\mathcal{A}_d$.

Where M is a classical model of $\mathcal{A}_s$, let for this $\mathcal{N}_{\mathcal{K}}(M) =_{\text{df}} \{A \in \mathcal{A}_d \mid M \models A\}$ be the *normal part* of M. We can then order the models by $\leq \subseteq \mathcal{M}(\mathcal{A}_s) \times \mathcal{M}(\mathcal{A}_s)$ as follows:

$$M \leq M' (M \text{ is at least as normal as } M') \text{ iff } \mathcal{N}_{\mathcal{K}}(M') \subseteq \mathcal{N}_{\mathcal{K}}(M).$$

In other words, the more defeasible assumptions a model verifies, the more normal it is. The most normal models will then be those in $\min_{\leq}(\mathcal{M}(\mathcal{A}_s))$. See for an illustration Fig. 11.

Example 21 (Example 9 cont.). We take another look at $\mathcal{K}'$ from Example 9. We have, among others, the classical models of $\mathcal{A}_s$ listed in Fig. 12 (left) whose ordering $\leq$ is illustrated on the right. The minimal models are M_1, M_2 and M_3. We therefore have, for instance, $\mathcal{K} \vdash_{\leq} p$ and $\mathcal{K} \vdash_{\leq} r \vee q$.

Semantic selections have also been used as a model of the closed-world assumption in McCarthy's circumscription (McCarthy, 1980).[31] In our presentation this is realized by letting $\mathcal{A}_d$ be a set of negated atoms.

Satoh (1989)) and adaptive logics (Batens, 2007) we proceed in an inverted manner: instead of interpreting the information such that as many defeasible assumptions in $\mathcal{A}_d$ are true as possible, one works with a set of negative assumptions which are interpreted false as much as possible.

[31] See Moinard and Rolland (1998) for an overview on circumscription.

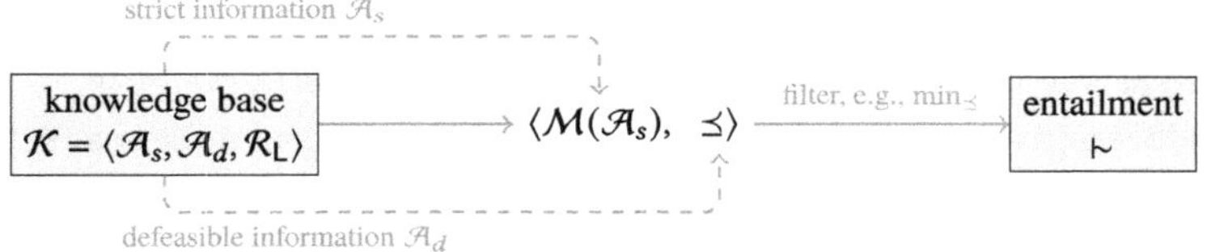

Figure 11 Nonmonotonic entailment by semantic selections.

		q		r	ab_1	ab_2	ab_3
M_1		1		1	0	0	1
M_2		1		0	0	1	0
M_3		0		1	1	0	0
M_4		1		0	1	1	0
M_4^i		0	$i \in \{0,1\}$	1	1	0
M_5^i		1	$i \in \{0,1\}$	0	1	1
M_6^i	$i \in \{0,1\}$			1	1	0	1
$M_7^{i,j}$	$i \in \{0,1\}$	$j \in \{0,1\}$		1	1	1

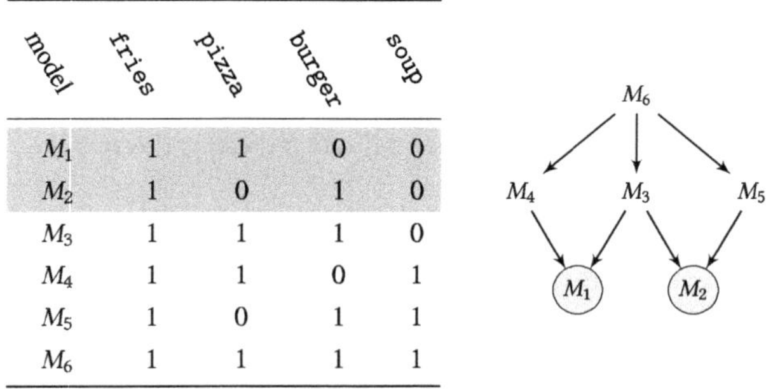

Figure 12 The order $\leq$ on the models of Example 21. Highlighted are the $\leq$-minimal models. The atoms p and s are true in every model of $\mathcal{A}_s$.

model	fries	pizza	burger	soup
M_1	1	1	0	0
M_2	1	0	1	0
M_3	1	1	1	0
M_4	1	1	0	1
M_5	1	0	1	1
M_6	1	1	1	1

Figure 13 Models of $\mathcal{A}_s$ in Example 22 with highlighted $\leq$-minimal models.

Example 22. Suppose Anne checks the online menu of the university canteen and finds the information that fries are served and that either pizza or burger is available. Consider the knowledge base $\mathcal{K}_{can} = \langle \mathcal{A}_s, \mathcal{A}_d, \mathcal{R}_{CL} \rangle$ where $\mathcal{A}_s = \{\texttt{fries}, \texttt{pizza} \vee \texttt{burger}\}$, $\mathcal{A}_d$ consists of $\{\neg A \mid A \in \text{Atoms}\}$, and Atoms $= \{\texttt{fries}, \texttt{pizza}, \texttt{burger}, \texttt{soup}\}$. In Fig. 13 we find the $\leq$-ordering of the models of $\mathcal{A}_s$. With $\vdash_\leq$ Anne concludes, for instance, $\neg\texttt{soup}$ and $\neg\texttt{pizza} \vee \neg\texttt{burger}$. This is in accordance with the closed-world assumption: what is not listed in the menu is assumed not to be offered.

6 A Roadmap

In this introduction we have explained the main ideas and concepts behind several core methods of NML. In what follows we will deepen our understanding of

- the *argumentation method* in which a reasoner analyzes the interplay between arguments and their counterarguments to determine coherent sets of arguments (Part II);
- the methods based on *consistent accumulation*, temperate and greedy, in which a reasoner gradually commits to more and more defeasible information from the given knowledge base (Part III); and
- the *semantic method* in which a reasoner determines the most normal interpretations of the given knowledge base (Part IV).

We will study metatheoretic properties that come with these methods and discuss central logics from the literature that implement them.

Given that the field of NML comes with such a variety of systems and methods, it will also be our task to provide links between the methods. As we will see, several classes of logics belonging to different methods give rise to the same class of nonmonotonic consequence relations (see Fig. 14 for an overview).

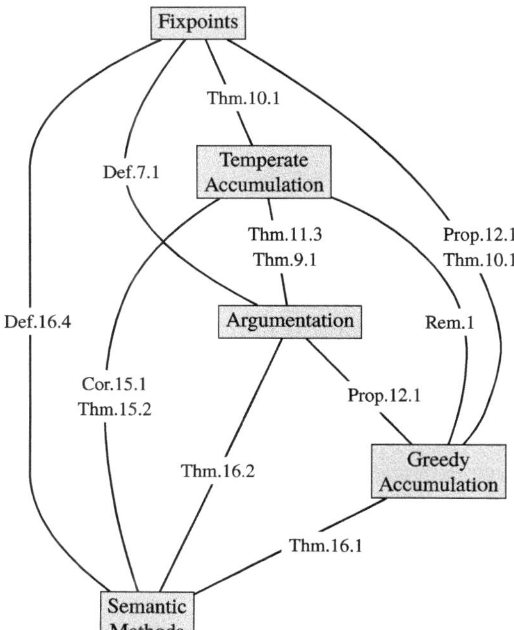

Figure 14 Links between the various methods studied in this Element.

PART II FORMAL ARGUMENTATION

Argumentation theory as a study of defeasible reasoning has been proposed already by Toulmin (1958). His book provides a critique of formal logic as a model of the defeasible nature of commonsense reasoning. While in the early 1980s many NMLs were proposed, we have to wait for the most influential pioneering works in formal argumentation such as Pollock (1991, 1995) and Dung (1995) until the 1990s. What distinguishes these approaches from earlier NMLs is the prominent status of arguments and defeat. The ambition is to provide both an intuitive and unifying account of defeasible reasoning. Recently, Mercier and Sperber (2017) have made a strong case for the argumentative nature of human reasoning. Together with the rich tradition in informal argumentation theory (e.g., Eemeren & Grootendorst, 2004; Walton et al., 2008) this strongly motivates formal argumentation as an account of defeasible reasoning which is close to human reasoning practices.

In this part we deepen our understanding of formal argumentation theory. In Section 7 we explain how Dung's abstract perspective provides a way to select arguments from an argumentation framework. In Sections 8 and 9, we present two ways of equipping arguments with logical structure.

7 Abstract Argumentation

In formal argumentation the question as to what follows from a given defeasible knowledge base $\mathcal{K}$ is answered by means of an argumentative analysis. It is the essential idea behind *abstract* argumentation (introduced by Dung (1995)) that as soon as the arguments induced by $\mathcal{K}$ are generated and collected in the set $\mathrm{Arg}_{\mathcal{K}}$, and as soon as the attacks between them are determined and collected in the relation att $\subseteq \mathrm{Arg}_{\mathcal{K}} \times \mathrm{Arg}_{\mathcal{K}}$, we can abstract from the concrete content of those arguments, focus on the directed graph given by $\langle \mathrm{Arg}_{\mathcal{K}}, \mathrm{att} \rangle$ and select arguments simply by means of analyzing this graph.[32] The latter is called the *argumentation framework* for $\mathcal{K}$. The *argumentation semantics* defined in the following definition offer criteria to select arguments that form a defendable and consistent stance. We call the selected sets of arguments *A-extensions* of $\mathcal{K}$. A-extensions form the basis of three types of nonmonotonic consequence relations: $\vdash_{\cap \mathrm{AExt}}, \vdash_{\cap \mathrm{PExt}}$, and $\vdash_{\cup \mathrm{Ext}}$ (see Table 3). Due to its strict division of labor between argument and attack generation, on the one hand, and argument selection with its induced notion of nonmonotonic consequence, on the other hand, formal argumentation offers a transparent and clean methodology.

---

[32] The reader is referred back to Section 5.1 where we introduced basic definitions such as the notion of an argument and the set $\mathrm{Arg}_{\mathcal{K}}$.

Table 4 Argumentation semantics.

$\mathcal{X}$ is	iff
conflict-free	for all $a, b \in \mathcal{X}$, $(a, b) \notin$ att
admissible	$\mathcal{X} \subseteq$ defended$(\mathcal{X})$
complete	$\mathcal{X} =$ defended$(\mathcal{X})$
grounded	$\mathcal{X}$ is the unique $\subseteq$-minimal complete set
preferred	$\mathcal{X}$ is $\subseteq$-maximal admissible
stable	$\mathcal{X}$ is conflict-free and for all $a \in$ Arg $\setminus \mathcal{X}$ there is a $b \in \mathcal{X}$ such that $(b, a) \in$ Arg

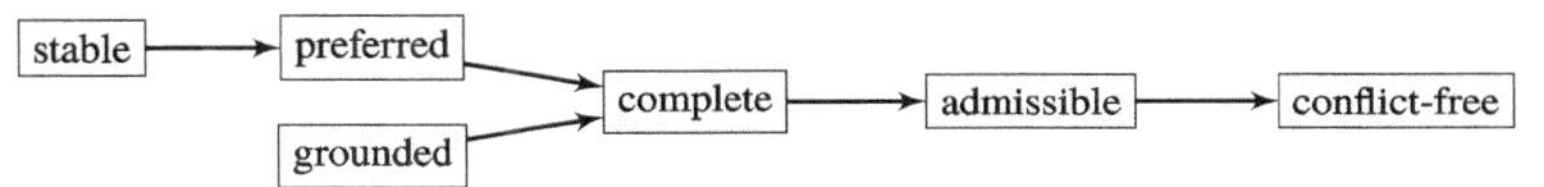

Figure 15 Relations between argumentation semantics. Every extension of the type left of an arrow is also an extension of the type to its right.

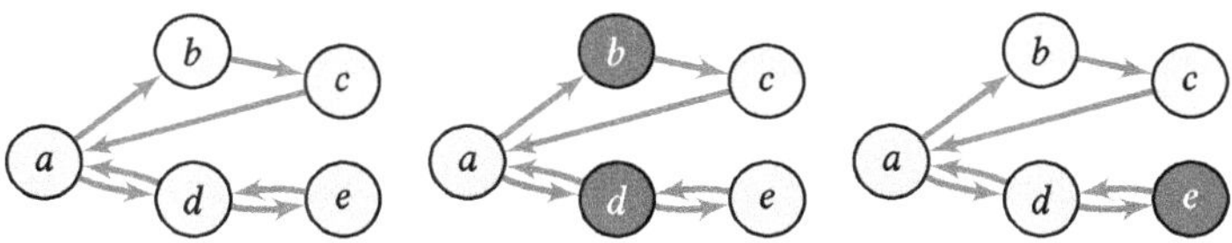

Figure 16 Left: An argumentation framework composed of five arguments. Highlighted in the center and on the right are its two preferred extensions. The extension in the center is the only stable extension. The grounded extension in this example is $\emptyset$.

Definition 7.1 (Argumentation Semantics, Dung (1995)). Let $\langle$Arg, att$\rangle$ be an argumentation framework and $\mathcal{X} \subseteq$ Arg a set of arguments. We say that $\mathcal{X}$ *defends* $a \in$ Arg if for all $b \in$ Arg, if $(b, a) \in$ att then there is a $c \in \mathcal{X}$ such that $(c, b) \in$ att. We write defended$(\mathcal{X})$ for the set of arguments that are defended by $\mathcal{X}$. In Table 4 we list several types of A-extensions.

In Fig. 15 we see the logical connections between the different argumentation semantics, all of which have been shown in Dung (1995). Dung also showed that, except for stable extensions, extensions of all other types always exist (they may be empty, though) and the grounded extension consists exactly of those arguments that are contained in every complete extension. Stable extensions often do not exist in frameworks that give rise to odd cycles: consider, for instance, $\mathcal{AF} = \langle \{a\}, \{(a, a)\} \rangle$ in which neither $\emptyset$ nor $\{a\}$ is stable. In Fig. 16 we find an argumentation framework with five arguments. Depicted are some of its extensions.

8 ASPIC$^+$

We now move from abstract to *structured argumentation.*[33] This means that our arguments will now get a logical form and attacks will be defined in terms of logical relations between arguments. ASPIC$^+$ is one of the most prominent and most expressive frameworks in formal argumentation (Modgil & Prakken, 2013). Arguments are generated on the basis of the inference rules and assumptions in a given knowledge base $\mathcal{K}$ of the form $\langle \mathcal{A}_s, \mathcal{A}_d, \mathcal{R}_s, \mathcal{R}_d, \leq \rangle$ (see Definition 5.1). We let $\mathsf{Arg}_{\mathcal{K}}$ denote the set of all arguments induced by $\mathcal{K}$. In the context of ASPIC$^+$ we frequently find three types of attacks. In order to define them, we need to enhance knowledge bases with two elements. (a) A *contrariness relation* $^{\overline{}}$ associates formulas with a set of contraries, for example, $\overline{A} = \{\neg A\}$ or $\overline{A} = \{B \mid B \rightarrow \neg A \in \mathcal{R}_s\}$. (b) A *naming function* name allows us to refer to defeasible rules $r \in \mathcal{R}_d$ in the object language by name(r). So our knowledge bases will have the extended form $\mathcal{K} = \langle \mathcal{A}_s, \mathcal{A}_d, \mathcal{R}_s, \mathcal{R}_d, \leq, ^{\overline{}}, \mathrm{name} \rangle$.

Definition 8.1. Where $a, b \in \mathsf{Arg}_{\mathcal{K}}$, we define three types of attacks:

Rebut: a rebuts b in $b' \in \mathsf{Sub}(b)$ iff b' is of the form $b_1, \ldots, b_n \Rightarrow B$ and $\mathsf{Con}(a) \in \overline{B}$.

Undercut: a undercuts b in $b' \in \mathsf{Sub}(b)$ iff b' is of the form $b_1, \ldots, b_n \Rightarrow B$ where the top rule is $r \in \mathcal{R}_d$ and $\mathsf{Con}(a) = \overline{\mathrm{name}(r)}$.

Undermining: a undermines b in a defeasible assumption $B \in \mathcal{A}_d$ in case $\mathsf{Con}(a) \in \overline{B}$ and $\langle B \rangle \in \mathsf{Sub}(b)$.

An informal example of a rebut is one where Peter calls upon weather report 1 to argue that it will rain, while Anne counters by calling upon weather report 2 that predicts the opposite. An undercut may occur in a case of specificity: while Peter argues that Tweety can fly based on the fact that Tweety is a bird and birds usually fly, Anne counters that the default "Birds fly" is not applicable to Tweety since Tweety is a penguin and, as such, Tweety is exceptional to "Birds fly." Undermining happens if Anne argues against one of Peter's basic (defeasible) assumptions: Peter may argue that they should go and buy groceries, since the shop is open, when Anne reminds him of the fact that it is a public holiday and therefore shops are closed.

Whenever the defeasible elements of a knowledge base differ in strength, not every attack may be successful. In the context of ASPIC$^+$ we refer to successful attacks as *defeats*. There are various ways defeats can be defined, but they are all based on a lifting of $\leq$ to the level of arguments (recall that

---

[33] For an overview on the state of the art in structured argumentation see Arieli et al. (2021a).

$\leq$ $\subseteq$ Def($\mathcal{K}$)$\times$Def($\mathcal{K}$) orders the defeasible elements of our knowledge base $\mathcal{K}$). We present here the most common approach, called *weakest link*. To simplify things, we also suppose that $\leq$ is a total preorder (so it is reflexive, transitive and total). Where $\mathcal{D}_1, \mathcal{D}_2 \subseteq$ Def($\mathcal{K}$), we let $\mathcal{D}_1 \leq \mathcal{D}_2$ if there is a $d_1 \in \mathcal{D}_1$ such that for all $d_2 \in \mathcal{D}_2$, $d_1 \leq d_2$. Then, for two arguments $a, b \in$ Arg$_{\mathcal{K}}$, we let $a \leq b$ iff Def(a) $\leq$ Def(b).[34] We now say that *a defeats b* iff *a* attacks *b* (Definition 8.1) and (i) $b \leq a$ or (ii) the attack is an undercut.[35]

In the special case in which no preference order $\leq$ is specified in the knowledge base, *a* defeats *b* iff *a* attacks *b*. If the naming function is left unspecified in $\mathcal{K}$, undercuts are omitted.

Definition 8.2. Let $\mathcal{K} = \langle \mathcal{A}_d, \mathcal{A}_s, \mathcal{R}_d, \mathcal{R}_s, \leq, \bar{\ }, \text{name} \rangle$ be a knowledge base. $\mathcal{AF}_{\mathcal{K}} = \langle \text{Arg}_{\mathcal{K}}, \rightsquigarrow \rangle$ is an *ASPIC$^+$-based argumentation framework*, where for $a, b \in$ Arg$_{\mathcal{K}}$, $a \rightsquigarrow b$ iff *a* defeats *b*.

A-extensions obtained via the different argumentation semantics s (grounded, preferred, stable, etc.) in Definition 7.1 can serve as a basis for the three types of consequences, defined exactly as in Definition 5.2 and Table 3 in Section 5.1.

Example 23. We consider the knowledge base $\mathcal{K} = \langle \mathcal{A}_s, \mathcal{A}_d, \mathcal{R}_s, \mathcal{R}_d, \leq, \bar{\ }, \text{name} \rangle$, where $\mathcal{A}_s = \{p\}$, $\mathcal{A}_d = \{q\}$, $\mathcal{R}_s = \{\neg q \rightarrow u, v \rightarrow u\}$,

$$\mathcal{R}_d = \{r_1 : p \Rightarrow^7 \neg t, p \Rightarrow^3 s, s \Rightarrow^5 \neg q, q \Rightarrow^3 t, t \Rightarrow^2 v, r_2 : p \Rightarrow^9 t\},$$

$\overline{\text{name}(r_1)} = \{s\}$, and $\overline{\text{name}(r_2)} = \{t\}$. In order to define $\leq$ we "rank" the members of Def($\mathcal{K}$) as indicated in the superscripts of the defaults and let the rank of the defeasible assumption q be 3. Where $d_1, d_2 \in$ Def($\mathcal{K}$), we then let $d_1 \leq d_2$ iff $\text{rank}(d_1) \leq \text{rank}(d_2)$.

The arguments induced by $\mathcal{K}$ and the corresponding argumentation framework are depicted in Fig. 17. We note that a_1 is defeated by b_1 despite the fact that b_1 is weaker than a_1 (by comparing their weakest links) since the attack is an undercut, for which the strength of the attacker plays no role. The defeat between b_2 and c_0 is symmetric. We have an undermine attack from b_2 to c_0, while the other way around it is a rebuttal. In Table 5 we list the different argumentation extensions and the corresponding consequence relations.

---

[34] See Beirlaen et al. (2018) for an overview of different accounts of argument strength.

[35] Our definition follows Modgil and Prakken (p. 364, 2013), according to whom preferences do not matter for defeats based on undercuts. See also Baroni et al. (2001) for more discussion.

Table 5 The various extensions and consequences for Example 23.

	Complete	Grounded	Preferred	Stable
	$\mathcal{X}_0 = \{a_0, b_1\}$	$\mathcal{X}_0$		
	$\mathcal{X}_1 = \{a_0, b_1, b_2, b_3\}$		$\mathcal{X}_1$	
	$\mathcal{X}_2 = \{a_0, b_1, c_0, c_1, c_2, c_3\}$		$\mathcal{X}_2$	$\mathcal{X}_2$
$\vdash_{\cap\mathsf{PExt}}$	$\{p, s\}$	$\{p, s\}$	$\{p, s, u\}$	$\{p, q, u, s, t, v\}$
$\vdash_{\cap\mathsf{AExt}}$	$\{p, s\}$	$\{p, s\}$	$\{p, s\}$	$\{p, q, u, s, t, v\}$
$\vdash_{\cup\mathsf{Ext}}$	$\mathcal{S} = \{p, q, \neg q, t, s, \neg s, u, v\}$	$\{p, s\}$	$\mathcal{S}$	$\{p, q, u, s, t, v\}$

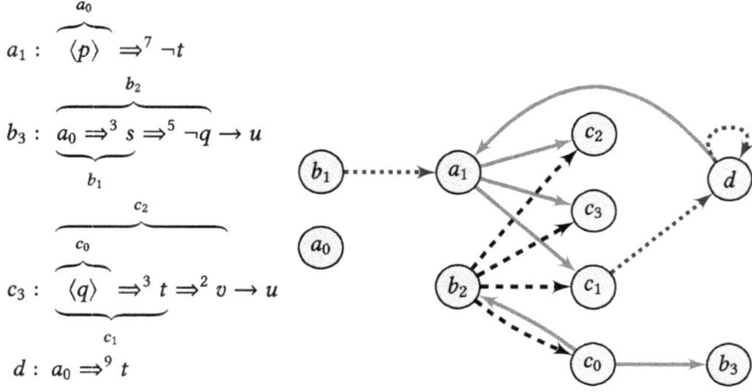

Figure 17 The argumentation framework for Example 23. Solid arrows represent rebuttals, dashed arrows undermining, and dotted arrows undercuts.

Example 24. Consider the knowledge base $\mathcal{K} = \langle \mathcal{A}_s, \mathcal{R}_{\mathsf{CL}}, \mathcal{R}_d \rangle$ (without preferences), where $\mathcal{R}_d = \{p \Rightarrow q, \; p \Rightarrow s, \; p \Rightarrow \neg(q \wedge s)\}$ and $\mathcal{A}_s = \{p\}$. We have, for instance, the following arguments:

$a_1 =$	$\langle p \rangle \Rightarrow q$		$a_4 =$	$a_1, a_2 \to q \wedge s$
$a_2 =$	$\langle p \rangle \Rightarrow s$		$a_5 =$	$a_1, a_3 \to \neg s$
$a_3 =$	$\langle p \rangle \Rightarrow \neg(q \wedge s)$		$a_6 =$	$a_2, a_3 \to \neg q$

The reader may be puzzled by on odd restriction in Definition 8.1, namely, when attacking an argument in which inference rules have been applied, only attacks in the heads of defeasible rules are allowed. Why did we not simply define: a attacks b iff $\vdash_{\mathsf{CL}} \mathrm{Con}(a) \equiv \neg\mathrm{Con}(b)$? Figure 18 features the resulting argumentation framework. We observe that there is now a preferred (and stable) extension with the conclusions p, s and $\neg(p \wedge s)$. This may be considered as unwanted if we want our A-extensions to represent rational and therefore consistent stances of debaters.

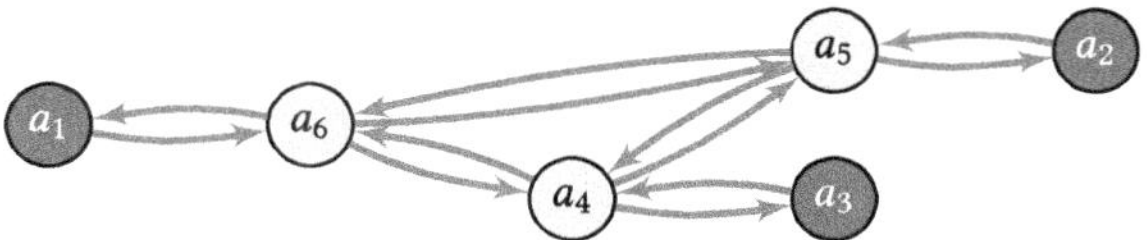

Figure 18 Example 24 with the inconsistent preferred and stable extension $\{a_1, a_2, a_3\}$.

Problems such as the one highlighted in our previous example show the need for a set of design desiderata, or *rationality postulates*, that argumentation-based NMLs should fulfill. The following have become standard in the literature (Caminada & Amgoud, 2007). Given a standard of consistency, a knowledge base $\mathcal{K} = \langle \mathcal{A}_s, \mathcal{A}_d, \mathcal{R}_s, \mathcal{R}_d, \leq, \bar{}, \text{name} \rangle$, an argumentation semantics, an A-extension $\mathcal{X}$ based on it, and the argumentation framework $\langle \text{Arg}_{\mathcal{K}}, \leadsto \rangle$, we define

Direct consistency. For all $a, b \in \mathcal{X}$, $\{\text{Con}(a), \text{Con}(b)\}$ is consistent.

Indirect consistency. $\text{Con}[\mathcal{X}]$ is consistent.

Strict closure. Where $a_1, \ldots, a_n \in \mathcal{X}$ and $\text{Con}(a_1), \ldots, \text{Con}(a_n) \to A \in \mathcal{R}_s$, also $a_1, \ldots, a_n \to A \in \mathcal{X}$.

In Example 24 we have seen that allowing in our simple framework for "unrestricted" rebut results in a violation of indirect consistency and strict closure,[36] unlike the unrestricted rebut of Definition 8.1.

Another rationality property has to do with syntactic relevance. We give an example to motivate it.

Example 25. Consider the knowledge base $\mathcal{K}_1 = \langle \mathcal{A}_s, \mathcal{R}_{\text{CL}}, \mathcal{R}_d^1, \bar{} \rangle$, where $\mathcal{A}_s = \{t\}$, $\mathcal{R}_d^1 = \{t \Rightarrow s\}$, and $\overline{A} = \{B \mid \vdash_{\text{CL}} A \equiv \neg B\}$. Clearly, the grounded extension will contain the argument $a : \langle t \rangle \Rightarrow s$ and therefore both t and s follow with $\vdash_{\cap \text{AExt}}$ and $\vdash_{\cap \text{PExt}}$.

We now extend our knowledge base to $\mathcal{K}_2 = \langle \mathcal{A}_s^2, \mathcal{R}_{\text{CL}}, \mathcal{R}_d^2, \bar{} \rangle$, where $\mathcal{A}_s^2 = \{t, p\}$ and $\mathcal{R}_d^2 = \{p \Rightarrow q, p \Rightarrow \neg q, t \Rightarrow s\}$. Figure 19 shows a relevant excerpt of the argumentation framework for $\mathcal{K}_2$. Argument c is obtained by the rule $q, \neg q \to \neg s$ that holds due to the classical explosion principle.

Note that we only added information to $\mathcal{K}_1$ that is syntactically irrelevant to both t and s. Nevertheless, the grounded extension of $\mathcal{K}_2$ only consists of arguments that do not involve defeasible rules (such as b_0 or $b_0' = b_0 \to p \vee q$). Therefore, a is not part of it. As a consequence, $\vdash_{\cap \text{PExt}}$ and $\vdash_{\cap \text{AExt}}$ will deliver only classical consequences of $\{p, t\}$, but not anymore s.

---

[36] Standard ASPIC$^+$ therefore disallows rebuttals in heads of strict rules. For alternative approaches to ASPIC$^+$ that lift this restriction see Caminada et al. (2014), and Heyninck and Straßer (2019).

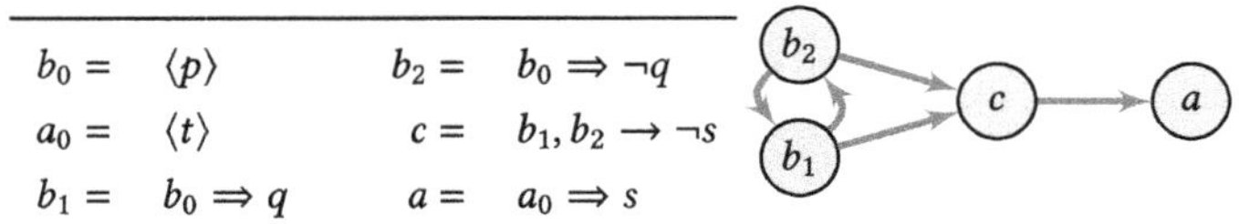

Figure 19 Excerpt of the argumentation framework of Example 25.

The rationality property *noninterference* (Caminada et al., 2012) expresses, informally, that adding syntactically irrelevant information to a knowledge base should not lead to the loss of consequences. Our example shows that this property does not hold for grounded extensions.

9 Logic-Based Argumentation

Another line of research within structured argumentation is logic-based (or deductive) argumentation. In what follows we will show that it has close connections to temperate accumulation and that, just as in the case of ASPIC$^+$, ill-conceived combinations of attack forms and argumentation semantics can lead to undesired metatheoretic behavior.

Logic-based argumentation has been proposed, for instance, in Arieli and Straßer (2015) and Besnard and Hunter (2001). Our presentation follows the approach in Arieli et al. (2023), but simplifies it in some respects.[37] Knowledge bases have the form $\mathcal{K} = \langle \mathcal{A}_d, \mathcal{A}_s, \mathcal{R}_\mathsf{L} \rangle$, where the set of strict rules $\mathcal{R}_\mathsf{L}$ is induced by an underlying Tarski logic L.

In Definition 5.1, arguments are proof trees. In the context of knowledge bases without defeasible rules and for which the strict rules are induced by a base logic L, arguments are often modeled more abstractly simply as premise-conclusion pairs.

Definition 9.1. Where $\mathcal{K} = \langle \mathcal{A}_s, \mathcal{A}_d, \mathcal{R}_\mathsf{L} \rangle$, we let $\mathsf{Arg}_\mathcal{K} = \{(\mathcal{S}, A) \mid \mathcal{S} \subseteq \mathcal{A}_s \cup \mathcal{A}_d$ is finite and $\mathcal{S} \vdash_\mathsf{L} A\}$. Where $a = (\mathcal{S}, A)$ is an argument in $\mathsf{Arg}_\mathcal{K}$, $\mathsf{Con}(a) = A$ and $\mathsf{Def}(a) = \mathcal{A}_d(a)$. Where $\mathcal{A} \subseteq \mathcal{A}_d$, $\mathsf{Arg}_\mathcal{K}(\mathcal{A}) = \{a \in \mathsf{Arg}_\mathcal{K} \mid \mathsf{Def}(a) \subseteq \mathcal{A}\}$.

Attacks between arguments can be defined in various ways. Some examples are given in Table 6.[38]

---

[37] There are some differences between these accounts; e.g., in Besnard and Hunter (2001) the premise set of an argument is supposed to be minimal and consistent, strict assumptions are not considered, and the approach is based on classical logic, whereas Arieli and Straßer (2015) allow for any Tarski base logic. Like Arieli et al. (2023) we here include defeasible assumptions, but we simplify the presentation in that we don't rely on an underlying sequent calculus.

[38] The terminology for attack forms in logical argumentation is incoherent with the one used in ASPIC$^+$. In order to not confuse the reader familiar with logical argumentation, we don't unify the terminology in this section.

Table 6 Attack types in logic-based argumentation.

Type	Attacker	Attacked	Conditions
Defeat	$\langle \mathcal{A}_1, \neg \wedge \mathcal{A}_2 \rangle$	$\langle \mathcal{A}_2 \cup \mathcal{A}_2', C \rangle$	$\mathcal{A}_2 \neq \emptyset, \mathcal{A}_2 \subseteq \mathcal{A}_d$
DirDefeat	$\langle \mathcal{A}_1, \neg A \rangle$	$\langle \mathcal{A}_2 \cup \{A\}, C \rangle$	$A \in \mathcal{A}_d$
ConDefeat	$\langle \mathcal{A}_1, \neg \wedge (\mathcal{A}_2 \setminus \mathcal{A}_s) \rangle$	$\langle \mathcal{A}_2, C \rangle$	$\mathcal{A}_1 \subseteq \mathcal{A}_s, \mathcal{A}_2 \cap \mathcal{A}_d \neq \emptyset$

Definition 9.2. Let α be a nonempty set of attack types based on the knowledge base $\mathcal{K} = \langle \mathcal{A}_s, \mathcal{A}_d, \mathcal{R}_L \rangle$ from Table 6, arguments be defined as in Definition 9.1, and att $\subseteq$ $\mathrm{Arg}_\mathcal{K} \times \mathrm{Arg}_\mathcal{K}$ be defined by $(a, b) \in$ att iff a attacks b in view of an attack type in α. We let $\mathcal{AF}_\alpha(\mathcal{K}) = \langle \arg(\mathcal{K}), \mathrm{att} \rangle$ be the argumentation framework induced by $\mathcal{K}$ and α. For a given argumentation semantics s $\in$ {grounded, preferred, stable} (see Table 4) and an attack type α, we denote the corresponding set of A-extensions by $\mathrm{AExt}_{s,\alpha}(\mathcal{K})$ and the underlying nonmonotonic consequences analogous to Table 3. For instance,

- $\mathcal{K} \vdash^{s,\alpha}_{\cap \mathrm{PExt}} A$ iff in every s-extension $\mathcal{X} \in \mathrm{AExt}_{s,\alpha}(\mathcal{K})$ there is an argument $\langle \mathcal{S}, A \rangle$.

Let in the following AttDir $= \{\{\mathrm{DirDefeat}\}, \{\mathrm{DirDefeat}, \mathrm{ConDefeat}\}\}$, and AttSet $= \{\{\mathrm{Defeat}\}, \{\mathrm{Defeat}, \mathrm{ConDefeat}\}\}$.

Example 26. We let $\mathcal{K} = \langle \mathcal{A}_s, \mathcal{A}_d, \mathcal{R}_{\mathsf{CL}} \rangle$, where $\mathcal{A}_s = \{s\}$ and $\mathcal{A}_d = \{p \wedge u, \neg p \wedge u, q, \neg s\}$. In Fig. 20 we see (a fragment of) the argumentation framework $\mathcal{AF}_\alpha(\mathcal{K})$. We note that for $\alpha \in$ AttSet the grounded extension concludes q, but not for $\alpha = \{\mathrm{DirDefeat}\}$. The latter is counterintuitive since q is syntactically unrelated to the conflicts in $p \wedge u$ and $\neg p \wedge u$ and the conflict in s and $\neg s$. On the right (center and bottom) we see the two stable resp. preferred extensions for this example. In both cases we can conclude q and the floating conclusion u.

We also note a correspondence between the argumentative extensions and selections based on maxicon sets of $\mathcal{K}$ (see Section 5.2.3). We have $\mathrm{maxcon}(\mathcal{K}) = \{\{p \wedge u, q\}, \{\neg p \wedge u, q\}\}$ and $\bigcap \mathrm{maxcon}(\mathcal{K}) = \{q\}$. So, in our example, the grounded semantics induces the same consequence relations $\vdash^{\mathrm{grounded},\alpha}_{\cap \mathrm{AExt}}$ and $\vdash^{\mathrm{grounded},\alpha}_{\cap \mathrm{PExt}}$ as $\vdash^{\mathrm{tem}}_{\cap \mathrm{AExt}}$ for $\alpha \in$ AttSet, while the stable and preferred semantics (s $\in$ {stable, preferred}) induce the same consequence relations $\vdash^{s,\alpha}_{\cap \mathrm{Ext}}$ as $\vdash^{\mathrm{tem}}_{\cap \mathrm{PExt}}$ for any $\alpha \in$ AttDir (recall Section 5.2.3 and Corollary 5.1). This is not coincidental, as we see with Theorem 9.1.

In fact, there is a close relation between logic-based argumentation and reasoning based on temperate accumulation.[39]

---

[39] For an overview on relations between methods based on maxicon sets and structured argumentation see Arieli et al. (2019).

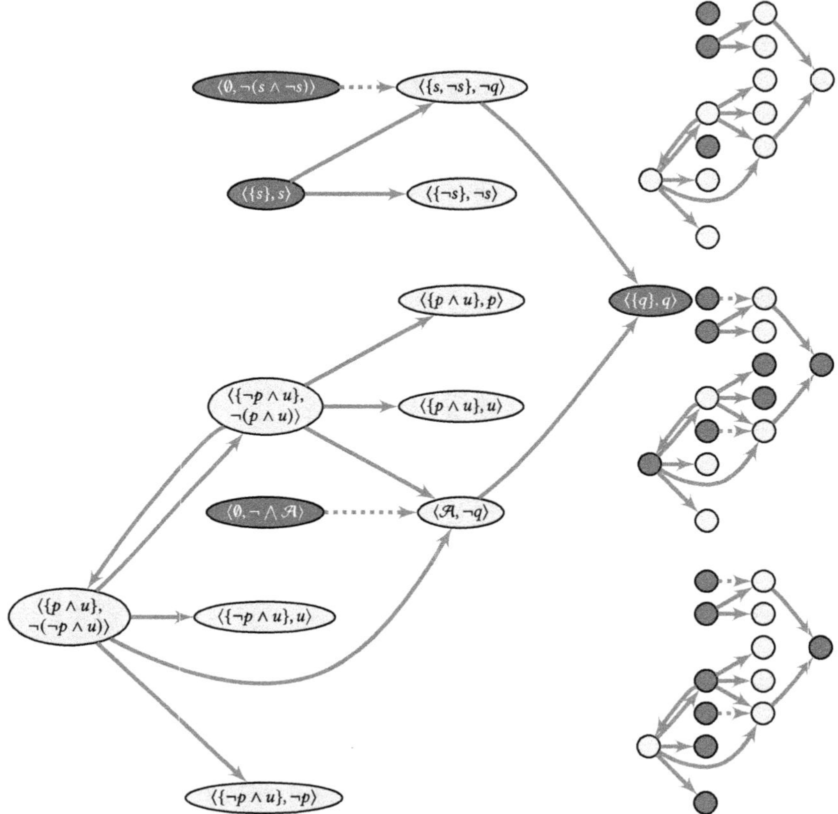

Figure 20 Example 26. Left: We let $\mathcal{A} = \{p \wedge u, \neg p \wedge u\}$. The black nodes represent the grounded extension. Dashed arrows correspond to those Defeats and ConDefeats that are not DirDefeats, while solid arrows are (also) DirDefeats. Right top: The grounded extension for $\alpha = \{\mathsf{DirDefeat}\}$. Right center and bottom: the two stable resp. preferred extensions.

Theorem 9.1 (Arieli et al., 2021b). *Let* $\mathcal{K} = \langle \mathcal{A}_s, \mathcal{A}_d, \mathcal{R}_\mathsf{L} \rangle$ *be a knowledge base. We have:*

1. $\mathsf{AExt}_{\mathsf{s},\alpha}(\mathcal{K}) = \{\mathsf{Arg}_\mathcal{K}(\mathcal{T}) \mid \mathcal{T} \in \mathsf{maxcon}(\mathcal{K})\}$ *and* $\vdash^{\mathsf{tem}}_{\cap\mathsf{PExt}} = \vdash^{\mathsf{s},\alpha}_{\cap\mathsf{PExt}}$, *for* $\alpha \in \mathsf{AttDir}$ *and* $\mathsf{s} \in \{\mathsf{stable}, \mathsf{preferred}\}$.
2. $\mathsf{AExt}_{\mathsf{s},\alpha}(\mathcal{K}) = \mathsf{Arg}_\mathcal{K}(\cap \mathsf{maxcon}(\mathcal{K}))$ *and* $\vdash^{\mathsf{tem}}_{\cap\mathsf{AExt}} = \vdash^{\mathsf{s},\alpha}_{\cap\mathsf{AExt}} = \vdash^{\mathsf{s},\alpha}_{\cap\mathsf{PExt}}$, *for* $\alpha \in \mathsf{AttSet}$ *and* $\mathsf{s} = \mathsf{grounded}$.

While Theorem 9.1 identifies well-behaved combinations of attack types and argumentation semantics, the following two examples show that one has to be careful in order to avoid counter-intuitive behavior. (Recall similar problems in the context of ASPIC$^+$ in Section 8.)

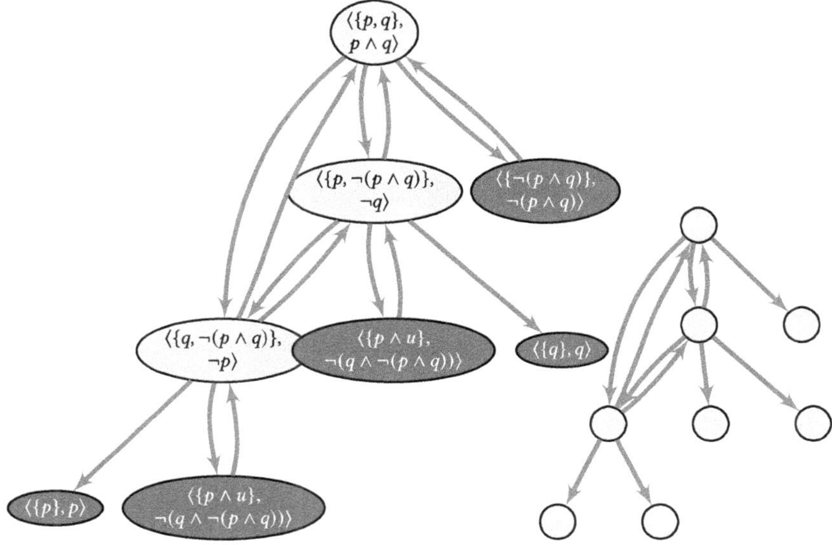

Figure 21 Example 27. Left: $\alpha \in$ AttSet. Right: $\alpha \in$ AttDir.

Example 27. We consider the knowledge base

$$\mathcal{K} = \langle \mathcal{A}_s : \emptyset, \ \mathcal{A}_d : \{p, q, \neg(p \wedge q)\}, \ \mathcal{R}_{\mathsf{CL}} \rangle.$$

In Fig. 21 we see that with $\alpha \in$ AttSet we obtain a problematic stable and preferred extension $\mathcal{X}$ featuring the inconsistent set of conclusions $\{p, q, \neg(p \wedge q)\}$ violating the indirect consistency property (see Section 8). On the right we find the argumentation framework with $\alpha \in$ AttDir where $\mathcal{X}$ is not anymore preferred (and therefore also not stable).

Selected Further Readings

An excellent overview on the state of the art in formal argumentation is provided by the handbook series *Handbook of Formal Argumentation* (Baroni et al. 2018) and *Handbook of Formal Argumentation* (Gabbay et al. 2021). Volume 5 of *Argument & Computation* contains several tutorials on central approaches, such as Modgil and Prakken (2014), and Toni (2014).

Already in the seminal Dung (1995) several embeddings of NMLs in abstract argumentation were provided, including default logic. A recent overview on structured argumentation can be found in Arieli et al., (2021a). Links to default logic with a special emphasis on preferences are established in, for example, Liao et al. (2018); Straßer and Pardo (2021), and Young et al. (2016), connections to maxicon sets are numerous (Arieli et al., 2019; Cayrol,

1995; Heyninck & Straßer, 2021b; Vesic, 2013), and links to adaptive logics are to be found in Borg (2020), Heyninck and Straßer (2016), and Straßer and Seselja (2010), and to logic programming in Caminada and Schulz (2017); Heyninck and Arieli (2019), and Schulz and Toni (2016). Nonmonotonic reasoning properties of several systems of structured argumentation are studied in Borg and Straßer (2018); Čyras and Toni (2015); Heyninck and Straßer (2021a), and Li et al. (2018). Probabilistic approaches can be found, for instance, in Haenni (2009); Hunter and Thimm (2017), and Straßer and Michajlova (2023). The *Handbook of Formal Argumentation* offers an excellent overview and detailed surveys of central topics in the area (see *Handbook of Formal Argumentation*, 2021).

PART III CONSISTENTLY ACCUMULATING DEFEASIBLE INFORMATION

10 Consistent Accumulation: General Setting

In this section we study in a systematic way the two variants of the consistent accumulation method: greedy and temperate accumulation. First, in Section 10.1 we present the algorithms GREEDYACC and TEMACC in the settings of knowledge bases in the general form of Section 4 (including preferences). Then, in Section 10.2 we present alternative characterizations in terms of fixed points. In Section 10.3 we study metatheoretic properties of extensions and nonmonotonic consequences. While this section provides a general perspective, we dive into particularities and concrete systems in Sections 11 and 12.

10.1 Greedy and Temperate Accumulation

We now consider knowledge bases with all components

$$\mathcal{K} = \langle \mathcal{A}_s, \mathcal{A}_d, \mathcal{R}_s, \mathcal{R}_d, \mathcal{R}_m, \leq \rangle$$

as introduced in Section 4, with the only restriction that the set of defeasible elements in $\mathcal{K}$, $\mathrm{Def}(\mathcal{K})(= \mathcal{A}_d \cup \mathcal{R}_d)$, is finite. As compared to Part I, we slightly generalize our two accumulation methods, greedy and temperate accumulation, by taking into account preferences among elements in $\mathrm{Def}(\mathcal{K})$. For this, we suppose there to be a reflexive and transitive order $\leq$ on $\mathrm{Def}(\mathcal{K})$.

In the following we suppose for any given nmL a formal language $\mathcal{L}$, a class of associated knowledge bases $\mathbf{K}_{\mathrm{nmL}}$, a notion of what it means that a set of sentences $\mathcal{S} \subseteq \mathrm{sent}_{\mathcal{L}}$ is (in)consistent, for each $\mathcal{K} \in \mathbf{K}_{\mathrm{nmL}}$ a set $\mathrm{Arg}_{\mathcal{K}}$ of arguments based on $\mathcal{K}$, and for each $a \in \mathrm{Arg}_{\mathcal{K}}$ a notion $\mathrm{Con}(a)$ of conclusion and $\mathrm{Def}(a)$ of the defeasible part of a (e.g., Definitions 5.1, 9.1 and 11.3).

Moreover, where $\mathcal{D} \subseteq \mathrm{Def}(\mathcal{K})$, $\mathrm{Arg}_{\mathcal{K}}(\mathcal{D}) =_{\mathrm{df}} \{a \in \mathrm{Arg}_{\mathcal{K}} \mid \mathrm{Def}(a) \subseteq \mathcal{D}\}$. Many of the results presented in this part of the Element (e.g., the metatheoretic insights in Sections 10.3 and 11.1) will not rely on a specific underlying notion of argument, but apply to many concrete logics from the literature (such as the ones presented in Sections 11.3.1 and 11.3.2).

We first discuss *greedy accumulation*. As explained in Section 5.2, the main idea behind the algorithm is to build a D-extension by accumulating (1) triggered and (2) consistent defeasible information $d \in \mathrm{Def}(\mathcal{K})$. Since we now consider prioritized defeasible information, we add the requirement (3) that d is $\leq$-maximal with properties (1) and (2). Let us make this precise.

Definition 10.1. For a defeasible rule $r = A_1, \ldots, A_n \Rightarrow B \in \mathcal{R}_d$, we let $\mathrm{Body}(r) =_{\mathrm{df}} \{A_1, \ldots, A_n\}$ and $\mathrm{Con}(r) =_{\mathrm{df}} B$. Similarly, for any $A \in \mathcal{A}_d$, we let $\mathrm{Body}(A) =_{\mathrm{df}} \emptyset$ and $\mathrm{Con}(A) =_{\mathrm{df}} A$. Then, where $\mathcal{D} \subseteq \mathrm{Def}(\mathcal{K})$ and $d \in \mathrm{Def}(\mathcal{K})$, we say that

- d is *triggered by* $\mathcal{D}$ iff $\mathrm{Body}(d) \subseteq \mathrm{Con}[\mathrm{Arg}_{\mathcal{K}}(\mathcal{D})]$.[40]
- d is *consistent with* $\mathcal{D}$ iff $\mathrm{Con}[\mathrm{Arg}_{\mathcal{K}}(\mathcal{D} \cup \{d\})]$ is consistent.
- $d \in \max_{\leq}(\mathcal{D})$ iff $d \in \mathcal{D}$ and for all $d' \in \mathcal{D}$, $d \not< d'$.

We write $\mathrm{Cons}_{\mathcal{K}}(\mathcal{D})$ for all the elements in $\mathrm{Def}(\mathcal{K})$ that are consistent with $\mathcal{D}$, $\mathrm{Trig}_{\mathcal{K}}(\mathcal{D})$ for all elements in $\mathrm{Def}(\mathcal{K})$ triggered by $\mathcal{D}$, and $\mathrm{Trig}_{\mathcal{K}}^{\top}(\mathcal{D})$ for all the elements in $\mathrm{Cons}_{\mathcal{K}}(\mathcal{D})$ that are triggered by $\mathcal{D}$.

Note that our definition implies that defeasible assumptions are automatically triggered. Algorithm GREEDYACC generates D-extensions for the greedy accumulation method. The A- resp. the P-extension associated with a D-extension $\mathcal{D}$ is defined by $\mathrm{Arg}_{\mathcal{K}}(\mathcal{D})$ resp. by $\mathrm{Con}[\mathrm{Arg}_{\mathcal{K}}(\mathcal{D})]$. We write $\mathrm{AExt}_{\mathrm{gr}}(\mathcal{K})$ resp. $\mathrm{PExt}_{\mathrm{gr}}(\mathcal{K})$ for the set of A-resp. P-extensions for $\mathcal{K}$. In this way we obtain the consequence relations $\vdash^{\mathrm{gr}}_{\cap\mathrm{AExt}}, \vdash^{\mathrm{gr}}_{\cap\mathrm{PExt}}$ and $\vdash^{\mathrm{gr}}_{\cup\mathrm{Ext}}$ (see Table 3), where the superscript indicates that the underlying extensions have been obtained via greedy accumulation.

Example 28 (The order puzzle, Example 11 cont.). We recall the knowledge base $\mathcal{K}_{\leq}$ containing the preference order: $(p \Rightarrow q) < (p \Rightarrow r) < (q \Rightarrow \neg r)$ (supposing reflexivity and transitivity). Our algorithm GREEDYACC has exactly one run in which in the first round of the loop $p \Rightarrow r$ is added to $\mathrm{Def}^{\star}$, since it is the $\leq$-preferred one among the two triggered and consistent defaults $p \Rightarrow r$

---

[40] We again use the notation with edgy brackets to denote the lifting of a function to sets of elements of its domain. E.g., where $\mathcal{A}$ is a set of arguments, $\mathrm{Con}[\mathcal{A}] = \{\mathrm{Con}(a) \mid a \in \mathcal{A}\}$.

and $p \Rightarrow q$. In the second round only $p \Rightarrow q$ is triggered and consistent. So we end up with $\mathrm{Def}^\star = \{p \Rightarrow r, p \Rightarrow q\}$ and GREEDYACC terminates since the remaining default $q \Rightarrow \neg r$ is inconsistent with the set of the already selected ones. This implies that $\mathcal{K}_\leq \vdash q$ for all $\vdash \in \{\vdash^{gr}_{\cap\mathrm{PExt}}, \vdash^{gr}_{\cap\mathrm{AExt}}, \vdash^{gr}_{\cup\mathrm{Ext}}\}$.

Algorithm 3 Greedy accumulation (general version)

1: **procedure** GREEDYACC($\mathcal{K}$) $\qquad\qquad$ ▷ where $\mathcal{K} = \langle \mathcal{A}_s, \mathcal{A}_d, \mathcal{R}_s, \mathcal{R}_d, \mathcal{R}_m, \leq \rangle$

2: $\qquad \mathrm{Def}^\star \leftarrow \emptyset$ $\qquad\qquad\qquad\qquad\qquad\qquad\qquad\qquad$ ▷ init D-extension

3: $\qquad$ **while** $\mathrm{Trig}^\top_\mathcal{K}(\mathrm{Def}^\star) \setminus \mathrm{Def}^\star \neq \emptyset$ **do**

4: $\qquad\qquad$ (nondeterministically) choose $d \in \max_\leq(\mathrm{Trig}^\top_\mathcal{K}(\mathrm{Def}^\star) \setminus \mathrm{Def}^\star)$

5: $\qquad\qquad \mathrm{Def}^\star \leftarrow \mathrm{Def}^\star \cup \{d\}$ $\qquad\qquad\qquad\qquad\qquad$ ▷ update D-extension

6: $\qquad$ **end while** $\qquad\qquad$ ▷ no more triggered and consistent defaults

7: $\qquad$ **return** $\mathrm{Def}^\star$ $\qquad\qquad\qquad\qquad\qquad\qquad$ ▷ return D-extension

8: **end procedure**

We now move to *temperate accumulation* which is characterized by the algorithm TEMACC. Recall that the main difference from greedy accumulation is that, when building D-extensions, temperate accumulation also considers non-triggered defaults that are consistent with the already accumulated defeasible elements. The set of D-, A-, and P-extension of $\mathcal{K}$ (denoted by $\mathrm{DExt}_{tem}(\mathcal{K})$, $\mathrm{AExt}_{tem}(\mathcal{K})$, and $\mathrm{PExt}_{tem}(\mathcal{K})$) and the consequence relations $\vdash^{tem}_{\cap\mathrm{AExt}}, \vdash^{tem}_{\cap\mathrm{PExt}}$, and $\vdash^{tem}_{\cup\mathrm{Ext}}$ are defined in analogy to the greedy case.

Algorithm 4 Temperate accumulation (general version)

1: **procedure** TEMACC($\mathcal{K}$) $\qquad\qquad$ ▷ where $\mathcal{K} = \langle \mathcal{A}_s, \mathcal{A}_d, \mathcal{R}_s, \mathcal{R}_d, \mathcal{R}_m, \leq \rangle$

2: $\qquad \mathrm{Def}^\star \leftarrow \emptyset$ $\qquad\qquad\qquad\qquad\qquad\qquad\qquad\qquad$ ▷ init D-extension

3: $\qquad$ **while** $\mathrm{Cons}_\mathcal{K}(\mathrm{Def}^\star) \setminus \mathrm{Def}^\star \neq \emptyset$ **do**

4: $\qquad\qquad$ (nondeterministically) choose $d \in \max_\leq(\mathrm{Cons}_\mathcal{K}(\mathrm{Def}^\star) \setminus \mathrm{Def}^\star)$

5: $\qquad\qquad \mathrm{Def}^\star \leftarrow \mathrm{Def}^\star \cup \{d\}$ $\qquad\qquad\qquad\qquad\qquad$ ▷ update D-extension

6: $\qquad$ **end while** $\qquad\qquad\qquad\qquad$ ▷ no more consistent defaults

7: $\qquad$ **return** $\mathrm{Def}^\star$ $\qquad\qquad\qquad\qquad\qquad\qquad$ ▷ return D-extension

8: **end procedure**

Example 29 (Example 28 cont.). We now apply TEMACC to $\mathcal{K}_\leq$. There is again only one possible run: in the first round we choose (the nontriggered) $q \Rightarrow \neg r$ as it is preferred over the other two defaults. In the second round we choose $p \Rightarrow r$ as it is preferred over $p \Rightarrow q$. This is when TEMACC terminates since the only remaining default $p \Rightarrow q$ is not consistent with $\{p \Rightarrow r, q \Rightarrow \neg r\}$. This implies that $\mathcal{K}_\leq \nvdash q$ for all $\vdash \in \{\vdash^{tem}_{\cap\mathrm{PExt}}, \vdash^{tem}_{\cap\mathrm{AExt}}, \vdash^{tem}_{\cup\mathrm{Ext}}\}$.

This shows that unlike in the nonprioritized setting, for knowledge bases with preferences there may be D-extensions for temperate accumulation that do not correspond to D-extensions for greedy accumulation.

10.2 Accumulation and Fixed Points

In this section we consider alternative characterizations of our two accumulation methods. Instead of using iterative algorithms such as TEMACC and GREEDYACC, we now describe these reasoning styles, that is, the D-extension they characterize, as fixed points of specific operations $\Pi : \wp(\mathsf{Def}(\mathcal{K})) \to \wp(\mathsf{Def}(\mathcal{K}))$. The underlying idea is that the possible final products of the reasoning process of a rational agent can be characterized as equilibrium states based on the given knowledge base $\mathcal{K}$. In what follows, we only consider knowledge bases without preferences.

Lemma 10.1. *Let $\mathcal{K}$ be a knowledge base. Then, $\mathcal{D} \in \mathsf{maxcon}(\mathcal{K})$ iff $\mathcal{D} = \mathsf{Cons}_{\mathcal{K}}(\mathcal{D})$.*

Proof. Let $\mathcal{D} \in \mathsf{maxcon}(\mathcal{K})$. By Definition 5.3 (i) and Definition 10.1, $\mathcal{D} \subseteq \mathsf{Cons}_{\mathcal{K}}(\mathcal{D})$. If $d \in \mathsf{Cons}_{\mathcal{K}}(\mathcal{D})$, then $d \in \mathcal{D}$ by Definition 5.3 (ii), and so $\mathsf{Cons}_{\mathcal{K}}(\mathcal{D}) \subseteq \mathcal{D}$. The other direction is similar. $\qquad\square$

Theorem 10.1. *Let $\mathcal{K}$ be a knowledge base and $\mathcal{D} \subseteq \mathsf{Def}(\mathcal{K})$.*

1. *$\mathcal{D}$ is a D-extension generated by TEMACC iff $\mathcal{D} = \mathsf{Cons}_{\mathcal{K}}(\mathcal{D})$.*
2. *$\mathcal{D}$ is a D-extension generated by GREEDYACC iff $\mathcal{D} = \mathsf{Trig}_{\mathcal{K}}^{\top}(\mathcal{D})$.*

Proof. Item 1 follows with Proposition 5.1 and Lemma 10.1.

Consider Item 2. ($\Rightarrow$) Let $\mathcal{D} = \bigcup_{i=0}^{n} \mathcal{D}_i$ be produced by GREEDYACC such that $\mathsf{Def}^{\star} = \mathcal{D}_i$ in round i and $\{d_{i+1}\} = \mathcal{D}_{i+1} \setminus \mathcal{D}_i$ for $0 \leq i < n$.

"$\subseteq$". Let $d \in \mathcal{D}$. So $d = d_{i+1}$ for some $0 \leq i < n$. We have to show that $d \in \mathsf{Trig}_{\mathcal{K}}^{\top}(\mathcal{D})$. Since $d \in \mathsf{Trig}_{\mathcal{K}}^{\top}(\mathcal{D}_i)$, $d \in \mathsf{Trig}_{\mathcal{K}}(\mathcal{D})$. Assume for a contradiction that $d \notin \mathsf{Cons}_{\mathcal{K}}(\mathcal{D})$. So, there is a $\subseteq$-minimal $\mathcal{D}' \subseteq \mathcal{D}$ such that $\mathcal{D}' \cup \{d\}$ is inconsistent in $\mathcal{K}$. Let d_j be the element in $\mathcal{D}'$ with maximal index. If $j > i+1$, $d_j \notin \mathsf{Cons}_{\mathcal{K}}(\mathcal{D}_{j-1}) \subseteq \mathsf{Trig}_{\mathcal{K}}^{\top}(\mathcal{D}_{j-1})$. If $j < i+1$, $d_{i+1} \notin \mathsf{Cons}_{\mathcal{K}}(\mathcal{D}_i) \subseteq \mathsf{Trig}_{\mathcal{K}}^{\top}(\mathcal{D}_i)$. Each case is a contradiction. So, $d \in \mathsf{Cons}_{\mathcal{K}}(\mathcal{D})$ and so $d \in \mathsf{Trig}_{\mathcal{K}}^{\top}(\mathcal{D})$.

"$\supseteq$". Let $d \in \mathsf{Def}(\mathcal{K}) \setminus \mathcal{D}$. By the guard of the **while**-loop (line 3), $d \notin \mathsf{Trig}_{\mathcal{K}}^{\top}(\mathcal{D})$.

($\Leftarrow$) Let now $\mathcal{D} = \mathsf{Trig}_{\mathcal{K}}^{\top}(\mathcal{D})$. It can easily be seen that $\mathcal{D}$ can be enumerated by $\langle d_i \rangle_{i=1}^{n}$ in such a way that $\mathcal{D}_0 = \emptyset$, $d_1 \in \mathsf{Trig}_{\mathcal{K}}^{\top}(\mathcal{D}_0)$, $\mathcal{D}_1 = \{d_1\}$, and $d_{i+1} \in \mathsf{Trig}_{\mathcal{K}}^{\top}(\mathcal{D}_i) \setminus \mathcal{D}_i$ and $\mathcal{D}_{i+1} = \mathcal{D}_i \cup \{d_{i+1}\}$. Moreover, there is a run of GREEDYACC in which each d_i is added to the scenario at round i for each $i = 1,\ldots,n$. Note that the algorithm terminates after round n since $\mathsf{Trig}_{\mathcal{K}}^{\top}(\mathcal{D}) \setminus \mathcal{D} = \emptyset$. $\square$

An advantage of the characterization of D-extensions in terms of fixed points as in Theorem 10.1 or with maxicon-sets as in Proposition 5.1 is that the restriction to finite sets of defeasible information $\mathsf{Def}(\mathcal{K})$ in our knowledge bases can be lifted. The restriction was necessary to warrant the termination of GREEDYACC and TEMACC.

10.3 More on Nonmonotonic Reasoning Properties

In this section we take another, more detailed look at abstract properties of nonmonotonic consequence relations (see Section 2.2). To simplify things, we will study them in a nonprioritized setting.

10.3.1 Knowledge Bases and Abstract Properties of Consequence Relations

Now that we have a better understanding of knowledge bases, let us have another look at the properties introduced in Section 2.2. Recall that consequence relations are used to study the question of what follows from a given defeasible knowledge base. An nmL gives an answer to this question on the basis of the coherent units of information provided by its underlying model of knowledge representation.[41] It gives rise to nonmonotonic consequence relations $\vdash\!\!\sim$ that hold between knowledge bases (in its associated class $\mathbf{K}_{\mathsf{nmL}}$) and sentences in its object language $\mathcal{L}$. In proof-theoretic approaches consequences will be determined by the given extensions of the knowledge base, while in semantic approach they will be based on (typically a selection of) its models.

In the remainder of the Element it will be our task to explain different central methods of knowledge representation and consequence underlying NMLs. Before doing so, we have to comment on what the introduction of knowledge bases means for the abstract study of nonmonotonic consequence presented in Section 2.2. There, the left-hand side of $\vdash\!\!\sim$ merely consisted of sets of sentences, but defeasible knowledge bases typically come with more structure. That means that the reasoning principles discussed in Section 2.2 need to be disambiguated. For example, one may distinguish between a strict and a defeasible form of cautious (or rational) monotonicity (see Fig. 22). Where

---

[41] Since the organization of conflicting knowledge bases into coherent units essentially underlies the reasoning process one should consider knowledge representation, reasoning, and the study of consequences as deeply interwoven. For analytic purposes we nevertheless present these aspects separately in this Element.

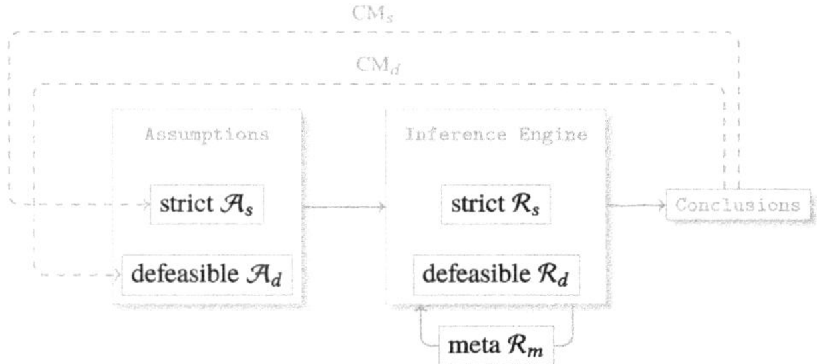

Figure 22 Versions of cautious monotonicity with defeasible knowledge bases

- $\langle \mathcal{A}_s, \mathcal{A}_d, \mathcal{R}_s, \mathcal{R}_d, \mathcal{R}_m \rangle \oplus_s A =_{df} \langle \mathcal{A}_s \cup \{A\}, \mathcal{A}_d, \mathcal{R}_s, \mathcal{R}_d, \mathcal{R}_m \rangle$,
- $\langle \mathcal{A}_s, \mathcal{A}_d, \mathcal{R}_s, \mathcal{R}_d, \mathcal{R}_m \rangle \oplus_d A =_{df} \langle \mathcal{A}_s, \mathcal{A}_d \cup \{A\}, \mathcal{R}_s, \mathcal{R}_d, \mathcal{R}_m \rangle$,

and where $i \in \{s, d\}$, we define:

$\mathrm{CM}_i(\vdash\!\!\sim)$	$\mathcal{K} \vdash\!\!\sim A$ and $\mathcal{K} \vdash\!\!\sim B$ implies $\mathcal{K} \oplus_i B \vdash\!\!\sim A$.
$\mathrm{CT}_i(\vdash\!\!\sim)$	$\mathcal{K} \vdash\!\!\sim A$ and $\mathcal{K} \oplus_i B \vdash\!\!\sim A$ implies $\mathcal{K} \vdash\!\!\sim B$.
$\mathrm{C}_i(\vdash\!\!\sim)$	$\mathrm{CM}_i(\vdash\!\!\sim)$ and $\mathrm{CT}_i(\vdash\!\!\sim)$ hold.
$\mathrm{M}_i(\vdash\!\!\sim)$	$\mathcal{K} \vdash\!\!\sim A$ implies $\mathcal{K} \oplus_i B \vdash\!\!\sim A$.
$\mathrm{OR}_i(\vdash\!\!\sim)$	$\mathcal{K} \oplus_i A \vdash\!\!\sim C$ and $\mathcal{K} \oplus_i B \vdash\!\!\sim C$ implies $\mathcal{K} \oplus_i (A \vee B) \vdash\!\!\sim C$.
$\mathrm{LLE}_i(\vdash\!\!\sim)$	$A \in \mathsf{Cn}_{\mathcal{R}_s}(\{B\})$, $B \in \mathsf{Cn}_{\mathcal{R}_s}(\{A\})$ and $\mathcal{K} \oplus_i A \vdash\!\!\sim C$ implies $\mathcal{K} \oplus_i B \vdash\!\!\sim C$.
$\mathrm{Ref}(\vdash\!\!\sim)$	$\mathcal{K} \oplus_s A \vdash\!\!\sim A$.
$\mathrm{RW}(\vdash\!\!\sim)$	$\mathcal{K} \vdash\!\!\sim A$ and $B \in \mathsf{Cn}_{\mathcal{R}_s}(\{A\})$ implies $\mathcal{K} \vdash\!\!\sim B$.

Since it seems not desirable to expect for defeasible assumptions to be derivable in just any given context, we didn't include reflexivity under the addition of defeasible assumptions ($\mathcal{K} \oplus_d A \vdash\!\!\sim A$). Similarly, we only stated the RW and LLE in the less demanding version relative to strict rules (as opposed to defeasible rules).

Definition 10.2. Let $i \in \{d, s\}$. A nonmonotonic consequence relation $\vdash\!\!\sim$ is *i-cumulative* if it satisfies $\mathrm{RW}(\vdash\!\!\sim)$, $\mathrm{LLE}_i(\vdash\!\!\sim)$, $\mathrm{Ref}(\vdash\!\!\sim)$, and $\mathrm{C}_i(\vdash\!\!\sim)$. It is *i-preferential* if it additionally satisfies $\mathrm{OR}_i(\vdash\!\!\sim)$.

10.3.2 Nonmonotonic Reasoning Properties and Extensions

So far, we have discussed cumulativity and related properties in the context of nonmonotonic consequence relations. We now consider these and similar properties from the perspective of extensions. The shift in perspective is well-motivated since, after all, nonmonotonic consequence is determined by the given extensions (see Table 3). In view of this, nonmonotonic reasoning properties should have counterparts from a perspective more focused on knowledge representation. E.g., where cautious monotonicity and transitivity concern the robustness of the consequence set under the addition of consequences to the knowledge base, we should expect a similar robustness of the set of extensions.

In this section we show that many metatheoretic properties hold for both accumulation methods if the underlying notion of argument satisfies some basic requirements.

Given a knowledge base $\mathcal{K} = \langle \mathcal{A}_s, \mathcal{A}_d, \mathcal{R}_s, \mathcal{R}_d, \mathcal{R}_m \rangle$, a sentence A, and a set $\mathcal{D} \subseteq \mathrm{Def}(\mathcal{K})$, we let $\mathcal{D} \oplus_d A =_{\mathrm{df}} \mathcal{D} \cup \{A\}$, $\mathcal{D} \oplus_s A =_{\mathrm{df}} \mathcal{D}$, $\mathcal{D} \ominus_s^{\mathcal{K}} A =_{\mathrm{df}} \mathcal{D}$, and

$$\mathcal{D} \ominus_d^{\mathcal{K}} A =_{\mathrm{df}} \begin{cases} \mathcal{D} \setminus \{A\} & \text{if } A \notin \mathcal{A}_d \\ \mathcal{D} & \text{else.} \end{cases}$$

Definition 10.3. Let nmL be an NML based on consistent accumulation with an associated class of knowledge bases $\mathbf{K}_{\mathrm{nmL}}$ and let $i \in \{s, d\}$. We define the following properties for nmL. For all $\mathcal{K} \in \mathbf{K}_{\mathrm{nmL}}$ and all sentences A, if $\mathcal{K} \vdash_{\cap \mathrm{PExt}} A$, then

- $\mathrm{CM}_i(\mathrm{PExt})$ holds, if $\mathcal{E} \in \mathrm{PExt}(\mathcal{K} \oplus_i A)$ implies $\mathcal{E} \in \mathrm{PExt}(\mathcal{K})$.
- $\mathrm{CM}_i(\mathrm{DExt})$ holds, if $\mathcal{D} \in \mathrm{DExt}(\mathcal{K} \oplus_i A)$ implies $\mathcal{D} \ominus_i^{\mathcal{K}} A \in \mathrm{DExt}(\mathcal{K})$.
- $\mathrm{CT}_i(\mathrm{PExt})$ holds, if $\mathcal{E} \in \mathrm{PExt}(\mathcal{K})$ implies $\mathcal{E} \in \mathrm{PExt}(\mathcal{K} \oplus_i A)$.
- $\mathrm{CT}_i(\mathrm{DExt})$ holds, if $\mathcal{D} \in \mathrm{DExt}(\mathcal{K})$ implies $\mathcal{D} \oplus_i A \in \mathrm{DExt}(\mathcal{K} \oplus_i A)$.

Moreover,

- $\mathrm{C}_i(\mathrm{PExt})$ holds, if $\mathrm{CT}_i(\mathrm{PExt})$ and $\mathrm{CM}_i(\mathrm{PExt})$ hold.
- $\mathrm{C}_i(\mathrm{DExt})$ holds, if $\mathrm{CT}_i(\mathrm{DExt})$ and $\mathrm{CM}_i(\mathrm{DExt})$ hold.

These notions are related as in Fig. 23 (see Theorem 10.2) for D-extensions induced by greedy or temperate accumulation and for any underlying notion of argument, as long as it fulfills the following requirements.

(arg-trans)   Let $\oplus \in \{\oplus_d, \oplus_s\}$ and $\mathcal{D} \subseteq \mathrm{Def}(\mathcal{K})$. If there is an $a \in \mathrm{Arg}_{\mathcal{K}}(\mathcal{D})$ with $\mathrm{Con}(a) = A$, then for all $b \in \mathrm{Arg}_{\mathcal{K} \oplus A}(\mathcal{D} \oplus A)$, there is a $c \in \mathrm{Arg}_{\mathcal{K}}(\mathcal{D})$ with $\mathrm{Con}(b) = \mathrm{Con}(c)$.

The criterion states that adding a conclusion $A \in \mathrm{Con}[\mathrm{Arg}_{\mathcal{K}}(\mathcal{D})]$ to $\mathcal{K}$ and $\mathcal{D}$ does not generate new conclusions: $\mathrm{Con}[\mathrm{Arg}_{\mathcal{K} \oplus A}(\mathcal{D} \oplus A)] \subseteq \mathrm{Con}[\mathrm{Arg}_{\mathcal{K}}(\mathcal{D})]$.

(arg-mono)   Let $\oplus \in \{\oplus_d, \oplus_s\}$ and $\mathcal{D} \subseteq \mathrm{Def}(\mathcal{K})$. We have $\mathrm{Arg}_{\mathcal{K}}(\mathcal{D}) \subseteq \mathrm{Arg}_{\mathcal{K} \oplus A}(\mathcal{D})$.

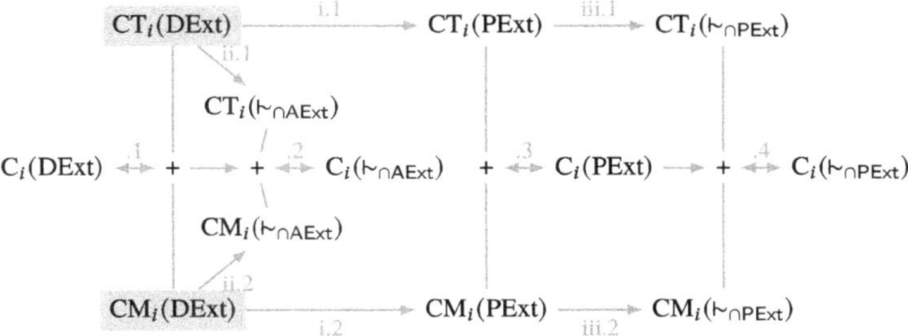

Figure 23 Relations between extensional and consequence-based notions of cumulativity, cautious transitivity and monotonicity (where $i \in \{s, d\}$).

The criterion expresses that adding assumptions to a knowledge base does not result in the loss of arguments.

(arg) (arg-trans) and (arg-mono).

Since by the definition of $\mathsf{Arg}_{\mathcal{K}}(\cdot)$, we have $\mathsf{Arg}_{\mathcal{K}}(\mathcal{D}) \subseteq \mathsf{Arg}_{\mathcal{K}}(\mathcal{D} \cup \mathcal{D}')$ for any $\mathcal{D}, \mathcal{D}' \subseteq \mathsf{Def}(\mathcal{K})$, by (arg-mono), $\mathsf{Arg}_{\mathcal{K}}(\mathcal{D}) \subseteq \mathsf{Arg}_{\mathcal{K} \oplus A}(\mathcal{D} \oplus A)$. Therefore, if (arg) holds and $A \in \mathsf{Con}[\mathsf{Arg}_{\mathcal{K}}(\mathcal{D})]$, then $\mathsf{Con}[\mathsf{Arg}_{\mathcal{K} \oplus A}(\mathcal{D} \oplus A)] = \mathsf{Con}[\mathsf{Arg}_{\mathcal{K}}(\mathcal{D})]$.

Lemma 10.2. *Definitions 5.1 and 9.1 satisfy (arg).*

Proof. In the case of Definition 9.1 this follows by the monotonicity and the transitivity of $\vdash_L$. (arg-mono) follows directly by Definition 5.1. For (arg-trans), let $b \in \mathsf{Arg}_{\mathcal{K} \oplus A}(\mathcal{D} \oplus A)$, where $A = \mathsf{Con}(a)$ for some $a \in \mathsf{Arg}_{\mathcal{K}}(\mathcal{D})$. Let c be the result of replacing every $\langle A \rangle \in \mathsf{Sub}(b)$ in b by a. Clearly $c \in \mathsf{Arg}_{\mathcal{K}}(\mathcal{D})$ and $\mathsf{Con}(c) = \mathsf{Con}(b)$. $\square$

$CT_i(\mathsf{DExt})$ and $CM_i(\mathsf{DExt})$ (highlighted in Fig. 23) have a central place. Instead of showing the corresponding properties $CT_i(\vdash)$ and $CT_i(\vdash)$ for the nonmonotonic consequence relations directly, one can show the corresponding extensional principles.[42]

Theorem⋆ 10.2. *Given (arg), the logical dependencies of Fig. 23 hold for both accumulation methods.*

Moreover, both accumulation methods satisfy $CT_i(\mathsf{DExt})$ if (arg) holds.

Proposition⋆ 10.1. *Let $i \in \{s, d\}$. Given (arg), $CT_i(DExt)$ holds for both accumulation methods.*

---

[42] Note that results marked with an asterisk are proven in the technical appendices.

Also LLE and RW hold given some intuitive requirements on the underlying notion of argument.

(arg-re) Let $\oplus_i \in \{\oplus_d, \oplus_s\}$. If $A \in \mathsf{Cn}_{\mathcal{R}_s}(B)$ and $B \in \mathsf{Cn}_{\mathcal{R}_s}(A)$, then for every $a \in \mathsf{Arg}_{\mathcal{K} \oplus_i A}$ there is a $b \in \mathsf{Arg}_{\mathcal{K} \oplus_i B}$ with $\mathsf{Con}(a) = \mathsf{Con}(b)$

$$\text{and} \begin{cases} \mathsf{Def}(a) = \mathsf{Def}(b) & \text{if } A \notin \mathcal{A}_d(a) \text{ or } i = s \\ (\mathsf{Def}(a) \setminus \{A\}) \cup \{B\} = \mathsf{Def}(b) & \text{else.} \end{cases}$$

The criterion expresses that if assumptions in the knowledge base are replaced with equivalent ones, we can still conclude the same sentences.

(arg-strict) For all $A \in \mathcal{A}_s$, (i) $\langle A \rangle \in \mathsf{Arg}_{\mathcal{K}}(\emptyset)$ and (ii) for all $A_1, \ldots, A_n \to B \in \mathcal{R}_s$ and all $\mathcal{D} \subseteq \mathsf{Def}(\mathcal{K})$, if $A_1, \ldots, A_n \in \mathsf{Con}[\mathsf{Arg}_{\mathcal{K}}(\mathcal{D})]$ then $B \in \mathsf{Con}[\mathsf{Arg}_{\mathcal{K}}(\mathcal{D})]$.

The criterion expresses that every strict assumption gives rise to an argument and arguments can be extended by strict rules.

Lemma 10.3. *Definitions 5.1 and 9.1 satisfy (arg-re), and (arg-strict).*

Proof. Consider Definition 5.1. (arg-strict) follows trivially. For (arg-re), let $A \in \mathsf{Cn}_{\mathcal{R}_s}(B)$ and $B \in \mathsf{Cn}_{\mathcal{R}_s}(A)$. So, there is a $c \in \mathsf{Arg}_{\mathcal{K} \oplus B}(\emptyset)$ of the form $\langle B \rangle \to \ldots \to A$. Let b be the result of replacing each $\langle A \rangle \in \mathsf{Sub}(a)$ in a by c. Then a and b satisfy the requirements of (arg-re). The proof for Definition 9.1 is similar, making use of the transitivity of $\vdash_\mathsf{L}$. $\qquad\square$

Proposition* 10.2. *Let $i \in \{s, d\}$, $\tau \in \{\mathtt{tem}, \mathtt{gr}\}$ and $\vdash \, \in \{\vdash^\tau_{\cap\mathsf{AExt}}, \vdash^\tau_{\cap\mathsf{PExt}}\}$. If (arg-re), $LLE_i(\vdash)$ holds.*

Proposition* 10.3. *Let $\tau \in \{\mathtt{tem}, \mathtt{gr}\}$ and $\vdash \, \in \{\vdash^\tau_{\cap\mathsf{AExt}}, \vdash^\tau_{\cap\mathsf{PExt}}, \vdash^\tau_{\cup\mathsf{Ext}}\}$. If (arg-strict), Ref$(\vdash)$ and RW$(\vdash)$ hold.*

11 Temperate Accumulation: Properties and Some Concrete Systems

In this section we study temperate accumulation in more detail. We show that it gives rise to preferential consequence relations (Section 11.1), if some basic conditions are met. Moreover, by "naming" default rules the structure of knowledge bases can be simplified (Section 11.2.1). Temperate accumulation can be characterized in terms of formal argumentation (Section 11.2.2).

Finally, we present two families of systems based on temperate accumulation: *reasoning with maxicon-sets* (Section 11.3.1) and *input–output logics* (Section 11.3.2) and apply the results from Section 11.1 to them.

11.1 Cumulativity and Preferentiality

The temperate accumulation method often yields cumulative or even preferential consequence relations. Table 7 gives an overview for the following two classes of knowledge bases:

- the "universal" class $\mathbf{K}_\Omega$ containing all knowledge bases of the form $\langle \mathcal{A}_s, \mathcal{A}_d, \mathcal{R}_s, \mathcal{R}_d, \mathcal{R}_m \rangle$;
- the class $\mathbf{K}_{\text{Ad}}$ containing all knowledge bases of the form $\langle \mathcal{A}_s, \mathcal{A}_d, \mathcal{R}_\mathsf{L} \rangle$ for a Tarski logic L. In this context we suppose that arguments are defined by Definition 9.1 and fulfill the following two properties:

    (arg-ex) it is *explosive* in the sense that a set of sentences is inconsistent iff its consequence set is trivial; and

    (arg-or) $\mathcal{A} \cup \{A \vee B\} \vdash_\mathsf{L} C_1 \vee C_2$ iff $\mathcal{A} \cup \{A\} \vdash_\mathsf{L} C_1$ and $\mathcal{A} \cup \{B\} \vdash_\mathsf{L} C_2$.[43]

As the reader may expect, the results in this section depend also on the underlying notion of argument construction (see Fig. 24 for an overview). In the following we show that any NML based on temperate accumulation and on the argument construction in Definition 5.1 or another definition satisfying (arg-re), (arg-strict), and (arg), satisfies $C_i(\text{DExt})$ (for $i \in \{s, d\}$) and is therefore cumulative, that is, $C_i(\mathrel{|\!\sim})$ holds for $\mathrel{|\!\sim} \in \{\mathrel{|\!\sim}^{\text{tem}}_{\cap\text{AExt}}, \mathrel{|\!\sim}^{\text{tem}}_{\cap\text{PExt}}\}$.

Proposition★ 11.1. *Let $i \in \{s, d\}$. Given (arg), $C_i(\text{DExt})$ holds for $\mathbf{K}_\Omega$.*

With Theorem 10.2 and Propositions 10.1 to 10.3 we get:

Corollary 11.1. *Let $i \in \{s, d\}$ and $\mathrel{|\!\sim}_\cap \in \{\mathrel{|\!\sim}^{\text{tem}}_{\cap\text{AExt}}, \mathrel{|\!\sim}^{\text{tem}}_{\cap\text{PExt}}\}$. Given (arg), (arg-re), and (arg-strict), $\mathrel{|\!\sim}_\cap$ is i-cumulative for $\mathbf{K}_\Omega$.*

Table 7 Two classes of knowledge bases and the properties of the associated consequence relations with the notion of argument from Definition 5.1.

	i-cumulativity		i-preferentiality	
	$\mathrel{|\!\sim}^{\text{tem}}_{\cap\text{PExt}}$	$\mathrel{|\!\sim}^{\text{tem}}_{\cap\text{AExt}}$	$\mathrel{|\!\sim}^{\text{tem}}_{\cap\text{PExt}}$	$\mathrel{|\!\sim}^{\text{tem}}_{\cap\text{AExt}}$
$\mathbf{K}_\Omega$	✓ (Cor. 11.1)	✓ (Cor. 11.1)		
$\mathbf{K}_{\text{Ad}}$	✓ (Cor. 11.1)	✓ (Cor. 11.1)	✓ (Thm. 11.1)	

---

[43] In particular we have: $\mathcal{A} \cup \{A \vee B\} \vdash_\mathsf{L} C$ iff $\mathcal{A} \cup \{A\} \vdash_\mathsf{L} C$ and $\mathcal{A} \cup \{B\} \vdash_\mathsf{L} C$.

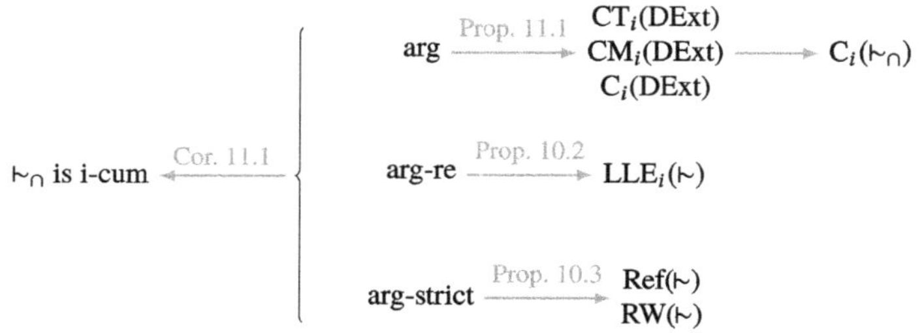

$$
\begin{array}{ccc}
& \xrightarrow{\text{Prop. 11.1}} & \begin{array}{l} \text{CT}_i(\text{DExt}) \\ \text{CM}_i(\text{DExt}) \longrightarrow \text{C}_i(\vdash_\cap) \\ \text{C}_i(\text{DExt}) \end{array} \\
\text{arg} & & \\
\end{array}
$$

$\vdash_\cap$ is i-cum $\xleftarrow{\text{Cor. 11.1}}$ { arg-re $\xrightarrow{\text{Prop. 10.2}}$ LLE$_i(\vdash)$

arg-strict $\xrightarrow{\text{Prop. 10.3}}$ $\begin{array}{l}\text{Ref}(\vdash) \\ \text{RW}(\vdash)\end{array}$

Figure 24 Nonmonotonic reasoning properties for temperate accumulation, where $i \in \{s, d\}$, $\vdash \in \{\vdash^{\text{tem}}_{\cap\text{AExt}}, \vdash^{\text{tem}}_{\cap\text{PExt}}, \vdash^{\text{tem}}_{\cup\text{Ext}}\}$, and $\vdash_\cap \in \{\vdash^{\text{tem}}_{\cap\text{AExt}}, \vdash^{\text{tem}}_{\cap\text{PExt}}\}$.

In the presence of defeasible rules OR($\vdash$) does not hold in general.

Example 30. Let $\vdash \in \{\vdash_{\cap\text{PExt}}, \vdash_{\cap\text{AExt}}\}$ and $\mathcal{K} = \langle \mathcal{A}_s, \mathcal{R}_{\text{CL}}, \mathcal{R}_d \rangle$ with $\mathcal{A}_s = \emptyset$ and $\mathcal{R}_d = \{p \Rightarrow s, q \Rightarrow s\}$. Clearly, $\mathcal{K} \oplus_s (p \vee q) \nvdash s$ while $\mathcal{K} \oplus_s p \vdash s$ and $\mathcal{K} \oplus_s q \vdash s$.

There are good news, however, for knowledge bases in $\mathbf{K}_{\text{Ad}}$, $\vdash^{\text{tem}}_{\cap\text{PExt}}$ is i-preferential for $i \in \{s, d\}$.

Theorem 11.1. *Let $i \in \{s, d\}$. $\vdash^{\text{tem}}_{\cap\text{PExt}}$ is i-preferential for* $\mathbf{K}_{\text{Ad}}$.

Proof. In view of Corollary 11.1 and Lemmas 10.2 and 10.3 we only have to show OR($\vdash$), where $\vdash = \vdash^{\text{tem}}_{\cap\text{PExt}}$. Suppose $\mathcal{K} \oplus_i A \vdash C$ and $\mathcal{K} \oplus_i B \vdash C$. We show the case $i = s$. Suppose $\mathcal{D} \in \text{DExt}(\mathcal{K} \oplus_s (A \vee B))$ and hence, by Theorem 10.1, $\mathcal{D} = \text{Cons}_{\mathcal{K} \oplus_s (A \vee B)}(\mathcal{D})$. If $\mathcal{D}$ is inconsistent in $\mathcal{K} \oplus_s A$, then $C \in \text{Con}[\text{Arg}_{\mathcal{K} \oplus_s A}(\mathcal{D})] = \text{Cn}_{\text{L}}(\mathcal{A}_s \cup \mathcal{D} \cup \{A\})$ by (arg-ex). Else, assume for a contradiction that there is a $\mathcal{D}'$ for which $\mathcal{D} \subsetneq \mathcal{D}' \subseteq \mathcal{A}_d$ that is consistent in $\mathcal{K} \oplus_s A$. So, $\text{Cn}_{\text{L}}(\mathcal{A}_d \cup \mathcal{D}' \cup \{A\})$ is nontrivial and by (arg-or) so is $\text{Cn}_{\text{L}}(\mathcal{A}_d \cup \mathcal{D}' \cup \{A \vee B\})$. So $\mathcal{D}' \subseteq \text{Cons}_{\mathcal{K} \oplus_s (A \vee B)}(\mathcal{D})$ which is a contradiction. So, $\mathcal{D} = \text{Cons}_{\mathcal{K} \oplus_s A}(\mathcal{D})$ and hence, by Theorem 10.1, $\mathcal{D} \in \text{DExt}(\mathcal{K} \oplus_s A)$. Thus, $C \in \text{Con}[\text{Arg}_{\mathcal{K} \oplus_s A}(\mathcal{D})] = \text{Cn}_{\text{L}}(\mathcal{A}_s \cup \mathcal{D} \cup \{A\})$ since $\mathcal{K} \oplus_s A \vdash C$. So, in any case $C \in \text{Cn}_{\text{L}}(\mathcal{A}_s \cup \mathcal{D} \cup \{A\})$.

For an analogous reason $C \in \text{Cn}_{\text{L}}(\mathcal{A}_s \cup \mathcal{D} \cup \{B\})$. By (arg-or), $C \in \text{Cn}_{\text{L}}(\mathcal{A}_s \cup \mathcal{D} \cup \{A \vee B\}) = \text{Con}[\text{Arg}_{\mathcal{K} \oplus_s (A \vee B)}(\mathcal{D})]$. Hence, $\mathcal{K} \oplus_s (A \vee B) \vdash C$. $\square$

The preceding result does not consider $\vdash^{\text{tem}}_{\cap\text{AExt}}$. We will show in Section 11.3.1 that OR($\vdash^{\text{tem}}_{\cap\text{AExt}}$) does not hold even for L = CL.

As a last result in this section we show that $\vdash^{\text{tem}}_{\cup\text{Ext}}$ is monotonic.

Proposition 11.2. *$M_d(\vdash^{\text{tem}}_{\cup\text{Ext}})$ (and so also $CM_d(\vdash^{\text{tem}}_{\cup\text{Ext}})$ and $RM_d(\vdash^{\text{tem}}_{\cup\text{Ext}})$) hold for* $\mathbf{K}_\Omega$.

Proof. Let $\vdash \; = \; \vdash^{\text{tem}}_{\cup\text{Ext}}$ and suppose $\mathcal{K} \vdash A$. Thus, there is a $\mathcal{D} \in \text{DExt}(\mathcal{K})$ for which there is an $a \in \text{Arg}_{\mathcal{K}}(\mathcal{D})$ with $\text{Con}(a) = A$. We have to show that $\mathcal{K} \oplus_d B \vdash A$ where B is an arbitrary sentence. We have, $\text{Arg}_{\mathcal{K}}(\mathcal{D}) = \text{Arg}_{\mathcal{K} \oplus_d B}(\mathcal{D})$. So, $\mathcal{D}$ is consistent in $\mathcal{K} \oplus_d B$. Thus, there is a maxicon-set $\mathcal{D}' \subseteq \text{Def}(\mathcal{K} \oplus_d B)$ for which $\mathcal{D} \subseteq \mathcal{D}'$. We have $a \in \text{Arg}_{\mathcal{K} \oplus_d B}(\mathcal{D}')$. Thus, $\mathcal{K} \oplus_d B \vdash A$. $\qquad \square$

11.2 Alternative Characterizations

In this section we present two alternative characterizations of temperate accumulation. First, in Section 11.2.1 we show that in temperate accumulation defeasible rules are dispensable in that a given knowledge base featuring defeasible rules can be translated into one without, in such a way that extensions and consequences are preserved. In Section 11.2.2 we show that temperate accumulation can be translated into formal argumentation.

11.2.1 Naming Defaults in Temperate Accumulation

We now show that, in the context of NMLs based on temperate accumulation, every knowledge base of the form $\mathcal{K} = \langle \mathcal{A}_s, \mathcal{A}_d, \mathcal{R}_s, \mathcal{R}_d \rangle$ can be translated into a knowledge base of the form $\mathcal{K}^\star = \langle \mathcal{A}_s, \mathcal{A}_d^\star, \mathcal{R}_s^\star \rangle$, which gives rise to the same D- and P-extensions (Theorem 11.2). The idea is to refer (or "name") the defaults in $\mathcal{R}_d$ in the object language, add a strict modus ponens–like rule, and a rule that expresses that a default is defeated in case its antecedents hold but its conclusion is false. This implies that genuinely defeasible rules can be "simulated" by strict rules in systems of temperate accumulation.

Suppose in the following that nmL is a NML based on a language $\mathcal{L}$ with a class of associated knowledge bases $\mathbf{K}_{\text{nmL}}$ of the form of $\mathcal{K}$. We assume that the notion of inconsistency underlying nmL satisfies for any set of sentences $\mathcal{S} \cup \{A\}$ the sufficient condition: $A, \neg A \in \mathcal{S}$ implies that $\mathcal{S}$ is inconsistent. Our translated knowledge bases $\mathcal{K}^\star$ make use of an enriched language: every sentence in $\mathcal{L}$ is a sentence in $\mathcal{L}^\star$, for every $r = A_1, \ldots, A_n \Rightarrow B \in \mathcal{R}_d$, $(A_1, \ldots, A_n \Rightarrow B)$ and $\neg(A_1, \ldots, A_n \Rightarrow B)$ are sentences in $\mathcal{L}^\star$, nothing else is a sentence in $\mathcal{L}^\star$. Note that $\Rightarrow$ is an object-level symbol in $\mathcal{L}^\star$ but not in $\mathcal{L}$. We write $\text{sent}_{\mathcal{L}}$ [resp. $\text{sent}_{\mathcal{L}^\star}$] for the set of all sentences in $\mathcal{L}$ [resp. in $\mathcal{L}^\star$].

Definition 11.1. Let the translation of a knowledge base $\mathcal{K} = \langle \mathcal{A}_s, \mathcal{A}_d, \mathcal{R}_s, \mathcal{R}_d \rangle$ to $\mathcal{K}^\star = \langle \mathcal{A}_s, \mathcal{A}_d^\star, \mathcal{R}_s^\star, \emptyset, \emptyset \rangle$ be given by:

$$\mathcal{A}_d^\star = \mathcal{A}_d \cup \mathcal{R}_d,$$
$$\mathcal{R}_s^\star = \mathcal{R}_s \cup \mathcal{R}_s^{\text{mp}} \cup \mathcal{R}_s^{\text{cp}}, \text{ where}$$
$$\mathcal{R}_s^{\text{mp}} = \{A_1, \ldots, A_n, r \rightarrow B \mid r = (A_1, \ldots, A_n \Rightarrow B) \in \mathcal{R}_d\}$$

$$\mathcal{R}_s^{\mathsf{cp}} = \{A_1, \ldots, A_n, \neg B \to \neg r \mid r = (A_1, \ldots, A_n \Rightarrow B) \in \mathcal{R}_d\}.$$

Note that $\mathsf{Def}(\mathcal{K}) = \mathcal{A}_d \cup \mathcal{R}_d = \mathsf{Def}(\mathcal{K}^\star)$.

Example 31. Recall the knowledge base from Example 9, $\mathcal{K} = \langle \mathcal{A}_s, \mathcal{A}_d, \mathcal{R}_d, \mathcal{R}_s \rangle$ with $\mathcal{A}_s = \{p\}$, $\mathcal{A}_d = \emptyset$, $\mathcal{R}_d = \{r_1 : p \Rightarrow q,\ r_2 : p \Rightarrow r,\ r_3 : q \Rightarrow \neg r\}$ and $\mathcal{R}_s = \{r \to s, \neg r \to s\}$. We translate it to $\mathcal{K}^\star = \langle \mathcal{A}_s, \mathcal{A}_d^\star, \mathcal{R}_s^\star \rangle$ with

- $\mathcal{A}_d^\star = \{r_1, r_2, r_3\}$ and
- $\mathcal{R}_s^\star = \mathcal{R}_s \cup \{p, r_1 \to q,\ p, r_2 \to r,\ q, r_3 \to \neg r\} \cup \{p, \neg q \to \neg r_1,\ p, \neg r \to \neg r_2,\ q, \neg\neg r \to \neg r_3\}$.

Theorem* 11.2. *Let* nmL *be based on temperate accumulation, let* $\mathcal{K} \in \mathbf{K}_{\mathsf{nmL}}$ *be of the form* $\langle \mathcal{A}_s, \mathcal{A}_d, \mathcal{R}_s, \mathcal{R}_d \rangle$, *and let* $\mathcal{K}^\star$ *be the translation defined in Definition 11.1. Then,* $\mathsf{DExt}(\mathcal{K}) = \mathsf{DExt}(\mathcal{K}^\star)$ *and* $\mathsf{PExt}(\mathcal{K}) = \mathsf{PExt}(\mathcal{K}^\star)$.

11.2.2 Temperate Accumulation as a Form of Argumentation

In the following we give an elegant argumentative characterization of NMLs based on temperate accumulation and on knowledge bases of the type $\mathcal{K} = \langle \mathcal{A}_s, \mathcal{A}_d, \mathcal{R}_s \rangle$.[44] We work under the assumption that (a) $\mathsf{Arg}_\mathcal{K}$ and $\mathsf{Arg}_\mathcal{K}(\cdot)$ are defined as in Definition 5.1 and (b) the inconsistency of a set of defeasible assumptions $\mathcal{A} \subseteq \mathcal{A}_d$ can be argumentatively expressed by

($\star$) $\mathcal{A}$ is inconsistent in $\mathcal{K}$ iff for every $A \in \mathcal{A}$ there is an $a \in \mathsf{Arg}_\mathcal{K}(\mathcal{A} \setminus \{A\})$ that concludes that the assumption A is false, that is, $\mathsf{Con}(a) = \neg A$.

($\star$) holds if $\mathcal{R}_s = \mathcal{R}_{\mathsf{CL}}$ or, more generally, if $\mathcal{R}_s = \mathcal{R}_{\mathsf{L}}$ for some logic L which has the property that $\mathcal{S}$ is inconsistent in L iff for all $A \in \mathcal{S}$, $\mathcal{S} \setminus \{A\} \vdash_{\mathsf{L}} \neg A$.

Definition 11.2. We define the argumentation framework $\mathcal{AF}_\mathcal{K} = \langle \mathsf{Arg}_\mathcal{K}, \leadsto \rangle$ where $a \leadsto b$ for $a, b \in \mathsf{Arg}_\mathcal{K}$ iff $\mathsf{Con}(a) = \neg B$ for some $B \in \mathcal{A}_d(b)$. Where $\mathsf{X} \in \{\mathsf{A}, \mathsf{P}\}$, we let, moreover, $\vdash_{\cap\mathsf{XExt}}^{\mathsf{stb}}$ be the consequence relation induced by the X-extensions and the stable argumentation semantics (see Definition 5.2) and $\mathsf{stable}(\mathcal{K})$ be the set of stable A-extensions of $\mathcal{K}$.

Example 32. We consider $\mathcal{K} = \langle \emptyset, \{p \wedge q, \neg p \wedge q, s\}, \mathcal{R}_{\mathsf{CL}} \rangle$. An excerpt from the argumentation framework $\mathcal{AF}_\mathcal{K}$ is illustrated in Fig. 25. We note that $\mathcal{K} \vdash_{\cap\mathsf{PExt}}^{\mathsf{tem}} q$ and $\mathcal{K} \vdash_{\cap\mathsf{PExt}}^{\mathsf{stb}} q$.

---

[44] In view of Section 11.2.1 (Theorem 11.2) this characterization, by translation, also covers knowledge bases of the form $\langle \mathcal{A}_s, \mathcal{A}_d, \mathcal{R}_s, \mathcal{R}_d \rangle$.

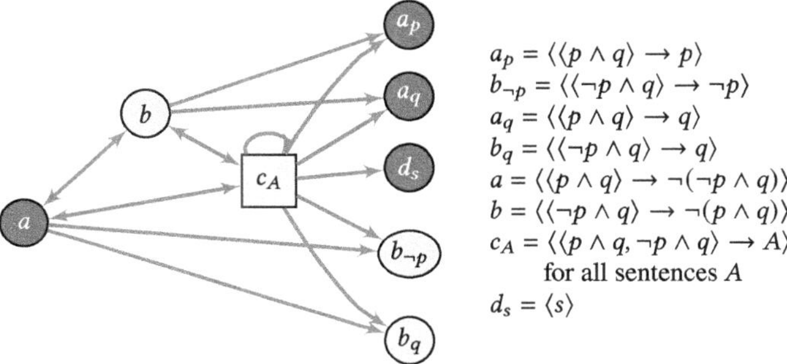

Figure 25 The argumentation framework for the knowledge base of Example 32 based on the arguments to the right. The rectangular node represents a class of arguments based on the inconsistent assumption set $\{p \wedge q, \neg p \wedge q\}$. An outgoing [resp. ingoing] arrow symbolizes an attack from [resp. to] some argument in the class.

We have, on the one hand, two D-extensions according to temperate accumulation, $\mathcal{X}_1 = \{p \wedge q, s\}$ and $\mathcal{X}_2 = \{\neg p \wedge q, s\}$, with the corresponding A-extensions $\mathsf{Arg}_\mathcal{K}(\mathcal{X}_1)$ and $\mathsf{Arg}_\mathcal{K}(\mathcal{X}_2)$ and the P-extensions $\mathsf{Cn}_{\mathsf{CL}}(\mathcal{X}_1)$ and $\mathsf{Cn}_{\mathsf{CL}}(\mathcal{X}_2)$. On the other hand, we have two stable A-extensions of $\mathcal{AF}_\mathcal{K}$ (highlighted in Fig. 25), namely $\mathsf{Arg}_\mathcal{K}(\mathcal{X}_1)$ and $\mathsf{Arg}_\mathcal{K}(\mathcal{X}_2)$, with the corresponding P-extensions $\mathsf{Cn}_{\mathsf{CL}}(\mathcal{X}_1)$ and $\mathsf{Cn}_{\mathsf{CL}}(\mathcal{X}_2)$.

The following theorem shows that the observed correspondences are not coincidental.

Theorem 11.2. *Let* nmL *be an NML based on temperate accumulation for which* $(\star)$ *holds and* $\mathcal{K} = \langle \mathcal{A}_s, \mathcal{A}_d, \mathcal{R}_s\rangle \in \mathbf{K}_{\mathsf{nmL}}$ *be a knowledge base.*

1. *If* $\mathcal{D} \in \mathsf{DExt}_{\mathsf{tem}}(\mathcal{K})$ *then* $\mathsf{Arg}_\mathcal{K}(\mathcal{D}) \in \mathsf{stable}(\mathcal{K})$.
2. *If* $\mathcal{X} \in \mathsf{stable}(\mathcal{K})$, *there is a* $\mathcal{D} \in \mathsf{DExt}_{\mathsf{tem}}(\mathcal{K})$ *such that* $\mathcal{X} = \mathsf{Arg}_\mathcal{K}(\mathcal{D})$.

Proof. For Item 1 suppose $\mathcal{D} \in \mathsf{DExt}_{\mathsf{tem}}(\mathcal{K})$. By Proposition 5.1, $\mathcal{D} \in \mathsf{maxcon}(\mathcal{K})$. Consider $a, b \in \mathsf{Arg}_\mathcal{K}$ such that $a \rightsquigarrow b$ and $a \in \mathsf{Arg}_\mathcal{K}(\mathcal{D})$. By $(\star)$ and the consistency of $\mathcal{D}$ in $\mathcal{K}$, $b \notin \mathsf{Arg}_\mathcal{K}(\mathcal{D})$. Thus, $\mathsf{Arg}_\mathcal{K}(\mathcal{D})$ is conflict-free.

Let now $a \in \mathsf{Arg}_\mathcal{K} \setminus \mathsf{Arg}_\mathcal{K}(\mathcal{D})$. So, there is an $A \in \mathcal{A}_d(a) \setminus \mathcal{D}$. Since $\mathcal{D} \in \mathsf{maxcon}(\mathcal{K})$, $\mathcal{D} \cup \{A\}$ is inconsistent in $\mathcal{K}$ and by $(\star)$ there is a $b \in \mathsf{Arg}_\mathcal{K}(\mathcal{D})$ with $\mathsf{Con}(b) = \neg A$. Thus, $\mathsf{Arg}_\mathcal{K}(\mathcal{D}) \in \mathsf{stable}(\mathcal{D})$.

For Item 2 let $\mathcal{X} \in \mathsf{stable}(\mathcal{AF}_\mathcal{K})$ and $(\dagger)$ $\mathcal{D} = \bigcup_{a \in \mathcal{X}} \mathcal{A}_d(a)$. Clearly, $\mathcal{X} \subseteq \mathsf{Arg}_\mathcal{K}(\mathcal{D})$. Assume for a contradiction that there is an $a \in \mathsf{Arg}_\mathcal{K}(\mathcal{D}) \setminus \mathcal{X}$. By stability, there is a $b \in \mathcal{X}$ such that $b \rightsquigarrow a$ and so $\mathsf{Con}(b) = \neg A$ for some $A \in \mathcal{A}_d(a)$. Since $A \in \mathcal{D}$ and $(\dagger)$, there is a $c \in \mathcal{X}$ for which $A \in \mathcal{A}_d(c)$ and so $b \rightsquigarrow c$ in contradiction to the conflict-freeness of $\mathcal{X}$. Thus, $\mathcal{X} = \mathsf{Arg}_\mathcal{K}(\mathcal{D})$.

By Proposition 5.1, we have to show that $\mathcal{D} \in \mathrm{maxcon}(\mathcal{K})$. In view of $(\star)$ and the conflict-freeness of $\mathcal{X}$, $\mathcal{D}$ is consistent in $\mathcal{K}$. Suppose $A \in \mathcal{A}_d$ is such that $\mathcal{D} \cup \{A\}$ is consistent. If $A \notin \mathcal{D}$, then $a = \langle A \rangle \in \mathrm{Arg}_{\mathcal{K}} \setminus \mathcal{D}$ and by stability, there is a $b \in \mathcal{X}$ such that $b \rightsquigarrow a$ and therefore $\mathrm{Con}(b) = \neg A$. But then, by $(\star)$, $\mathcal{D} \cup \{A\}$ is inconsistent in $\mathcal{K}$. So, $A \in \mathcal{D}$ and therefore $\mathcal{D} \in \mathrm{maxcon}(\mathcal{K})$. $\square$

11.3 Two Families of NMLs from the Literature

In this section we will introduce two well-known families of NMLs, both based on the idea of forming maxicon sets of defeasible information from the given knowledge base.

11.3.1 Reasoning with Maxicon Sets of Sentences

A time-honored family of NMLs has been proposed by Rescher and Manor (1970). These NMLs model reasoning scenarios in which an agent is confronted with reliable but not infallible information (e.g., resulting from testimonies, weather reports, and so on) that may give rise to contradictions. Such information is encoded by sets of defeasible assumptions. Clearly, due to the possibility of logical explosion, classical logic cannot be applied to such sets, at least not naively. The basic idea behind Rescher's and Manor's approach is to form ($\subseteq$-maximal) consistent sets of defeasible assumptions and reason on their basis. In our terminology these maxicon sets of defeasible assumptions form D-extensions and their classical closures are P-extensions induced by temperate accumulation. We obtain the three types of consequences that have been introduced in Definition 5.2.

While Rescher and Manor considered knowledge bases of the form $\langle \emptyset, \mathcal{A}_d, \mathcal{R}_{\mathsf{CL}} \rangle$, Makinson's system of Default Assumptions (Makinson (2005)) also considered strict assumptions and so generalized the considered class of knowledge bases to those of the form $\langle \mathcal{A}_s, \mathcal{A}_d, \mathcal{R}_{\mathsf{CL}} \rangle$.[45] Of course, one may consider other Tarski-logics L instead of classical logic. Let the class $\mathbf{K}_{\mathrm{mcon}}$ consist of all knowledge bases of the form $\langle \mathcal{A}_s, \mathcal{A}_d, \mathcal{R}_{\mathsf{L}} \rangle$. We let:[46]

---

[45] A related family of logics is Adaptive Logics (Batens, 2007). They have been shown to give rise to the same consequence relations as Makinson's default assumptions (Van De Putte, 2013). Instead of working with "positive" assumptions, the knowledge bases of adaptive logics consider negative assumptions, so-called "abnormalities" (see Section 2.3). Adaptive logics have found many applications, from abductive reasoning (Beirlaen & Aliseda, 2014), to inductive generalizations (Batens, 2011), from normative reasoning (Van De Putte et al., 2019) to default logic (Straßer, 2009a). For a book-length introduction see Straßer (2014).

[46] The consequence relation $\vdash^{\mathrm{mcon}}_{\cap\mathrm{ext}}$ is also called the *strong* or *universal* entailment, $\vdash^{\mathrm{mcon}}_{\cap\mathrm{arg}}$ the *free* consequence, and $\vdash^{\mathrm{mcon}}_{\cup}$ the *existential* consequence. See Benferhat et al. (1997) for a detailed study of these consequence relations.

Table 8 Overview on properties of the consequence relations based on maxicon sets. All positive results follow from the general results for NMLs based on temperate accumulation in Section 11.1 (see also Corollary 11.2 below).

	M_d	M_s	CM_d	CM_s	CT_d	CT_s	RM_d	RM_s	OR_d	OR_s
$\vdash^{mcon}_{\cap PExt}$			✓	✓	✓	✓			✓	✓
$\vdash^{mcon}_{\cap AExt}$			✓	✓	✓	✓				
$\vdash^{mcon}_{\cup Ext}$	✓		✓				✓	✓		

1. $\mathcal{K} \vdash^{mcon}_{\cap Pext} A$ iff $A \in \mathsf{Cn_L}(\mathcal{S} \cup \mathcal{A}_s)$ for every $\mathcal{S} \in \mathsf{maxcon}(\mathcal{K})$.
2. $\mathcal{K} \vdash^{mcon}_{\cap AExt} A$ iff there is a $\mathcal{S} \subseteq \bigcap \mathsf{maxcon}(\mathcal{K})$ for which $A \in \mathsf{Cn_L}(\mathcal{S} \cup \mathcal{A}_s)$.
3. $\mathcal{K} \vdash^{mcon}_{\cup Ext} A$ iff there is a $\mathcal{S} \in \mathsf{maxcon}(\mathcal{K})$ such that $A \in \mathsf{Cn_L}(\mathcal{S} \cup \mathcal{A}_s)$.

In what follows we let arguments be defined as in Definition 9.1.

Example 33. Consider the knowledge base $\mathcal{K} = \langle \mathcal{A}_s, \mathcal{A}_d, \mathcal{R}_{CL} \rangle$ where $\mathcal{A}_s = \{\neg u\}$ and $\mathcal{A}_d = \{p \wedge q, \neg p \wedge t, s, u\}$. We have $\mathsf{maxcon}(\mathcal{K}) = \{\mathcal{X}_1, \mathcal{X}_2\}$ where $\mathcal{X}_1 = \{p \wedge q, s\}$, and $\mathcal{X}_2 = \{\neg p \wedge t, s\}$. Note that the defeasible assumption u conflicts with the strict assumption $\neg u$.

We first observe that $q \vee t$ is a floating conclusion in view of the conflicting arguments $(\{p \wedge q\}, q \vee t) \in \mathsf{Arg}(\mathcal{X}_1)$ and $(\{\neg p \wedge t\}, q \vee t) \in \mathsf{Arg}(\mathcal{X}_2)$. Indeed, $\mathcal{K} \vdash^{mcon}_{\cap PExt} q \vee t$ while $\mathcal{K} \not\vdash^{mcon}_{\cap AExt} q \vee t$.

In view of Proposition 5.1 the three consequence relations $\vdash^{mcon}_{\cap PExt}, \vdash^{mcon}_{\cap AExt}$, and $\vdash^{cmon}_{\cup Ext}$ are identical to $\vdash^{tem}_{\cap PExt}, \vdash^{tem}_{\cap AExt}$, and $\vdash^{tem}_{\cup Ext}$ on the class $\mathbf{K}_{mcon}$. Therefore, the results from Section 11.1 are applicable (Table 8).

Proposition 11.3. *Let $\mathcal{K} \in \mathbf{K}_{mcon}$. Then, (i) $\mathcal{K} \vdash^{tem}_{\cap PExt} A$ iff $\mathcal{K} \vdash^{mcon}_{\cap PExt} A$, (ii) $\mathcal{K} \vdash^{tem}_{\cap AExt} A$ iff $\mathcal{K} \vdash^{mcon}_{\cap AExt} A$, and (iii) $\mathcal{K} \vdash^{tem}_{\cup Ext} A$ iff $\mathcal{K} \vdash^{mcon}_{\cup Ext} A$.*

Proof. We show case (ii). The others are analogous and left to the reader. $\mathcal{K} \vdash^{tem}_{\cap AExt} A$, iff, there is an $a \in \bigcap \{\mathsf{Arg}_{\mathcal{K}}(\mathcal{D}) \mid \mathcal{D} \in \mathsf{DExt}(\mathcal{K})\}$ with $\mathsf{Con}(a) = A$, iff, $A \in \mathsf{Cn_L}(\bigcap \{\mathcal{D} \mid \mathcal{D} \in \mathsf{DExt}(\mathcal{K})\} \cup \mathcal{A}_s)$, iff [by Proposition 5.1], $A \in \mathsf{Cn_L}(\bigcap \{\mathcal{D} \mid \mathcal{D} \in \mathsf{maxcon}(\mathcal{K})\} \cup \mathcal{A}_s)$, iff, $\mathcal{K} \vdash^{mcon}_{\cap AExt} A$. $\square$

In view of Corollary 11.1, Theorem 11.1, and Lemmas 10.2 and 10.3 we therefore get:

Corollary 11.2. *Let $i \in \{s, d\}$. $\vdash^{mcon}_{\cap Aext}$ is i-cumulative. If (arg-ex) and (arg-or) hold, $\vdash^{mcon}_{\cap Pext}$ is i-preferential.*

Table 9 Counterexamples to $\mathrm{OR}_i(\vdash)$. Where $j \in \{1,2,3\}$ let $\mathcal{K}_j = \langle \emptyset, \mathcal{A}_j, \mathcal{R}_{\mathsf{CL}} \rangle$, $\mathcal{A}_1 = \{\neg p \wedge r, \neg q \wedge r\}$, $\mathcal{A}_2 = \{\neg p, \neg q, \neg p \supset r, \neg q \supset r\}$, $\mathcal{A}_3 = \mathcal{A}_3^u \cup \mathcal{A}_3^{\neg u}$, $\mathcal{A}_3^u = \{u \wedge (p \supset r)\}$, $\mathcal{A}_3^{\neg u} = \{\neg u \wedge (q \supset r)\}$, and $\mathcal{A}_2^A = \mathcal{A}_2 \cup \{A\}$.

	$\mathcal{K}^\star =$	$\mathcal{K} \oplus_i p$	$\mathcal{K} \oplus_i q$	$\mathcal{K} \oplus_i (p \vee q)$
$i = s,$ $\mathcal{K} = \mathcal{K}_1$	$\mathrm{maxcon}(\mathcal{K}^\star)$	$\{\neg q \wedge r\}$	$\{\neg p \wedge r\}$	$\{\neg q \wedge r\}, \{\neg p \wedge r\}$
	$\bigcap \mathrm{DExt}(\mathcal{K}^\star)$	$\{\neg q \wedge r\}$	$\{\neg p \wedge r\}$	$\emptyset$
	$\mathcal{K}^\star \vdash^{\mathrm{mcon}}_{\cap\mathsf{AExt}} r$?	✓	✓	✗
$i = d,$ $\mathcal{K} = \mathcal{K}_2$	$\mathrm{maxcon}(\mathcal{K}^\star)$	$\mathcal{A}_2^p \setminus \{\neg p\}$ $\mathcal{A}_2$	$\mathcal{A}_2^q \setminus \{\neg q\}$ $\mathcal{A}_2$	$\mathcal{A}_2^{p\vee q} \setminus \{\neg p\}$ $\mathcal{A}_2^{p\vee q} \setminus \{\neg q\}$ $\mathcal{A}_2$
	$\bigcap \mathrm{DExt}(\mathcal{K}^\star)$	$\mathcal{A}_2 \setminus \{\neg p\}$	$\mathcal{A}_2 \setminus \{\neg q\}$	$\mathcal{A}_2 \setminus \{\neg p, \neg q\}$
	$\mathcal{K}^\star \vdash^{\mathrm{mcon}}_{\cap\mathsf{AExt}} r$?	✓	✓	✗
$i \in \{s,d\}$ $\mathcal{K} = \mathcal{K}_3$	$\mathrm{maxcon}(\mathcal{K}^\star)$	$\mathcal{A}_3^u \oplus_i p$ $\mathcal{A}_3^{\neg u} \oplus_i p$	$\mathcal{A}_3^u \oplus_i q$ $\mathcal{A}_3^{\neg u} \oplus_i q$	$\mathcal{A}_3^u \oplus_i (p \vee q)$ $\mathcal{A}_3^{\neg u} \oplus_i (p \vee q)$
	$\mathcal{K}^\star \vdash^{\mathrm{mcon}}_{\cup\mathsf{Ext}} r$?	✓	✓	✗

Example 34. Where $i \in \{s, d\}$, in Table 9 we list counter-examples to (OR) and therefore to the i-preferentiality of $\vdash^{\mathrm{mcon}}_{\cap\mathsf{AExt}}$ and $\vdash^{\mathrm{cmon}}_{\cup\mathsf{Ext}}$. In Table 10 we find counterexamples to $\mathrm{RM}_i(\vdash)$ for $\vdash \in \{\vdash^{\mathrm{mcon}}_{\cap\mathsf{PExt}}, \vdash^{\mathrm{mcon}}_{\cap\mathsf{AExt}}\}$.

We end this section with two simple counterexamples concerning the cautious monotonicity and transitivity of $\vdash^{\mathrm{cmon}}_{\cup\mathsf{Ext}}$ and a positive result concerning its rational monotonicity.

Example 35. Let $\vdash = \vdash^{\mathrm{mcon}}_{\cup\mathsf{Ext}}$. We first let $\mathcal{K}_1 = \langle \emptyset, \{p, \neg p\}, \mathcal{R}_{\mathsf{CL}} \rangle$. Then, $\mathcal{K}_1 \vdash p$ and $\mathcal{K}_1 \vdash \neg p$, but $\mathcal{K}_1 \oplus_s p \not\vdash \neg p$. Note for this that $\{\neg p\} \in \mathrm{maxcon}(\mathcal{K}_1) \setminus \mathrm{maxcon}(\mathcal{K}_1 \oplus_s p)$. This shows that $\mathrm{CM}_s(\vdash^{\mathrm{cmon}}_{\cup\mathsf{Ext}})$ and $\mathrm{M}_s(\vdash^{\mathrm{cmon}}_{\cup\mathsf{Ext}})$ don't hold.

Let now $\mathcal{K}_2 = \langle \emptyset, \{p \wedge q, \neg p, (\neg p \wedge q) \supset s\}, \mathcal{R}_{\mathsf{CL}} \rangle$ and $i \in \{s, d\}$. We note that $\mathcal{K}_2 \vdash q$ (since $\{p \wedge q, (\neg p \wedge q) \supset s\} \in \mathrm{maxcon}(\mathcal{K}_2)$) and $\mathcal{K}_2 \oplus_i q \vdash s$ (since $\{\neg p, (\neg p \wedge q) \supset s\} \oplus_i q \in \mathrm{maxcon}(\mathcal{K}_2 \oplus_i q)$). However, $\mathcal{K}_2 \not\vdash s$. This shows that $\mathrm{CT}_i(\vdash^{\mathrm{mcon}}_{\cup\mathsf{Ext}})$ does not hold.

Proposition 11.4. *Let* $\mathcal{K} = \langle \mathcal{A}_s, \mathcal{A}_d, \mathcal{R}_{\mathsf{CL}} \rangle \in \mathbf{K}_{\mathrm{mcon}}$, $i \in \{s, d\}$, *and* $\vdash = \vdash^{\mathrm{mcon}}_{\cup\mathsf{Ext}}$. *Then,* $\mathrm{RM}_i(\vdash)$ *holds.*

Table 10 Counterexamples to $\mathrm{RM}_i(\vdash)$ where $\mathcal{K} = \langle \emptyset, \mathcal{A}_d, \mathcal{R}_{\mathrm{CL}} \rangle$ with $\mathcal{A}_d = \{p, \neg p, q \wedge r\}$. We have: $\mathcal{K} \vdash r$ and $\mathcal{K} \not\vdash \neg\neg(p \wedge r)$, while $\mathcal{K} \oplus \neg(p \wedge r) \not\vdash r$.

$\mathcal{K}^\star =$	$\mathcal{K}$	$\mathcal{K} \oplus_s \neg(p \wedge r)$	$\mathcal{K} \oplus_d \neg(p \wedge r)$
$\mathrm{maxcon}(\mathcal{K}^\star)$	$\{p, q \wedge r\},$ $\{\neg p, q \wedge r\}$	$\{p\},$ $\{\neg p, q \wedge r\}$	$\{p, \neg(p \wedge r)\},$ $\{p, q \wedge r\},$ $\{\neg p, q \wedge r, \neg(p \wedge r)\}$
$\bigcap \mathrm{DExt}(\mathcal{K}^\star)$	$\{q \wedge r\}$	$\emptyset$	$\emptyset$
$\mathcal{K}^\star \vdash^{\mathrm{mcon}}_{\cap\mathrm{AExt}} r$?	✓	✗	✗
$\mathcal{K}^\star \not\vdash^{\mathrm{mcon}}_{\cap\mathrm{AExt}} \neg\neg(p \wedge r)$?	✓		
$\mathcal{K}^\star \vdash^{\mathrm{mcon}}_{\cap\mathrm{PExt}} r$?	✓	✗	✗
$\mathcal{K}^\star \not\vdash^{\mathrm{mcon}}_{\cap\mathrm{PExt}} \neg\neg(p \wedge r)$?	✓		

Sketch of the Proof. Suppose $\mathcal{K} \vdash A$ and $\mathcal{K} \not\vdash \neg B$ and let $\oplus \in \{\oplus_s, \oplus_d\}$. In view of $\mathcal{K} \not\vdash \neg B$ every $\mathcal{D} \in \mathrm{maxcon}(\mathcal{K})$ is consistent with B. It is therefore easy to see that $\mathcal{D} \in \mathrm{maxcon}(\mathcal{K})$ iff $\mathcal{D} \oplus B \in \mathrm{maxcon}(\mathcal{D} \oplus B)$ and therefore also $\mathcal{K} \oplus B \vdash A$. $\qquad\square$

11.3.2 Reasoning with Consistent Sets of Defaults and Metarules: Input–Output Logic

Input–output logics (in short, IO-logics) have been first presented in Makinson and Van Der Torre (2000) and in a nonmonotonic setting in 2001. We work with the class of knowledge bases $\mathbf{K}_{\mathrm{io}}$ of the type $\mathcal{K} = \langle \mathcal{A}_s, \mathcal{R}_{\mathrm{L}}, \mathcal{R}_d, \mathcal{R}_m \rangle$, where the strict rules are provided by a Tarski base logic L (such as classical or intuitionistic logic).[47] Instead of Definition 5.1, arguments in IO-logic are constructed according to the following "two-phase" definition in which (a) the derivation of information from strict assumptions by the strict rules and (b) the derivation of defeasible rules from strict and defeasible rules by means of metarules are separated. The detachment of argument conclusions is applied to the results of (a) and (b).

Definition 11.3 (Arguments, Consistency, and Consequences in IO-logic). Let $\mathcal{K} = \langle \mathcal{A}_s, \mathcal{R}_{\mathrm{L}}, \mathcal{R}_d, \mathcal{R}_m \rangle \in \mathbf{K}_{\mathrm{io}}$. Where $\mathcal{D} \subseteq \mathrm{Def}(\mathcal{K})$, $(A, B) \in \mathrm{Arg}^{\mathrm{io}}_{\mathcal{K}}(\mathcal{D})$ iff (a)

---

[47] Input–output logics have two characterizations, a semantic and a syntactic, proof-theoretic one. We here focus on the latter, since it coheres better with our overall presentation.

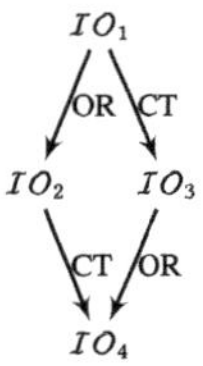

	nmL, where	$\mathbf{K}_{\mathsf{nmL}}$, where
	$i \in \{1,\dots,4\}$	$\mathcal{R}_m = \mathcal{IO}_i$
	IO_i	$\langle \mathcal{A}_s, \mathcal{R}_{\mathsf{L}}, \mathcal{R}_d, \mathcal{R}_m \rangle$
	IO_i^+	$\langle \mathcal{A}_s, \mathcal{R}_{\mathsf{L}}, \mathcal{R}_d \cup \mathcal{R}_d^{\mathsf{id}}, \mathcal{R}_m \rangle$
	$\mathsf{IO}_i^\star$	$\langle \mathcal{A}_s, \mathcal{R}_{\mathsf{L}}, \mathcal{R}_d, \mathcal{R}_m \cup \{\mathsf{ID}\} \rangle$

Figure 26 The basic input–output logics and their associated knowledge bases where $\mathcal{IO}_1 = \{\mathsf{RW}, \mathsf{LS}, \mathsf{AND}\}$ and $\mathcal{R}_d^{\mathsf{id}} = \{A \Rightarrow A \mid A \in \mathsf{sent}_{\mathcal{L}}\}$.

$A \in \mathsf{Cn}_{\mathsf{L}}(\mathcal{A}_s)$ and (b) $A \Rightarrow B \in \mathsf{Cn}_{\mathcal{R}_m}(\mathcal{D} \cup \mathcal{R}_s)$. We let $\mathsf{Con}((A,B)) = B$ and $\mathsf{Arg}^{\mathsf{io}}_{\mathcal{K}} = \mathsf{Arg}^{\mathsf{io}}_{\mathcal{K}}(\emptyset)$.

$\mathcal{D}$ is *consistent* in $\mathcal{K}$ iff there is no sentence B for which $B, \neg B \in \mathsf{Con}[\mathsf{Arg}^{\mathsf{io}}_{\mathcal{K}}(\mathcal{D})]$.

We define D-, A-, and P-extensions as usual (see Section 10). Where $X \in \{\cap\mathsf{PExt}, \cap\mathsf{AExt}, \cup\mathsf{Ext}\}$, we will write $\vdash^{\mathsf{io}}_X$ for the induced consequence relation (see Definition 5.2) on the class of knowledge bases $\mathbf{K}_{\mathsf{io}}$.

In IO-logic metarules play a central role. Paradigmatic rules are:

Right Weakening (RW)	$(A \to B), (C \Rightarrow A) \mapsto (C \Rightarrow B)$
Left Strengthening (LS)	$(A \to C), (C \Rightarrow B) \mapsto (A \Rightarrow B)$
Right Conjunction (AND)	$(A \Rightarrow B), (A \Rightarrow C) \mapsto (A \Rightarrow B \wedge C)$
Cumulative Transitivity (CT)	$(A \Rightarrow B), (A \wedge B \Rightarrow C) \mapsto (A \Rightarrow C)$
Left Disjunction (OR)	$(A \Rightarrow C), (B \Rightarrow C) \mapsto (A \vee B \Rightarrow C)$
Identity (ID)	$\mapsto A \Rightarrow A$

Depending on the underlying class of knowledge bases, we have 12 base systems, summarized in Fig. 26.

Example 36. Let $\mathcal{K} = \langle \mathcal{A}_s, \mathcal{R}_{\mathsf{CL}}, \mathcal{R}_d, \mathcal{R}_m \rangle$ where $\mathcal{R}_d = \{p \Rightarrow q,\ p \Rightarrow \neg s,\ q \Rightarrow s\}$, $\mathcal{A}_s = \{p\}$, and $\mathcal{R}_m = \mathcal{IO}_3 = \{\mathsf{RM}, \mathsf{LS}, \mathsf{AND}, \mathsf{CT}\}$. We have three maxicon sets for $\mathcal{K}$: $\mathcal{X}_1 = \{p \Rightarrow q, p \Rightarrow \neg s\}$, $\mathcal{X}_2 = \{p \Rightarrow q, q \Rightarrow s\}$, and $\mathcal{X}_3 = \{p \Rightarrow \neg s, q \Rightarrow s\}$. By Proposition 5.1, we know that these correspond to the D-extension generated by TEMACC. We have $\mathcal{K} \nvdash^{\mathsf{io}}_{\cap\mathsf{Pext}} q$ since $\mathcal{X}_3$ doesn't contain an argument for q.

Note that $\mathcal{R}_d$ is not consistent since it contains the argument $(p, \neg s)$ for $\neg s$ and (p, s) for s based on the $\mathcal{R}_m$-derivation

$$\frac{p \Rightarrow q \quad \dfrac{p \wedge q \to q \quad q \Rightarrow s}{p \wedge q \Rightarrow s}\ \mathsf{LS}}{p \Rightarrow s}\ \mathsf{CT}\ .$$

IO-logics have found applications in deontic logic where the rules in $\mathcal{R}_d$ are interpreted as conditional norms: $A \Rightarrow B \in \mathcal{R}_d$ is read as "A commits us/you/etc. to bring about B" (Parent & van der Torre, 2013). The right side of the consequence relation $\vdash$ encodes the obligations derivable from a knowledge base, where the latter represents the information available about the actual situation $\mathcal{A}_s$ and the given conditional norms $\mathcal{R}_d$. In deontic logic, conflicts between norms can occur in various ways, for example, in terms of contrary-to-duty situations.

Example 37. Let h stand for "helping the neighbor," and n for "notifying the neighbor" (Chisholm, 1963). Consider $\mathcal{A}_s = \{\neg h\}$, $\mathcal{R}_d = \{\top \Rightarrow h, h \Rightarrow n, \neg h \Rightarrow \neg n\}$ and $\mathcal{R}_m = \mathcal{IO}_3$. We have three maxicon sets, namely $\mathcal{X}_1 = \{\top \Rightarrow h, h \Rightarrow n\}$, $\mathcal{X}_2 = |, \{\top \Rightarrow h, \neg h \Rightarrow \neg n\}$, and $\mathcal{X}_3 = \{\neg h \Rightarrow \neg n, h \Rightarrow n\}$. One may object to $\top \Rightarrow h$ being part of the D-extensions since our strict assumptions express that our agent already determined the outcome $\neg h \in \mathcal{A}_s$ and so $\top \Rightarrow h$ would not be action-guiding. Moreover, in $\mathcal{X}_2$ this leads to a pragmatic oddity according to which an agent should help and also not notify the neighbor. To deal with this problem, knowledge bases have been extended with a set of constraints (such as here $\{\neg h\}$) on the output in Makinson and Van Der Torre (2001). In order to simplify the presentation, we have omitted constraints in this section.

We will now consider some of the properties studied in Section 10.3. We say that L *has a proper conjunction* $\wedge$ iff (a) $\{A_1, \ldots, A_n\} \vdash_\mathsf{L} B$ iff $\{\bigwedge_{i=1}^n A_i\} \vdash_\mathsf{L} B$ and (b) $\{A_1, \ldots, A_n\} \vdash_\mathsf{L} B_1, \ldots, \{A_1, \ldots, A_n\} \vdash_\mathsf{L} B_m$ implies $\{A_1, \ldots, A_n\} \vdash_\mathsf{L} \bigwedge_{i=1}^m B_i$. In the following we assume that L has a proper conjunction.

Lemma 11.1. *An IO-logic whose metarules include LS and CT satisfies (arg-re) and (arg).*

Proof. For (arg-trans) consider a $\mathcal{D} \subseteq \mathcal{R}_d$ for which there is an $(B, A) \in \mathsf{Arg}_\mathcal{K}(\mathcal{D})$ and suppose $(C, D) \in \mathsf{Arg}_{\mathcal{K} \oplus_s A}(\mathcal{D})$. Thus, there are proofs P_1 resp. P_2 based on the rules in $\mathcal{R}_m$ of $B \Rightarrow A$ resp. of $C \Rightarrow D$ from $\mathcal{D} \cup \mathcal{R}_\mathsf{L}$. Moreover, $B \in \mathsf{Cn}_\mathsf{L}(\mathcal{A}_s)$ and $C \in \mathsf{Cn}_\mathsf{L}(\mathcal{A}_s \cup \{A\})$. So, there are $A_1, \ldots, A_n \in \mathcal{A}_s$ for which $A, A_1, \ldots, A_n \vdash_\mathsf{L} C$. By the monotonicity of L and since $\wedge$ is a proper conjunction, $B \wedge \bigwedge_{i=1}^n A_i \to B$ and $B \wedge \bigwedge_{i=1}^n A_i \wedge A \to C$. Consider the following proof based on the metarules $\mathcal{R}_m$:

$$
\cfrac{\cfrac{B \wedge \bigwedge_{i=1}^n A_i \to B \quad \cfrac{\vdots}{(B \Rightarrow A)}\,\mathsf{P}_1}{(B \wedge \bigwedge_{i=1}^n A_i \Rightarrow A)}\,\mathsf{LS} \quad \cfrac{B \wedge \bigwedge_{i=1}^n A_i \wedge A \to C \quad \cfrac{\vdots}{(C \Rightarrow D)}\,\mathsf{P}_2}{(B \wedge \bigwedge_{i=1}^n A_i \wedge A \Rightarrow D)}\,\mathsf{LS}}{(B \wedge \bigwedge_{i=1}^n A_i \Rightarrow D)}\,\mathsf{CT}
$$

Note that $B \wedge \bigwedge_{i=1}^{n} A_i \in \mathsf{Cn_L}(\mathcal{A}_s)$ and so $B \wedge \bigwedge_{i=1}^{n} A_i \Rightarrow D \in \mathsf{Arg}_{\mathcal{K}}(\mathcal{D})$.

The simple proofs of (arg-re) and (arg-mono) are left to the reader. $\qquad\square$

Corollary 11.3. *Let* $\vdash \; \in \; \{\vdash^{io}_{\cap\mathsf{AExt}}, \vdash^{io}_{\cap\mathsf{PExt}}\}$*. Any IO-logic whose metarules include LS and CT satisfies* $C_s(\vdash)$ *and* $LLE_s(\vdash)$*.*

In view of Corollary 11.1 the logics $\mathsf{IO}_i^{\star}$ with $i \in \{3,4\}$ from Fig. 26 are s-cumulative, since their notions of argument satisfy (arg-strict).

Lemma 11.2. *Any IO-logic* $\mathsf{IO}_i^{\star}$ *from Fig. 26 satisfies (arg-strict).*

Proof. Concerning (i) we note that if $A \in \mathcal{A}_s$, since $\mathrm{ID} \in \mathcal{R}_m$, also $(A,A) \in \mathsf{Arg}_{\mathcal{K}}(\emptyset)$. Concerning (ii), where $\mathcal{D} \subseteq \mathcal{R}_d$, suppose $A_1, \ldots, A_n \to B \in \mathcal{R}_\mathsf{L}$ and there are $(B_1, A_1), \ldots, (B_n, A_n) \in \mathsf{Arg}_{\mathcal{K}}(\mathcal{D})$. So, $B_i \in \mathsf{Cn_L}(\mathcal{A}_s)$ for each $i = 1, \ldots, n$. So, $C \in \mathsf{Cn_L}(\mathcal{A}_s)$ where $C = \bigwedge_{i=1}^{n} B_i$. By (LS), $(C, A_i) \in \mathsf{Arg}_{\mathcal{K}}(\mathcal{D})$ for each $i = 1, \ldots, n$. By AND, $(C, D) \in \mathsf{Arg}_{\mathcal{K}}(\mathcal{D})$ where $D = \bigwedge_{i=1}^{n} A_i$. Since $D \to B \in \mathcal{R}_\mathsf{L}$ and by RW, $(C, B) \in \mathsf{Arg}_{\mathcal{K}}(\mathcal{D})$. $\qquad\square$

By Corollary 11.1 and Lemmas 11.1 and 11.2 we get:

Corollary 11.4. *Let* $\mathsf{X} \in \{\mathsf{A}, \mathsf{P}\}$ *and* $i \in \{3,4\}$*.* $\vdash^{io}_{\cap\mathsf{XExt}}$ *satisfies s-cumulativity for* $\mathsf{IO}_i^{\star}$*.*

Example 38. s-cumulativity is not satisfied for IO_i^{+} since Ref does not hold. Consider $\mathcal{K} = \langle \{p\}, \mathcal{R}_\mathsf{CL}, \mathcal{R}_d^{id} \cup \{\top \Rightarrow \neg p\}, \mathcal{IO}_4 \rangle$. Clearly, there are maxicon sets including $\top \Rightarrow \neg p$ in view of which $\mathcal{K} \not\vdash p$, where $\vdash \; \in \; \{\vdash^{io}_{\cap\mathsf{AExt}}, \vdash^{io}_{\cap\mathsf{PExt}}\}$.

The situation is different when considering $\mathcal{K}' = \langle \{p\}, \mathcal{R}_\mathsf{CL}, \{\top \Rightarrow \neg p\}, \mathcal{IO}_4 \cup \{\mathrm{ID}\} \rangle$. Now, the only D-extension is $\emptyset$ and therefore $\mathcal{K}' \vdash p$ since $(p,p) \in \mathsf{Arg}_{\mathcal{K}'}(\emptyset)$ due to the presence of the metarule $\mapsto p \Rightarrow p$.

The following example demonstrates that the OR metarule allows for a form of disjunctive reasoning that is not available in systems without.

Example 39. Let $\mathcal{K} = \langle \mathcal{A}_s, \mathcal{R}_\mathsf{CL}, \mathcal{R}_d, \mathcal{IO}_4 \rangle$, where $\mathcal{R}_d = \{p \Rightarrow q \vee t, q \Rightarrow s, t \Rightarrow s\}$ and $\mathcal{A}_s = \{p\}$. Note that $(p,s) \in \mathsf{Arg}_{\mathcal{K}}(\mathcal{R}_d)$ in view of the proof: $(q \Rightarrow s), (t \Rightarrow s) \mapsto (q \vee t \Rightarrow s) \mapsto (p \wedge (q \vee t) \Rightarrow s)$ (by OR and LS) and $(p \Rightarrow q \vee t), (p \wedge (q \vee t) \Rightarrow s) \mapsto (p \Rightarrow s)$ by CT. Note also that $\mathcal{R}_d$ is consistent. Therefore, $\mathcal{K} \vdash^{io}_{\cap\mathsf{PExt}} s$ and $\mathcal{K} \vdash^{io}_{\cap\mathsf{AExt}} s$. The situation is different for weaker logics; for example, if we let $\mathcal{R}'_m = \mathcal{IO}_i$ where $i \in \{1,2,3\}$ and

$\mathcal{K}' = \langle \mathcal{A}_s, \mathcal{R}_{CL}, \mathcal{R}_d, \mathcal{R}'_m \rangle$, then $(p,s) \notin \mathrm{Arg}_{\mathcal{K}'}(\mathcal{R}_d)$ and so $\mathcal{K}' \not\vdash^{io}_{\cap PExt} s$ and $\mathcal{K}' \not\vdash^{io}_{\cap AExt} s$.

If OR is available, we get $\mathrm{OR}_s(\vdash^{io}_{\cap PExt})$ for base logics that satisfy (arg-or) and (arg-ex) (such as CL, see Section 11.1).

Proposition 11.5. *Let* $i \in \{2,4\}$ *and* $\vdash \, = \, \vdash^{io}_{\cap PExt}$. *If (arg-or) and (arg-ex), we have* $\mathrm{OR}_s(\vdash)$ *for* $\mathrm{IO}_i, \mathrm{IO}_i^+, \mathrm{IO}_i^\star$.

Proof. Let $\vdash \, = \, \vdash^{io}_{\cap PExt}$. Suppose $\mathcal{K} \oplus_s A \vdash C$ and $\mathcal{K} \oplus_s B \vdash C$ and consider $\mathcal{D} \in \mathrm{DExt}(\mathcal{K} \oplus_s A \vee B)$. Assume for a contradiction that $\mathcal{D}$ is inconsistent in both $\mathcal{K} \oplus_s A$ and $\mathcal{K} \oplus_s B$. So, there are $(D,E),(D',\neg E) \in \mathrm{Arg}_{\mathcal{K}\oplus_s A}(\mathcal{D})$ and $(F,G),(F',\neg G) \in \mathrm{Arg}_{\mathcal{K}\oplus_s B}(\mathcal{D})$. By (arg-ex) and LS, $(G,E),(G',\neg E) \in \mathrm{Arg}_{\mathcal{K}\oplus_s B}(\mathcal{D})$ for some $G, G' \in \mathrm{Cn}_{\mathcal{L}}(\mathcal{A}_s \cup \{B\})$. By (arg-or), $D \vee G, D' \vee G' \in \mathrm{Cn}_L(\mathcal{A}_s \cup \{A \vee B\})$. So, by OR, $(D \vee G, E),(D' \vee G', \neg E) \in \mathrm{Arg}_{\mathcal{K}\oplus_s A \vee B}(\mathcal{D})$. This shows that $\mathcal{D}$ is inconsistent in $\mathcal{K} \oplus_s A \vee B$, which is a contradiction.

So, $\mathcal{D} \subseteq \mathrm{Cons}_{\mathcal{K}\oplus_s A}(\mathcal{D})$ or $\mathcal{D} \subseteq \mathrm{Cons}_{\mathcal{K}\oplus_s B}(\mathcal{D})$. Without loss of generality, assume the former. Thus, there is a $\mathcal{D}' \in \mathrm{maxcon}_{\mathcal{K}\oplus_s A}(\mathcal{K})$ for which $\mathcal{D} \subseteq \mathcal{D}'$. Assume for a contradiction that $\mathcal{D}'$ is inconsistent in $\mathcal{K} \oplus_s A \vee B$. So, there are $(D,E),(D',\neg E) \in \mathrm{Arg}_{\mathcal{K}\oplus_s(A\vee B)}(\mathcal{D}')$. Since $D, D' \in \mathrm{Cn}_{CL}(\mathcal{A}_s \oplus_s A \vee B)$ and by (arg-or), also $D, D' \in \mathrm{Cn}_{CL}(\mathcal{A}_s \oplus_s A)$. But then $\mathcal{D}'$ is not consistent in $\mathcal{K} \oplus_s A$, which is a contradiction. So, $\mathcal{D}'$ is consistent in $\mathcal{K} \oplus_s A \vee B$ and by the $\subseteq$-maximally of $\mathcal{D}$, $\mathcal{D} = \mathcal{D}'$. Since $\mathcal{K} \oplus_s A \vdash C$, $C \in \mathrm{Con}[\mathrm{Arg}_{\mathcal{K}\oplus_s A}(\mathcal{D})]$.

Altogether this shows that $\mathcal{K} \oplus_s A \vee B \vdash C$. $\square$

An immediate consequence of Corollary 11.4 and Proposition 11.5 is:[48]

Corollary 11.5. *Let* $i \in \{3,4\}$. *If (arg-or) and (arg-ex),* $\vdash^{io}_{\cap PExt}$ *satisfies* s-*preferentiality for* $\mathrm{IO}_i^\star$.

12 Greedy Accumulation: Properties and Reiter's Default Logic

In this section we take a closer look at greedy accumulation. We start by considering some of the properties of nonmonotonic inference for greedy accumulation in Section 12.1. We then investigate Reiter's more general formulation of default rules in Section 12.2. In Section 12.3 we show that default logic can be considered a form of formal argumentation.

---

[48] The situation is different for $\vdash^{io}_{\cap AExt}$ and the systems $\mathcal{IO}_i^\star$ (for $i \in \{2,4\}$). For instance, the knowledge base $\mathcal{K}_2$ in Table 9 can easily be adjusted for input–output logics to serve as a counterexample.

12.1 Properties of Nonmonotonic Reasoning

As we have seen in Section 10.3, some properties of nonmonotonic inference (Propositions 10.1 to 10.3, in particular CT, LLE, Ref, and RW) hold for greedy accumulation. In this section we present some negative results.

Example 40 (Makinson, 2003)**.** We consider the default theory

$$\mathcal{K} = \langle \mathcal{A}_s : \emptyset, \mathcal{A}_d : \emptyset, \mathcal{R}_{\mathsf{CL}}, \mathcal{R}_d : \{ \Rightarrow q, p \lor q \Rightarrow \neg q \} \rangle.$$

We get one D-extension, namely $\{ \Rightarrow q \}$ with corresponding P-extension $\mathsf{Cn}_{\mathsf{CL}}(\{q\})$ and so $\mathcal{K} \mathrel{\vdash_{\cap\mathsf{AExt}}} q$, $\mathcal{K} \mathrel{\vdash_{\cap\mathsf{AExt}}} p \lor q$, $\mathcal{K} \mathrel{\vdash_{\cap\mathsf{PExt}}} q$, and $\mathcal{K} \mathrel{\vdash_{\cap\mathsf{PExt}}} p \lor q$.

When considering $\mathcal{K} \oplus_s (p \lor q)$ resp. $\mathcal{K} \oplus_d (p \lor q)$ the situation changes. We now have the additional D-extension $\{ p \lor q \Rightarrow \neg q \}$ resp. $\{ p \lor q, p \lor q \Rightarrow \neg q \}$ with the corresponding P-extension $\mathsf{Cn}_{\mathsf{CL}}(\{p, \neg q\})$. Thus, where $\oplus \in \{\oplus_s, \oplus_d\}$, $\mathcal{K} \oplus (p \lor q) \mathrel{\not\vdash_{\cap\mathsf{AExt}}} q$ and $\mathcal{K} \oplus (p \lor q) \mathrel{\not\vdash_{\cap\mathsf{PExt}}} q$.

The example shows that CM does not hold for greedy accumulation. The next example shows that also OR fails (it is analogous to Example 30 for temperate accumulation).

Example 41. Let $\oplus \in \{\oplus_s, \oplus_d\}$, $\vdash \in \{\vdash_{\cap\mathsf{AExt}}, \vdash_{\cap\mathsf{PExt}}\}$, and

$$\mathcal{K} = \langle \mathcal{A}_s : \emptyset, \mathcal{A}_d : \emptyset, \mathcal{R}_{\mathsf{CL}}, \mathcal{R}_d : \{ p \Rightarrow r, q \Rightarrow r \} \rangle.$$

We note that $\mathcal{K} \oplus p \vdash r$ and $\mathcal{K} \oplus q \vdash r$, although $\mathcal{K} \oplus (p \lor q) \not\vdash r$ (since the only D-extension of $\mathcal{K} \oplus (p \lor q)$ is $\emptyset$).

It is not surprising that several alternative formulations of default logic have been introduced to obtain CT or OR, a discussion of which goes beyond the scope of this Element (see Section 12.3).

12.2 Nonnormal Defaults

Reiter's default logic is one of the most prominent NMLs to reason with default rules such as "Birds usually fly." In Reiter's original account defaults are more expressive in the sense that they allow one to express additional consistency assumptions. They have the following general form:

$$r = \frac{A_1, \ldots, A_n \quad B_1, \ldots, B_m}{C}. \tag{12.2.1}$$

Besides the body $\mathsf{Body}(r) = \{A_1, \ldots, A_n\}$ and a head $\mathsf{Head}(r) = C$, each default rule also comes with *justifications* $\mathsf{Just}(r) = \{B_1, \ldots, B_m\}$. Where $\mathcal{R}_d$ is a set of generalized defaults we call knowledge bases of the form $\langle \mathcal{A}_s, \mathcal{R}_s, \mathcal{R}_d \rangle$ *Reiter default theories.*[49]

Example 42. We compare the following two defaults:

$$d_1 = \frac{\texttt{hasMotive} \quad \texttt{guilty} \wedge \texttt{suspect}}{\texttt{suspect}}$$

$$d_2 = \frac{\texttt{hasMotive} \quad \texttt{guilty} \wedge \texttt{suspect}}{\texttt{guilty} \wedge \texttt{suspect}}$$

Defaults of the form d_2, for which the justification is identical to the conclusion, are called *normal defaults*. Both, d_1 and d_2 have the same conditions of defeat: defeat happens if we learn that a person is not guilty or not suspect. However, d_1 has a weaker conclusion in that it only allows one to infer that the person who has a motive is suspect, but unlike d_2 it does not warrant the inference to the person's guilt as well. The use of nonnormal defaults is motivated by cases in which the conclusion is logically weaker than the justification. From the perspective of argumentation these are cases in which we do not only want to retract inferences when being rebutted, but also allow other forms of defeat which are expressed in terms of richer justifications (one may think of these justifications as anchors for undercuts).

Definition 12.1. Let $\mathcal{K} = \langle \mathcal{A}_s, \mathcal{R}_d, \mathcal{R}_s \rangle$ be a Reiter default theory and $\mathcal{D} \subseteq \mathcal{R}_d$. We let $\mathsf{Arg}_\mathcal{K}$ and $\mathsf{Arg}_\mathcal{K}(\mathcal{D})$ be defined similar to Definition 5.1: $a \in \mathsf{Arg}_\mathcal{K}$ iff

- $a = \langle A \rangle_\emptyset$, where $A \in \mathcal{A}_s$. We let $\mathsf{Con}(a) = A$, $\mathsf{Sub}(a) = \{a\}$, and $\mathcal{R}_d(a) = \emptyset$.
- $a = \langle a_1, \ldots, a_n \Rightarrow A \rangle_\mathcal{D}$, where $a_1, \ldots, a_n \in \mathsf{Arg}_\mathcal{K}$, $\mathcal{D} = \bigcup_{i=1}^n \mathcal{R}_d(a_i) \cup \{r\}$, and

$$r = \frac{\mathsf{Con}(a_1), \ldots, \mathsf{Con}(a_n) \quad B_1, \ldots, B_m}{A} \in \mathcal{R}_d.$$

  We let $\mathsf{Con}(a) = A$, $\mathsf{Sub}(a) = \bigcup_{i=1}^n \mathsf{Sub}(a_i) \cup \{a\}$, and $\mathcal{R}_d(a) = \mathcal{D}$.
- $a = \langle a_1, \ldots, a_n \rightarrow A \rangle_\mathcal{D}$, where $a_1, \ldots, a_n \in \mathsf{Arg}_\mathcal{K}$, $\mathsf{Con}(a_1), \ldots, \mathsf{Con}(a_n) \rightarrow A \in \mathcal{R}_s$, and $\mathcal{D} = \bigcup_{i=1}^n \mathcal{R}_d(a_i)$.
  We let $\mathsf{Con}(a) = A$, $\mathsf{Sub}(a) = \bigcup_{i=1}^n \mathsf{Sub}(a_i) \cup \{a\}$, and $\mathcal{R}_d(a) = \mathcal{D}$.

Where $a \in \mathsf{Arg}_\mathcal{K}$ and $\mathcal{D} \subseteq \mathcal{R}_d$, we let $\mathsf{Def}(a) =_{\mathsf{df}} \mathcal{R}_d(a)$ and $\mathsf{Arg}_\mathcal{K}(\mathcal{D}) =_{\mathsf{df}} \{a \in \mathsf{Arg}_\mathcal{K} \mid \mathsf{Def}(a) \subseteq \mathcal{D}\}$. We let $\mathsf{Trig}_\mathcal{K}(\mathcal{D})$ be the set of all $r \in \mathcal{R}_d$ such that

---

[49] In order to simplify things, we omit, e.g., priorities from the presentation in this section.

for all $A \in \mathrm{Body}(r)$ there is an $a \in \mathrm{Arg}_{\mathcal{K}}(\mathcal{D})$ with $\mathrm{Con}(a) = A$. Where $\mathcal{E}$ is a set of $\mathcal{L}$-sentences, we let $\mathrm{Cons}_{\mathcal{K}}(\mathcal{E})$ be the set of all $r \in \mathcal{R}_d$ for which each $B \in \mathrm{Just}(r)$ is consistent with $\mathcal{E}$. We let $\mathrm{Trig}_{\mathcal{K}}^{\top}(\mathcal{E}, \mathcal{D}) = \mathrm{Trig}_{\mathcal{K}}(\mathcal{D}) \cap \mathrm{Cons}_{\mathcal{K}}(\mathcal{E})$.

D-extensions of Reiter default theories are generated by an algorithm, similar to `GreedyAcc`. However, we need to accommodate the consistency check (in the loop guard, line 3) to the additional ingredient of defaults, their justifications. Since justifications need not be implied by the heads of their respective defaults, the consistency check cannot proceed iteratively anymore. This is to avoid that a justification of a default added earlier conflicts with the head of one added later on in the procedure. Reiter solved this problem by means of a semi-inductive procedure in which the reasoner has to first guess the outcome. Consistency checks are then performed relative to the guessed set of sentences. This results in the algorithm GREEDYACCGEN.[50]

Algorithm 5 Generalized Greedy Accumulation

```
 1: procedure GREEDYACCGEN(K, D)      ▷ where K = ⟨As, Rd, Rs⟩ and D ⊆ Rd
 2:     D* ← ∅                                                            ▷ init
 3:     E ← Con[ArgK(D)]                             ▷ the guessed P-extension
 4:     while ∃r ∈ Trig┬K(E, D*) \ D* do           ▷ scan triggered and consistent
                                                                        defaults
 5:         D* ← D* ∪ {r}                                      ▷ update scenario
 6:     end while                      ▷ no more triggered and consistent defaults
 7:     if D = D* then
 8:         return(D*)                                            ▷ correct guess
 9:     else
10:         return(failure)                                    ▷ incorrect guess
11:     end if
12: end procedure
```

Definition 12.2. A *Reiter D-extension* of a Reiter default theory $\mathcal{K} = \langle \mathcal{A}_s, \mathcal{R}_d, \mathcal{R}_s \rangle$ is a set $\mathcal{D} \subseteq \mathcal{R}_d$ for which $\mathcal{D} = \mathrm{GREEDYACCGEN}(\mathcal{K}, \mathcal{D})$. Its corresponding A-extension is $\mathrm{Arg}_{\mathcal{K}}(\mathcal{D})$, and its corresponding P-extension is $\mathrm{Con}[\mathrm{Arg}_{\mathcal{K}}(\mathcal{D})]$. We write again $\mathrm{DExt}(\mathcal{K})$ [resp. $\mathrm{AExt}(\mathcal{K})$, $\mathrm{PExt}(\mathcal{K})$] for the set of Reiter D- [resp. A-,P-]extensions of $\mathcal{K}$.

Example 43. We consider $\mathcal{K} = \langle \mathcal{A}_s, \mathcal{R}_d, \mathcal{R}_{\mathrm{CL}} \rangle$, where

$$\mathcal{A}_s = \{t, t'\} \qquad \text{and} \qquad \mathcal{R}_d = \left\{ r_1 : \frac{t \quad p, \neg s}{p}, \; r_2 : \frac{t' \quad s}{s} \right\}.$$

We simulate two runs of GREEDYACCGEN.

---

50 An alternative algorithm without the need to guess has been proposed in Łukaszewicz (1988). It also avoids the problem of nonexisting extensions in Example 44.

1. When running GREEDYACCGEN($\mathcal{K}, \{r_1\}$), $\mathcal{E}$ is the set $\{t, t', p\}$ closed under classical logic. In the first round of the **while**-loop we add r_1 to $\mathcal{D}^\star$. In the second round we add r_2 since its justification is also consistent with $\mathcal{E}$. This leads to `failure` since $\mathcal{D}^\star \neq \{r_1\}$.

2. We consider GREEDYACCGEN($\mathcal{K}, \{r_2\}$). Now $\mathcal{E}$ is the set $\{t, t', s\}$ closed under classical logic. Since r_1 is inconsistent with $\mathcal{E}$, the loop terminates with $\mathcal{D}^\star = \{r_2\}$ and therefore returns the only D-extension of $\mathcal{K}$.

Reiter's format of defaults and the GREEDYACCGEN algorithm generalize greedy accumulation as presented in Section 5.2.1. Suppose we have a knowledge base $\mathcal{K} = \langle \mathcal{A}_s, \mathcal{R}_d, \mathcal{R}_s \rangle$ with only defaults of the form $r = A_1, \ldots, A_n \Rightarrow B$. We can translate $\mathcal{K}$ to a Reiter default theory $\mathcal{K}'$ by translating each default r to a Reiter default

$$\frac{A_1, \ldots, A_n \quad B}{B}$$

Applying GREEDYACC to $\mathcal{K}$ and GREEDYACCGEN to $\mathcal{K}'$ will lead to the same D-extensions (under the translation) and therefore the same P-extensions (Łukaszewicz, 1988).

Nevertheless, the introduction of generalized defaults may lead to scenarios in which no D-extensions exist.

Example 44. Consider $\mathcal{K} = \langle \mathcal{A}_s, \mathcal{R}_d, \mathcal{R}_{\mathsf{CL}} \rangle$ where $\mathcal{A}_s = \{p\}$ and $\mathcal{R}_d$ only contains the default $r = \frac{p \quad \neg q}{q}$. We have two possible guesses to run GREEDYACCGEN: $\mathcal{D}_1 = \{r\}$ and $\mathcal{D}_2 = \emptyset$. Note that with the first guess the algorithm never enters the **while**-loop, since the justification $\neg q$ of r is inconsistent with $\mathsf{Con}[\mathsf{Arg}_{\mathcal{K}}(\mathcal{D}_1)] = \mathsf{Cn}_{\mathsf{CL}}(\{p, q\})$ and it therefore returns `failure`. With the second guess, however, since $\neg q$ is consistent with $\mathsf{Con}[\mathsf{Arg}_{\mathcal{K}}(\emptyset)] = \mathsf{Cn}_{\mathsf{CL}}(\{p\})$, the **while**-loop is entered and r is added to $\mathcal{D}^\star$, again leading to `failure`.

Similarly as described in Section 10.2 for normal default theories, also Reiter D-extensions can be characterized in terms of fixed-points.

Proposition* 12.1. *Let $\mathcal{K} = \langle \mathcal{A}_s, \mathcal{R}_d, \mathcal{R}_s \rangle$ be a Reiter default theory, $\mathcal{D} \subseteq \mathcal{R}_d$, and $\mathcal{E} = \mathsf{Con}[\mathsf{Arg}_{\mathcal{K}}(\mathcal{D})]$. $\mathcal{D}$ is a Reiter D-extension of $\mathcal{K}$ iff $\mathcal{D} = \mathsf{Trig}_{\mathcal{K}}^{\top}(\mathcal{E}, \mathcal{D})$.*

12.3 An Argumentative Characterization of Reiter's Default Logic

In this section we demonstrate that there is a natural argumentative characterization of extensions of Reiter default theories.[51] For this we use a slightly

---

$$a_0 = \Diamond p$$
$$a_1 = \Diamond \neg s$$
$$b_0 = \Diamond s$$
$$a = \langle t \rangle, a_0, a_1 \rightarrow p$$
$$b = \langle t' \rangle, b_0 \rightarrow s \rightarrow \neg\neg s$$

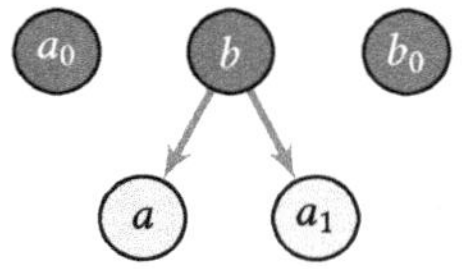

Figure 27 Illustration of Example 45.

generalized language $\text{sent}_{\mathcal{L}}^{\Diamond} = \text{sent}_{\mathcal{L}} \cup \{\Diamond A \mid A \in \text{sent}_{\mathcal{L}}\}$. The unary operator $\Diamond$ will track the consistency assumptions underlying the justifications in generalized defaults. For this, it need not get equipped with logical properties, but it will be used when defining argumentative attacks.

Definition 12.3. Given a Reiter default theory $\mathcal{K} = \langle \mathcal{A}_s, \mathcal{R}_d, \mathcal{R}_s \rangle$, we define the argumentation framework $\mathcal{AF}_{\mathcal{K}} = \langle \text{Arg}(\mathcal{K}'), \rightsquigarrow \rangle$, where $\mathcal{K}' = \langle \mathcal{A}_s, \mathcal{A}'_d, \mathcal{R}_s \cup \mathcal{R}'_s \rangle$, $\mathcal{A}'_d$ contains $\Diamond B$ for every sentence B, and $r' = A_1, \ldots, A_n, \Diamond B_1, \ldots, \Diamond B_n \rightarrow C \in \mathcal{R}'_s$ iff

$$r = \frac{A_1, \ldots, A_n \quad B_1, \ldots, B_m}{C} \in \mathcal{R}_d. \tag{12.3.1}$$

We let $a \rightsquigarrow b$ if there is a $b' \in \text{Sub}(b)$ such that $\text{Con}(a) \in \overline{\text{Con}(b')}$, where $\overline{\Diamond A} = \{\neg A\}$ for all sentences A.

Example 45 (Ex. 43 cont.). We recall $\mathcal{K} = \langle \mathcal{A}_s, \mathcal{R}_d, \mathcal{R}_{\text{CL}} \rangle$ from Example 43. In Fig. 27 we see an excerpt of $\mathcal{AF}_{\mathcal{K}}$. The only Reiter D-extension of $\mathcal{K}$ is $\mathcal{D} = \{\frac{t' \quad s}{s}\}$. Its induced P-extension corresponds exactly to the consequences of the arguments in the only stable A-extension of $\mathcal{K}'$ (highlighted).

The following result shows that the correspondence between Reiter extensions and stable A-extensions is not coincidental.

Theorem* 12.1 *Let $\mathcal{K} = \langle \mathcal{A}_s, \mathcal{R}_d, \mathcal{R}_s \rangle$ be a general default theory and $\mathcal{K}'$ as in Definition 12.3. Then*

1. *for every Reiter P-extension $\mathcal{E}$ of $\mathcal{K}$, there is a stable A-extension $\mathcal{X}$ of $\mathcal{K}'$ for which $\text{Con}[\mathcal{X}] \cap \text{sent}_{\mathcal{L}} = \mathcal{E}$,*
2. *for every stable A-extension $\mathcal{X}$ of $\mathcal{K}'$, $\text{Con}[\mathcal{X}] \cap \text{sent}_{\mathcal{L}}$ is a Reiter P-extension of $\mathcal{K}$.*

Selected Further Readings

Metatheoretic properties of reasoning on the basis of maxicon sets in the style of Rescher and Manor have been thoroughly studied in Benferhat et al. (1997). A well-known prioritized version is provided in Brewka (1989).

An overview on the state of the art in input–output logic can be found in Parent and van der Torre (2013). Input–output logics have also been applied to causal and explanatory reasoning in many works by Bochman: Bochman (2005) is a good starting point. Proof theories for input–output logics that allow for Boolean combinations of defeasible conditionals are presented in Straßer et al. (2016) and van Berkel and Straßer (2022). The latter also provides a translation of input/output logic to formal argumentation. Hansen's approach to (prioritized) deontic conditionals falls within temperate accumulation (Hansen, 2008), while Horty's follows the greedy approach of deontic logic (Horty, 2012).

An overview on many variants of default logic can be found in Antoniou and Wang (2009). Due to the problems indicated in Section 12.1, some cumulative variants have been proposed (Antonelli, 1999; Brewka, 1991) as well as disjunctive versions (Gelfond et al., 1991). In Poole (1985) special attention is paid to specificity.

Moore's autepistemic logic has close links to default logic (Denecker et al., 2011; Konolige, 1988) and to logic programming (Gelfond & Lifschitz, 1988). The equi-expressivity of adaptive logics and default assumptions have been shown in Van De Putte (2013). A modal selection semantics (as presented in Sections 5.3 and Section 15) for default logic has been studied in Lin and Shoham (1990).

PART IV SEMANTIC METHODS

In this final part of the Element we move the focus from syntax to semantics. The main underlying method will be based on imposing preference orders on interpretations and selecting specific interpretations of the given information. In Section 13 we will study a well-known semantics for defaults (Kraus et al., 1990) based on the idea of preferring more "normal" models over less "normal" ones. In particular, we investigate a sophisticated method to determine the set of defaults that are entailed by a given set of defaults, the Rational Closure (Lehmann & Magidor, 1992). Section 14 provides an overview on some quantitative methods for providing meaning to defaults, including probabilistic methods. In Section 15 we use the idea of ordering models to obtain a semantics for temperate accumulation. Finally, in Section 16 we introduce one of the central paradigms in logic programming, answer set programming, and show how it is closely related to both default logic and formal argumentation. In this way, we once more demonstrate that although the underlying formal methods of NMLs are quite diverse, they often result in the same consequence relations and extensions (recall Fig. 14).

13 A Semantics for Defaults

In Section 1.1 we proposed to interpret defaults $A \Rightarrow B$ as "If A then normally/typically/usually/etc. B". The argumentation (Part II) and accumulation methods (Part III) model reasoning with defaults by focusing on inference rules: arguments are formed by treating $\Rightarrow$ as a defeasible inference rule and the notions of consistency and conflict are used to obtain nonmonotonic consequence relations. In this way the meaning of $\Rightarrow$ is characterized in a syntax-based, proof-theoretic way.

In what follows, we will interpret $A \Rightarrow B$ in a semantic, model-theoretic way, by:

($\star$) *B holds under the most normal/plausible/etc. situations in which A holds.*

This interpretation naturally leads to nonmonotonicity: while Anne jogs most mornings (`morning` $\Rightarrow$ `jog`), rainy mornings are exceptional (`morning` $\wedge$ `rain` $\not\Rightarrow$ `jog`).

The proposed interpretation can be made precise by using models of the form $M = \langle \mathcal{S}, \prec, v \rangle$ with a nonempty set of situations $\mathcal{S}$ which are interpreted by means of an assignment function $v : \text{Atoms} \to \wp(\mathcal{S})$ that associates atoms with the set of those situations (also referred to as states) in which they hold, and an order $\prec \subseteq \mathcal{S} \times \mathcal{S}$ that orders situations according to their normality. We read $s \prec s'$ (where $s, s' \in \mathcal{S}$) as expressing that s' is less normal than s. Where $s \in \mathcal{S}$ we let

- $(M, s) \models \top$
- $(M, s) \models A$ for an atom A iff $s \in v(A)$
- $(M, s) \models \neg A$ iff $(M, s) \not\models A$
- $(M, s) \models A \wedge B$ iff $(M, s) \models A$ and $(M, s) \models B$
- $(M, s) \models A \vee B$ iff $(M, s) \models A$ or $(M, s) \models B$.

We let $[\![A]\!]_M =_{\text{df}} \{s \in \mathcal{S} \mid (M, s) \models A\}$ be the set of all situations which validate A and skip the subscript whenever the context disambiguates. Such sets of situations are called *propositions*. Following the idea expressed in ($\star$), we let:[52]

- $M \models A \Rightarrow B$ iff in all $s \in \min_{\prec}([\![A]\!])$, $(M, s) \models B$.

---

[52] The idea of using semantic selections to give meaning to conditionals predates NMLs. Stalnaker used a selection function to give meaning to counterfactuals (R. F. Stalnaker, 1968), while Lewis used semantic spheres (Lewis, 1973).

Note that validity for $A \Rightarrow B$ is defined globally, not relative to a given state. In the following we write $\Rightarrow_M$ for the set of all $A \Rightarrow B$ for which $M \models A \Rightarrow B$, and we write $A \Rightarrow_M B$ in case $A \Rightarrow B \in \Rightarrow_M$. We will call $\Rightarrow_M$ the *conditional theory induced by M*.

By letting $A <_M B =_{df} A \vee B \Rightarrow_M \neg B$ we can express that A is "more normal" than B. Indeed, if in all minimal states of $A \vee B$, $A \wedge \neg B$ holds, then the minimal states of A are $<$-lower than those of B.

One may think of M as a model of the belief state of an agent. $A \Rightarrow_M B$ expresses that if the agent were to learn A, she would believe B, where $\top \Rightarrow_M B$ means that, absent new information, the agent believes B. If $A <_M B$, the agent would be less surprised when learning A than when learning B.

Example 46. Let $M = \langle \mathcal{S}, <, v \rangle$ where $\mathcal{S} = \{s_1, s_2, s_3\}$, $v(p) = \mathcal{S}$, $v(q) = \{s_1, s_3\}$, $v(r) = \{s_1, s_2\}$, $v(s) = \{s_3\}$, and $< = \{(s_2, s_3)\}$. We have, for instance, $\min_<(\llbracket p \rrbracket) = \{s_1, s_2\}$, $\min_<(\llbracket q \rrbracket) = \{s_1, s_3\}$, $\min_<(\llbracket p \vee q \rrbracket) = \{s_1, s_2\}$, $\min_<(\llbracket r \vee s \rrbracket) = \{s_1, s_2\}$, and $\min_<(\llbracket p \wedge q \rrbracket) = \{s_1, s_3\}$. Thus,

1. $p \Rightarrow_M r$ and $p \vee q \Rightarrow_M r$,
2. $r \vee s \Rightarrow_M \neg s$ and so $r <_M s$,
3. but $p \not\Rightarrow_M \neg q$ and $p \wedge q \not\Rightarrow_M r$.

In models with infinite sequences of more and more normal states we may face situations in which $\min_<(\llbracket A \rrbracket)$ is empty, although $\llbracket A \rrbracket$ is not. To exclude such scenarios, we restrict the focus on only those models for which it holds that for all sentences A and all $s \in \llbracket A \rrbracket \setminus \min_<(\llbracket A \rrbracket)$ there is an $s' \in \min_<(\llbracket A \rrbracket)$ such that $s' < s$. Models that satisfy this requirement are called *smooth* (Kraus et al., 1990) or *stuttered* (Makinson, 2003). In what follows we will discuss some other basic properties one may impose on $<$, such as transitivity (if $s_1 < s_2$ and $s_2 < s_3$, then also $s_1 < s_3$) or irreflexivity ($s \not< s$).

In particular, we will study two classes of well-behaved models by only considering models for which the underlying order $<$ has specific properties.

13.1 Preferential Models

Let us now state properties one may expect from the conditional theory $\Rightarrow_M$ induced by a model M. For this, we adjust the properties from Section 4 to statements of the form $A \Rightarrow B$.

The properties are to be read as closure conditions on a set of defaults $\mathcal{D}$. For example, REF states that $A \Rightarrow A \in \mathcal{D}$ for all sentences A, or CM states that if $A \Rightarrow B, A \Rightarrow C \in \mathcal{D}$, then also $A \wedge B \Rightarrow C \in \mathcal{D}$ for all sentences A, B, C.

LLE	If $\vdash_{CL} A \equiv B$, then $A \Rightarrow C$ iff $B \Rightarrow C$.
RW	If $A \vdash_{CL} B$ and $C \Rightarrow A$ implies $C \Rightarrow B$.
REF	$A \Rightarrow A$.
OR	If $A \Rightarrow C$ and $B \Rightarrow C$, then $A \vee B \Rightarrow C$.
CM	If $A \Rightarrow B$ and $A \Rightarrow C$, then $A \wedge B \Rightarrow C$.
CT	If $A \Rightarrow B$ and $A \wedge B \Rightarrow C$, then $A \Rightarrow C$.

We call a set of defaults $\mathcal{D}$ *preferential theory* in case it is closed under these properties.

Given the intuitive nature of the previously mentioned properties, a natural question is: what kinds of models give rise to preferential theories? With Kraus et al. (1990) we call $M = \langle \mathcal{S}, <, v \rangle$ a *preferential model* in case $<$ is smooth, irreflexive, and transitive. It is an easy exercise to confirm that the preceding properties hold for $\Rightarrow_M$, where M is a preferential model. We paradigmatically consider CM (for which smoothness is needed) and OR.

For CM, suppose that $A \Rightarrow_M B$ and $A \Rightarrow_M C$. In case $\min_<([\![A \wedge B]\!]) = \emptyset$, trivially $A \wedge B \Rightarrow C$. Otherwise, consider some $s \in \min_<([\![A \wedge B]\!])$. Assume for a contradiction that $s \notin \min_<([\![A]\!])$. Thus, by smoothness, there is a $s' \in \min_<([\![A]\!])$ such that $s' < s$. Since $s' \in \min_<([\![A]\!])$ and $A \Rightarrow_M B$, $(M,s) \models B$ and so $(M,s) \models A \wedge B$. But then s was not $<$-minimal in $[\![A \wedge B]\!]$, a contradiction. So, $s \in \min_<([\![A]\!])$ and so $(M,s) \models C$ since $A \Rightarrow_M C$. Thus, $A \wedge B \Rightarrow_M C$.

For OR suppose that $A \Rightarrow_M C$ and $B \Rightarrow_M C$. If $\min_<([\![A \vee B]\!]) = \emptyset$, trivially $A \vee B \Rightarrow C$. Otherwise consider an $s \in \min_<([\![A \vee B]\!])$. Assume for a contradiction that $s \notin \min_<([\![A]\!]) \cup \min_<([\![B]\!])$. Then, there is a $s' \in [\![A]\!] \cup [\![B]\!]$ such that $s' < s$. Since $s' \in [\![A \vee B]\!]$, this contradicts the $<$-minimality of s. So, $s \in \min_<([\![A]\!]) \cup \min_<([\![B]\!])$ and so, by the supposition, $(M,s) \models C$. So, $A \vee B \Rightarrow_M C$.

Altogether, it can be shown that:

Theorem 13.1 (Kraus et al., 1990). *If $M = \langle \mathcal{S}, <, v \rangle$ is a preferential model, $\Rightarrow_M$ is a preferential theory.*

Also the inverse holds, that is, any preferential $\Rightarrow$ can be characterized by a preferential model. As a result, preferential models provide an adequate semantic characterization of preferential theories.

Theorem 13.2 (Kraus et al., 1990). *If $\mathcal{D}$ is a preferential theory, then there is a preferential model M for which $\Rightarrow_M = \mathcal{D}$.*

13.2 Ranked Models

Preferential models do not, in general, validate the rational monotonicity property:[53]

RM   If $A \Rightarrow B$ and $A \not\Rightarrow \neg C$ then $A \wedge C \Rightarrow B$.

RM has in $A \not\Rightarrow \neg C$ a negative condition. A set of defaults $\mathcal{D}$ is closed under RM if for all sentences A, B, C, if $A \Rightarrow B \in \mathcal{D}$ and $A \Rightarrow \neg C \notin \mathcal{D}$, then $A \wedge C \Rightarrow B \in \mathcal{D}$. A preferential theory $\mathcal{D}$ that is closed under RM is called *rational*.

Example 47 (Example 46 cont.).   In our example we have: $p \Rightarrow_M r$ and $p \not\Rightarrow_M \neg q$, but $p \wedge q \not\Rightarrow_M r$. So, $\Rightarrow_M$ does not validate RM, although it is preferential.

As Example 47 shows, preferential models M do not, in general, give rise to rational theories $\Rightarrow_M$. What kind of models are such that their induced conditional theories are rational? The key will be to let all states be comparable.

Preferential models allow for incomparabilities of states in the following sense: there are s_1, s_2, s_3 for which $s_2 < s_3$ but s_1 is not comparable to s_2 and s_3. We have such a situation in Example 46. We notice that this is responsible for a violation of RM by $\Rightarrow_M$.

The RM property holds if the set of minimal states of $A \wedge C$ is contained in the set of minimal states of A, in case there are some minimal states of A that validate C. In view of $A \not\Rightarrow \neg C$, one may expect them to be, since there are indeed minimal states of A that do not satisfy $\neg C$ and in which therefore C holds. In our example the outlier is $s_3 \in \min_<(\llbracket p \wedge q \rrbracket) \setminus \min_<(\llbracket p \rrbracket)$. The situation improves if s_1 is comparable to s_2 and/or to s_3. In the rightmost model of Fig. 28 we have $p \Rightarrow_M r$, $p \not\Rightarrow_M \neg q$, and $p \wedge q \Rightarrow_M r$ (while in the model in the center we have $p \Rightarrow_M \neg q$).

A *ranked model* $M = \langle \mathcal{S}, <, v \rangle$ is a preferential model for which $<$ is *modular*, that is, for all s_1, s_2, s_3, if $s_2 < s_3$, then $s_1 < s_3$ or $s_2 < s_1$. It can easily be seen that an order is modular in case its states can be "ranked" by a function $r : \mathcal{S} \to \mathcal{T}$ to a total order $\langle \mathcal{T}, < \rangle$ in such a way that $s < s'$ iff $r(s) < r(s')$. So, any states s_1 and s_2 in a ranked model are comparable in that $r(s_1) \leq r(s_2)$ or $r(s_2) < r(s_1)$. Ranked models provide an adequate semantic characterization of rational theories.

---

[53] RM has a corresponding principle CV in Lewis's logic VC, as studied in the context of counterfactuals (Lewis, 1973).

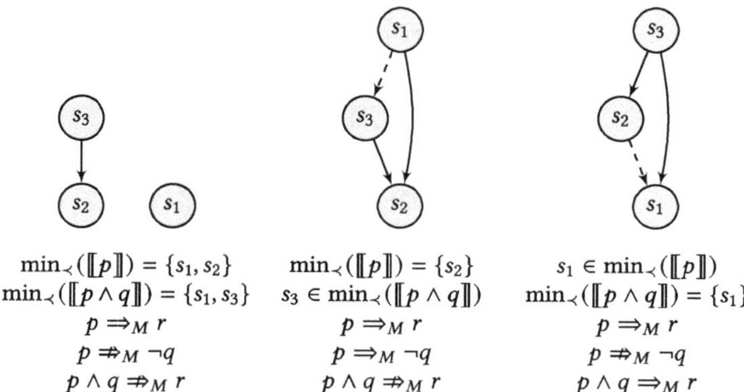

Figure 28 (Left) The preferential model $M = \langle \mathcal{S}, <, v \rangle$ of Example 46. (Middle and Right) Ranked models $M' = \langle \mathcal{S}, <', v \rangle$ based on modular extension $<'$ of $<$. The dashed arrow is optional.

Theorem 13.3 (Lehmann and Magidor (1992)). *(i) If M is a ranked model, $\Rightarrow_M$ is a rational theory. (ii) If $\mathcal{D}$ is a rational theory, there is a ranked model M for which $\Rightarrow_M = \mathcal{D}$.*

13.3 What Does a Conditional Knowledge Base Entail?

While so far our focus has been on semantic characterizations of defaults, we now turn to a different, although related question. Given a set of defaults $\mathcal{D}$ (of the form $A \Rightarrow B$): what other defaults follow from them? To answer this question, one may take the principles LLE, RW, REF, OR, CM, and CT (and RM) underlying preferential (resp. rational) consequence relations and use them as metarules $\mathcal{R}_m$, just like we have seen metarules being applied to defeasible rules in the context of input–output logic (see Section 11.3.2).

The set of metarules consisting of LLE, RW, REF, OR, CM and CT is often referred to as system P, while adding RM to P results in system R. Where $S \in \{P, R\}$, we write $A \Rightarrow B \in \mathrm{Cn}_S(\mathcal{D})$ if $A \Rightarrow B$ is derivable from $\mathcal{D}$ by means of the metarules in S.

Example 48. Suppose we have the set of defaults $\mathcal{D} = \{$`environmentalist` $\Rightarrow$ `vegan`; `environmentalist` $\Rightarrow$ `avoidsFlying`$\}$. Then, `environmentalist`$\wedge$ `vegan` $\Rightarrow$ `avoidsFlying` follows from $\mathcal{D}$ in both system P and system R (by means of CM).

Given the representational results Theorems 13.1 to 13.3 from Sections 13.1 and 13.2 concerning the adequacy of preferential resp. of ranked models, it is easy to see that P- and R-entailment can be semantically expressed. We say that a preferential model M is a model of $\mathcal{D}$ iff for all $A \Rightarrow B \in \mathcal{D}$, $A \Rightarrow_M B$.

Theorem 13.4 (Lehmann and Magidor, 1992). *Where $\mathcal{D}$ is a set of defaults, $A \Rightarrow B \in \mathrm{Cn_P}(\mathcal{D})$ iff for all preferential models M of $\mathcal{D}$, $A \Rightarrow_M B$.*

The preferential theory $\mathrm{Cn_P}(\mathcal{D})$ is called the *preferential closure of* $\mathcal{D}$. It is interesting, and maybe somewhat disappointing, to observe that for any $\mathcal{D}$, P-entailment and R-entailment are identical, that is, $\mathrm{Cn_P}(\mathcal{D}) = \mathrm{Cn_R}(\mathcal{D})$. This is for a rather trivial reason: the rule RM is also applied to negated defaults, no set of defaults $\mathcal{D}$ contains such objects, and so RM is never applied. In fact, the question is, what is a more rewarding interpretation of $\not\Rightarrow$ in the context of RM? It seems reasonable to consider RM as a closure principle, that is, a principle that extends $\mathrm{Cn_R}(\mathcal{D})$ to a set $\mathsf{RatClosure}(\mathcal{D})$ for which:

($\dagger$) if

$\quad (\alpha_1) \quad A \Rightarrow B \in \mathsf{RatClosure}(\mathcal{D})$ and

$\quad (\alpha_2) \quad A \Rightarrow \neg C \notin \mathsf{RatClosure}(\mathcal{D})$,

(γ) then $A \wedge C \Rightarrow C \in \mathsf{RatClosure}(\mathcal{D})$.

But, how to find such a set $\mathsf{RatClosure}(\mathcal{D})$? A first idea could be to simply take the theory provided by the intersection of the theories induced by ranked models of $\mathcal{D}$. But, as the following example shows, this does not work.

Example 49 (Example 48 cont.). We now show that, although

(α_1) in all ranked models of $\mathcal{D}$, d_1 : `environmentalist` $\Rightarrow$ `vegan` holds; and
(α_2) there are ranked models of $\mathcal{D}$ in which d_2 : `environmentalist` $\Rightarrow$ `¬drummer` doesn't hold; but
($\overline{\gamma}$) there are ranked models of $\mathcal{D}$ in which d_3 : `environmentalist` $\wedge$ `drummer` $\Rightarrow$ `vegan` doesn't hold.

Given $\mathcal{D}$, in view of d_2, being a drummer is irrelevant to the question whether environmentalists are usually vegans (d_1). If Anne is an environmentalist who happens to be a drummer, this should still allow us to infer that she (likely) is a vegan (d_3). While from an intuitive point of view the rule RM seems to exactly allow for the strengthening of an antecedent with information that is not atypical for the antecedent (like being a drummer for being an environmentalist), the example demonstrates that it doesn't fulfill this role. For this we consider the following states (where $i, j, k \in \{0, 1\}$ and in the case of $s_3^{i,j,k}$ we let $(i, j, k) \notin \{(1, 0, 1), (1, 1, 1)\}$):

Figure 29 shows two ranked models of $\mathcal{D}$. Only M_2 validates d_3. Not so M_1, since

$$s_3^{0,1,1} \in \min{}_{<}(\llbracket \texttt{environmentalist} \wedge \texttt{drummer} \rrbracket) \text{ and } (M_1, s_3^{0,1,1}) \not\models \texttt{vegan}.$$

	s_1	s_2	$s_3^{i,j,k}$	$s_4^{i,j,k}$
environmentalist	1	1	1	0
vegan	1	1	i	i
drummer	0	1	j	j
avoidsFlying	1	1	k	k

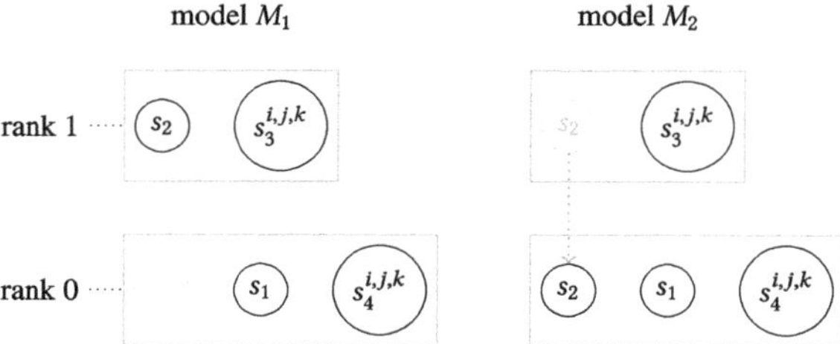

Figure 29 Two ranked models of Example 49.

The problem with M_1 is that it validates d_2 due to the fact that

$$\min_{\prec}(\llbracket\texttt{environmentalist}\rrbracket) = \{s_1\}$$

and in s_1, $\neg\texttt{drummer}$ is true. In contrast, in M_2,

$$\min_{\prec}(\llbracket\texttt{environmentalist}\rrbracket) = \{s_1, s_2\}$$

and since in s_2 $\texttt{drummer}$ holds, d_2 is invalid in this model, and by means of RM it has to be the case that d_3 holds. Indeed, in M_2 we have:

$$\min_{\prec}(\llbracket\texttt{environmentalist}\rrbracket) \supseteq \min_{\prec}(\llbracket\texttt{environmentalist}\wedge\texttt{drummer}\rrbracket).$$

In sum, although each ranked model M satisfies RM for its induced theory $\Rightarrow_M$, RM as interpreted in (†) is not satisfied for the consequence relation induced by the ranked models. We need another approach.

In order to let RM fulfill this role, it would seem that we need to interpret sentences $\neg B$ as *not* being default entailed by A (i.e., $A \Rightarrow \neg B$) as much as possible, in order to allow for the inference from $A \Rightarrow C$ to $A \wedge B \Rightarrow C$ via RM. After all, in all ranked models M of $\mathcal{D}$ in which d_2 doesn't hold, d_3 holds (unlike in our M_1). So, our strategy is to somehow trade in the invalidity of more general defaults ($A \Rightarrow \neg B$) for the validity of more specific defaults ($A \wedge B \Rightarrow C$). How to execute this tricky task?

Figure 29 gives a hint at a procedure for this: when moving from model M_1 to M_2 we ranked one state, namely s_2, more normal. We can generalize this: our goal is to rank each state as normal as possible. This intuitive idea can be made precise in terms of imposing an order $\sqsubset$ on the ranked models of a given set of defaults $\mathcal{D}$ and to select the best model. The way two ranked models M and M' of $\mathcal{D}$ are compared has an argumentative interpretation. Suppose there are two discussants, one arguing in favor of M, the other one in favor of M'. Each discussant produces attacks against the model favored by the other agent and defends her model against such attacks. M is *preferred* to M' (written: $M \sqsubset M'$) if the proponent of M can attack M' such that the proponent of M' cannot defend M', and M can be defended from every attack by the latter. But, how are attacks and defenses supposed to work?

A proponent of M may *attack* the model M' favored by the other agent by accusing it of validating too many inferential relations, that is, by pointing to a default $A \Rightarrow B$ that holds in M' but not in M. Recall that our goal is to invalidate for arbitrary A and B the default $A \Rightarrow B$, if possible. There is a trade-off though, since invalidating some $A \Rightarrow \neg B$ may lead, via RM, to the strengthening of the antecedent of others, for example, from $A \Rightarrow C$ to $A \wedge B \Rightarrow C$.

In Fig. 29, the discussant arguing in favor of M_1 may attack the proponent of M_2 by stating that

$$\texttt{environmentalist} \wedge \texttt{drummer} \Rightarrow_{M_2} \texttt{vegan,}$$

$$\texttt{while environmentalist} \wedge \texttt{drummer} \not\Rightarrow_{M_1} \texttt{vegan.}$$

However, a way to *defend* M_1 is to point out that (a)

$$\texttt{environmentalist} \Rightarrow_{M_1} \neg\texttt{drummer,} \tag{a}$$

$$\texttt{while environmentalist} \not\Rightarrow_{M_2} \neg\texttt{drummer,}$$

and (b) $\texttt{environmentalist}$ is according to M_1's standards even more normal than $\texttt{environmentalist} \wedge \texttt{drummer}$ (formally, $\texttt{environmentalist} <_{M_1} \texttt{environmentalist} \wedge \texttt{drummer}$).

Altogether, our informal discussion motivates the following definition of an order $\sqsubset$ between models of a set of defaults $\mathcal{D}$. For this we let

$$\Rightarrow_M^{\downarrow A} =_{\mathsf{df}} \{C \Rightarrow D \in \,\Rightarrow_M \mid C <_M A\}.$$

Definition 13.1. Where M and M' are two ranked models, $M \sqsubset M'$ iff the following two conditions hold:

(defeat) there is an $A \Rightarrow B \in (\Rightarrow_{M'} \setminus \Rightarrow_M)$ such that $\Rightarrow_M^{\downarrow A} \subseteq \,\Rightarrow_{M'}$, and

(defense) for all $A \Rightarrow B \in (\Rightarrow_M \setminus \Rightarrow_{M'})$, $(\Rightarrow_{M'}^{\downarrow A} \setminus \Rightarrow_M) \neq \emptyset$.

(defeat) expresses that there is an attack from M to M' which is undefendable, while **(defense)** expresses that every attack from M' to M can be defended. In terms of the preceding described argumentative reading, the two conditions describe winning conditions for the proponent of M when arguing with an opponent favoring M'.

Definition 13.2. In case there is a unique $\sqsubset$-minimal model M among all ranked models of a given set of defaults $\mathcal{D}$, $\Rightarrow_M$ is called the *rational closure* of $\mathcal{D}$.[54]

Example 50 (Example 49 cont.). We consider models M_1 and M_2 in Fig. 29. We have $M_2 \sqsubset M_1$. (**defeat**) holds since

$$\texttt{environmentalist} \Rightarrow \neg\texttt{drummer} \in (\Rightarrow_{M_1} \setminus \Rightarrow_{M_2})$$
$$\text{and } \Rightarrow_{M_2}^{\downarrow\texttt{environmentalist}} = \emptyset \subseteq \Rightarrow_{M_1}.$$

Also (**defense**) holds, for example, where $A = \texttt{environmentalist} \wedge \texttt{drummer}$, although $A \Rightarrow \texttt{vegan} \in \Rightarrow_{M_2} \setminus \Rightarrow_{M_1}$, there is

$$\texttt{environmentalist} \Rightarrow \neg\texttt{drummer} \in (\Rightarrow_{M_1}^{\downarrow A} \setminus \Rightarrow_{M_2}).$$

We now discuss an alternative characterization of the rational closure in terms of ranking sentences according to their normality (relative to $\mathcal{D}$). This will also help defining a significant class of sets of defaults for which the rational closure exists, so-called admissible sets (see Proposition 13.1). For this we inductively associate sentences with ordinals via a function rank. We say that a sentence A is *exceptional* for $\mathcal{D}$ in case $\top \Rightarrow \neg A \in \mathrm{Cn_P}(\mathcal{D})$, so in case $\mathcal{D}$ expresses that normally A is false. Similarly, $A \Rightarrow B \in \mathcal{D}$ is exceptional for $\mathcal{D}$ if A is exceptional for $\mathcal{D}$. We collect the exceptional defaults in $\mathcal{D}$ in the set $\mathrm{Exc}(\mathcal{D})$. Where $\mathcal{D}_0 = \mathcal{D}$, we let $\mathcal{D}_{\tau+1} = \mathrm{Exc}(\mathcal{D}_\tau)$ for all successor ordinals $\tau + 1$ and $\mathcal{D}_\tau = \bigcup_{\tau' < \tau} \mathcal{D}_{\tau'}$ for all limit ordinals τ. Now, some sentence A has a rank for $\mathcal{D}$ in case there is a least ordinal τ for which A is not exceptional for $\mathcal{D}_\tau$, in which case the rank of A is τ. Otherwise, A has *no rank*.[55]

Example 51 (Example 50 cont.). For all $A \in \{\texttt{environmentalist}, \texttt{vegan}, \texttt{avoidsFlying}, \texttt{drummer}\}$, A and $\neg A$ are not exceptional for $\mathcal{D}$ and so have rank 0. Exceptional for $\mathcal{D}$ are, for instance, $\texttt{environmentalist} \wedge \neg\texttt{vegan}$ and $\texttt{environmentalist} \wedge \texttt{vegan} \wedge \neg\texttt{avoidsFlying}$. These formulas have rank 1.

We call a set $\mathcal{D}$ *admissible* if for every sentence A that has no rank, $A \Rightarrow \bot \in \mathrm{Cn_P}(\mathcal{D})$. Examples for admissible sets are sets $\mathcal{D}$ based on a finite language

---

[54] An equivalent approach to Rational Closure has been defined on the basis of ϵ-semantics (see Section 14.1) under the name of system **Z** (Goldszmidt & Pearl, 1990; Pearl, 1990).

[55] In case our language only contains finitely many atoms, say n many, there is an upper limit to the rank, namely 2^n.

(a language with only finitely many atoms), or for which the preferential closure has no infinite sequences of more and more normal sentences.

Proposition 13.1 (Lehmann and Magidor (1990)). *Where $\mathcal{D}$ is admissible, the rational closure of $\mathcal{D}$ exists and it consists of all $A \Rightarrow B$ for which $A \wedge \neg B$ has no rank, or for which* $\mathrm{rank}(A) < \mathrm{rank}(A \wedge \neg B)$.

Example 52 (Example 51 cont.). In view of Proposition 13.1, for instance, `environmentalist` $\wedge$ `vegan` $\Rightarrow$ `avoidsFlying` is in the rational closure of $\mathcal{D}$ since `environmentalist` $\wedge$ `vegan` has rank 0 while `environmentalist` $\wedge$ `vegan` $\wedge$ `¬avoidsFlying` has rank 1.

However, `environmentalist` $\wedge$ `¬vegan` $\Rightarrow$ `avoidsFlying` is not in the rational closure of $\mathcal{D}$ since

$$\text{environmentalist} \wedge \neg\text{vegan}$$
$$\text{and} \quad \text{environmentalist} \wedge \neg\text{vegan} \wedge \neg\text{avoidsFlying}$$

have the same rank, namely 1. This shows that rational closure "suffers" from the drowning problem (see Section 1.2): since nonvegans are exceptional with respect to `environmentalist` $\Rightarrow$ `vegan`, they turn out exceptional also with respect to `environmentalist` $\Rightarrow$ `avoidsFlying`.[56]

14 Quantitative Methods

So far, we have interpreted $A \Rightarrow B$ as B holds in the most normal situations in which A holds (recall ($\star$)). According to a similar idea:

($\star'$) $A \Rightarrow B$ holds if, given A, B is more normal/plausible/etc. than $\neg B$.

The notion of normality was rendered precise in terms of a preference order on the logically possible situations. Instead of this qualitative approach, one may follow the idea behind ($\star'$) but proceed quantitatively and interpret $A \Rightarrow B$ in terms of probabilities: given A, B is more probable than $\neg B$. In what follows we introduce the central approach to probabilistic semantics by Adams (1975), which corresponds to system P.[57]

---

[56] Some follow-up work tackles this problem by penalizing models in the comparison of models for violations of defaults (where M violates $A \Rightarrow B$ if A holds in M but B does not) such that the penalty is the higher the more specific the default is (Goldszmidt et al., 1993; Lehmann, 1995).

[57] In Eagle (2024) the reader finds an introduction to inductive logics which are used to probabilistically study the support that some evidence provides for a claim.

Table 11 The states and probability functions for Example 53.

situation s	$s \models b$	$s \models f$	$s \models w$	P_1	P_2
s_1	✓			.2	.1
s_2	✓		✓	.2	.1
s_3	✓	✓		.2	.2
s_4	✓	✓	✓	.4	.2
s_1'				0	.1
s_2'			✓	0	.1
s_3'		✓		0	.1
s_4'		✓	✓	0	.1

14.1 Adams' Approach: ϵ-Semantics

We again consider a set of situations $\mathcal{S}$ interpreted via an assignment v : Atoms $\to \{0, 1\}$.[58]

We now equip $\wp(\mathcal{S})$ with a probability function P which maps sets of situations into $[0, 1]$ such that (1) $P(\mathcal{S}) = 1$ and (2) for any pairwise disjoint $\mathcal{S}_1, \ldots, \mathcal{S}_n \in \wp(\mathcal{S})$, $P(\mathcal{S}_1 \cup \ldots \cup \mathcal{S}_n) = \sum_{i=1}^{n} P(\mathcal{S}_i)$. We call each $M = \langle \mathcal{S}, P, v \rangle$ a *probabilistic model*. For every formula A, a probabilistic model provides information of how probable it is to be in a situation consistent with A. Where $[\![A]\!]_M = \{s \in \mathcal{S} \mid (M, s) \models A\}$ (we skip the subscript when the context disambiguates), we will write $P(A)$ instead of $P([\![A]\!])$ for the formal expression of this information. The conditional probability $P(A \mid B)$ is, as usual, defined by $\frac{P(A \wedge B)}{P(A)}$ in case $P(A) > 0$ (otherwise, it is undefined). It expresses the probability of being in a situation in which A holds, given that B holds.

Example 53. Let Atoms $= \{b, f, w\}$, where b stands for 'being a bird', f for 'flying' and w for 'having wings'. The probabilistic models $M_1 = \langle \mathcal{S}, P_1, v_1 \rangle$ and $M_2 = \langle \mathcal{S}, P_2, v_2 \rangle$ are given by Table 11.

We have, for instance, $P_1(b) = P_1(\{s_1, \ldots, s_4\}) = 1$, $P_1(b \wedge f) = P_1(\{s_3, s_4\}) = .6$ and therefore $P_1(f \mid b) = {\cdot}6/1 = .6$, while $P_2(b) = .6$, $P_2(b \wedge f) = .4$ and $P_2(f \mid b) = {\cdot}4/.6 = 2/3$.

We now define when a default $A \Rightarrow B$ holds in a given probabilistic model $M = \langle \mathcal{S}, P, v \rangle$ (in signs, $A \Rightarrow_M B$). A consequence relation can then be defined as follows. Where $\mathcal{D}$ is a set of defaults: $A \Rightarrow B \in \mathsf{Cn}_\epsilon(\mathcal{D})$ iff for all

---

[58] In order to slightly simplify the discussion, we stick to a finite language.

probabilistic models M of $\mathcal{D}$, $A \Rightarrow_M B$.[59] Before moving to Adams' approach, we state three naive ideas. Let $M = \langle \mathcal{S}, P, v \rangle$.

Naive 1 $A \Rightarrow_M^1 B$, iff $P(A \wedge B) > P(A \wedge \neg B)$ or if $P(A) = 0$.[60]

Naive 2 $A \Rightarrow_M^2 B$, iff $P(B \mid A) > P(\neg B \mid A)$ or if $P(A) = 0$.

Naive 3 $A \Rightarrow_M^3 B$, iff $P(B \mid A) > \tau$ for some threshold value τ (such as $\tau = .5$), or if $P(A) = 0$.[61]

We note that approaches **Naive 1** and **Naive 2** are equivalent since, in case $P(A) > 0$: $P(B \mid A) > P(\neg B \mid A)$, iff $\frac{P(A \wedge B)}{P(A)} > \frac{P(A \wedge \neg B)}{P(A)}$, iff $P(A \wedge B) > P(A \wedge \neg B)$. The weakness of the preceding naive approaches can be illustrated by applying them to our example.

Example 54 (Example 53 cont.). Let $i \in \{1, 2, 3\}$. In model M_1 we have $P_1(b \wedge w) = P_1(\{s_2, s_4\}) = .6 > P_1(b \wedge \neg w) = P_1(\{s_1, s_3\}) = .4$ which is why $b \Rightarrow_{M_1}^i w$. Similarly, $P_1(b \wedge f) = P(\{s_3, s_4\}) = .6 > P_1(b \wedge \neg f) = P_1(\{s_1, s_2\}) = .4$, which is why $b \Rightarrow_{M_1}^i f$. However, since $P_1(b \wedge f \wedge w) = P_1(\{s_4\}) = .4 < P_1(b \wedge \neg(f \wedge w)) = P_1(\{s_1, s_2, s_3\}) = .6$, we also have $b \not\Rightarrow_{M_1}^i f \wedge w$, even $b \Rightarrow_{M_1}^i \neg(f \wedge w)$.

This means that **AND** is violated for the induced consequence relation. This model allows for a situation where $b \Rightarrow_{M_1} f, b \Rightarrow_{M_1} w, b \Rightarrow_{M_1} \neg(f \wedge w)$, albeit $\{b, f, \neg(f \wedge w)\}$ is an inconsistent set. Similarly, other central properties of nonmonotonic entailment, such as **CT**, fail in our naive approaches.

In view of these weaknesses, Adams introduced another approach. In his semantics the degree of assertability of $A \Rightarrow B$ is modelled by the conditional probability $P(B \mid A)$. In a nutshell, the central idea is that some $A \Rightarrow B$ is entailed by a set of defaults $\mathcal{D}$ in case its assertability approximates 1 when the elements of $\mathcal{D}$ are being interpreted as increasingly assertable. In formal terms, let P be a *proper probability function for* $\mathcal{D}$ in case $P(B \mid A) > 0$ for all $A \Rightarrow B \in \mathcal{D}$. We define:

Definition 14.1 (ϵ-entailment, Adams, 1975; Pearl 1989)**.** Let $\mathcal{D} \cup \{A \Rightarrow B\}$ be a set of defaults. We define: $A \Rightarrow B \in \mathsf{Cn}_\epsilon(\mathcal{D})$, iff, for any $\epsilon \in (0, 1]$, there

---

[59] Adams considers knowledge bases of the form $\langle \mathcal{A}_d, \mathcal{R}_d \rangle$. Our restriction to knowledge bases consisting of sets of defaults $\mathcal{D}$ is without loss of generality since, in Adams' system, factual assumptions A are equivalent to $\top \Rightarrow A$.

[60] In Section 14.2 we show, however, that when utilizing other types of quantitative measures, this idea does not suffer from the problems discussed later for probability measures.

[61] By using big-stepped probabilities, the problems indicated later for approaches based on probabilistic thresholds can be avoided (see Benferhat et al. (1999)).

is a $\delta \in (0, 1]$ such that for all proper probability functions P for $\mathcal{D}$: if, for all $C \Rightarrow D \in \mathcal{D}, P(D \mid C) \geq 1 - \delta$, then $P(B \mid A) \geq 1 - \epsilon$.

Does this approach lead to a more well-behaved entailment relation and what are characteristic properties of ϵ-entailment? Let us have another look at our example.

Example 55 (Example 54 cont.). Where $\mathcal{D} = \{b \Rightarrow \neg f, b \Rightarrow w\}$, we have, for instance, $b \Rightarrow \neg f \wedge w \in \mathsf{Cn}_\epsilon(\mathcal{D})$. In order to show this, let $\epsilon \in (0, 1]$ be arbitrary and consider a probability function P. We need to find a $\delta \in (0, 1]$ such that if $P(\neg f \mid b), P(w \mid b) \geq 1 - \delta$, then $P(\neg f \wedge w \mid b) \geq 1 - \epsilon$. Let $\delta = \epsilon/2$ and suppose that $P(\neg f \mid b), P(w \mid b) \geq 1 - \delta$. Then,

$$P(\neg f \wedge w \mid b) = 1 - P(f \vee \neg w \mid b)$$

$$= 1 - \frac{P((f \vee \neg w) \wedge b)}{P(b)} \leq 1 - \left(\frac{P(f \wedge b)}{P(b)} + \frac{P(\neg w \wedge b)}{P(b)} \right)$$

$$= 1 - (P(f \mid b) + P(\neg w \mid b))$$

$$= 1 - ((1 - P(\neg f \mid b)) + (1 - P(w \mid b))) = P(\neg f \mid b) + P(w \mid b) - 1$$

$$\geq 2(1 - \delta) - 1 = 2 - 2\delta - 1 = 1 - 2\delta = 1 - \epsilon$$

What we have just shown in the context of our example is not coincidental. Indeed, the proof of **AND** for ϵ-entailment follows exactly the structure of the proof in Example 55. What is more, ϵ-entailment can be shown to coincide with system P for finite knowledge bases (Geffner, 1992; Lehmann & Magidor, 1990): a remarkable correspondence between two rather different perspectives on the meaning of $\Rightarrow$.

14.2 Other Quantitative Approaches

We close this section with some pointers to related approaches. While in Adams' approach we find a probabilistic characterization of P-entailment, the reader may wonder whether also R-entailment can be represented by a quantitative approach. Indeed, utilizing a nonstandard probabilistic approach including infinitesimal values, Lehmann and Magidor (1992) present a variant of Adams' system that characterizes rational entailment.

Instead of probability measures other quantitative measures have been utilized in the literature to give meaning to defaults. We let $\mathcal{S}$ again be a finite set of situations and $v : \mathsf{Atoms} \to \wp(\mathcal{S})$ an assignment function.

- A *possibility measure* (Dubois & Prade, 1990) $\mathsf{Poss} : \wp(\mathcal{S}) \to [0, 1]$ determines the possibility of a set of situations, from impossible (0) to maximally possible (1).[62] It is required that $\mathrm{Poss}(\emptyset) = 0$, $\mathrm{Poss}(\mathcal{S}) = 1$, and for any $\mathcal{S}' \subseteq \mathcal{S}$, $\mathrm{Poss}(\mathcal{S}') = \max_{s \in \mathcal{S}'}(\mathrm{Poss}(\{s\}))$. A *possibilistic model M* is of the form $\langle \mathcal{S}, \mathrm{Poss}, v \rangle$.

- An *ordinal ranking function* (Goldszmidt & Pearl, 1992; Spohn, 1988) $\kappa : \wp(\mathcal{S}) \to \{0, 1, \ldots, \infty\}$ associates each set of situations with a level of surprise, from unsurprising (0) to shocking (∞). It is required that $\kappa(\mathcal{S}) = 0$, $\kappa(\emptyset) = \infty$, and, for any $\mathcal{S}' \subseteq \mathcal{S}$, $\kappa(\mathcal{S}') = \min_{s \in \mathcal{S}'}(\kappa(\{s\}))$. An *ordinal ranking model M* is of the form $\langle \mathcal{S}, \kappa, v \rangle$.

It is easy to see that letting $s < s'$ iff $\mathrm{Poss}(\{s\}) > \mathrm{Poss}(\{s'\})$ in the context of a possibilistic model $M = \langle \mathcal{S}, \mathrm{Poss}, v \rangle$ [resp. iff $\kappa(s) < \kappa(s')$ in the context of an ordinal ranking model $M = \langle \mathcal{S}, \kappa, v \rangle$] gives rise to a ranked model $M' = \langle \mathcal{S}, <, v \rangle$.

In each of these approaches the meaning of defaults in a given model is defined analogous to the underlying idea of $(\star')$:

- Where $M = \langle \mathcal{S}, \mathrm{Poss}, v \rangle$ is a possibilistic model, we let $A \Rightarrow_M B$ iff $\mathrm{Poss}([\![A]\!]) = 0$ or $\mathrm{Poss}([\![A \wedge B]\!]) > \mathrm{Poss}([\![A \wedge \neg B]\!])$
- Where $M = \langle \mathcal{S}, \kappa, v \rangle$ is an ordinal ranking model, we let $A \Rightarrow_M B$ iff $\kappa([\![A]\!]) = \infty$ or $\kappa([\![A \wedge \neg B]\!]) > \kappa([\![A \wedge B]\!])$.

We say that a possibilistic model [resp. an ordinal ranking model] M is a model of a set of defaults $\mathcal{D}$ in case $A \Rightarrow_M B$ for all $A \Rightarrow B \in \mathcal{D}$.

For instance, a possibilistic model verifies $A \Rightarrow B$ just in case A is impossible, or if $A \wedge B$ is strictly more possible than $A \wedge \neg B$. Since ranking functions model the level of surprise an agent would face when learning that some A is true, according to a ranking function $A \Rightarrow B$ is valid in case A would cause maximal surprise or if learning about $A \wedge B$ would cause strictly less surprise than learning about $A \wedge \neg B$.

Example 56 (Ex. 53 cont.). We consider the set of states $\mathcal{S}$ in Example 53. Fig. 30 shows a cardinal ranking function κ and a possibility function Poss. Recall that for $\mathcal{S}' \subseteq \mathcal{S}$,

$$\kappa(\mathcal{S}') = \min_{s \in \mathcal{S}'}(\kappa(\{s\})) \quad \text{and} \quad \mathrm{Poss}(\mathcal{S}') = \max_{s \in \mathcal{S}'}(\mathrm{Poss}(\{s\})),$$

which is why the figure fully characterizes κ and Poss by illustrating what values are assigned to single states. Where $M_\kappa = \langle \mathcal{S}, \kappa, v \rangle$ and $M_{\mathrm{Poss}} = \langle \mathcal{S}, \mathrm{Poss}, v \rangle$, we have:

---

[62] Necessity is a separate technical notion in possibility theory, defined by $\mathrm{Nec}(\mathcal{S}') = 1 - \mathrm{Poss}(\mathcal{S} \setminus \mathcal{S}')$.

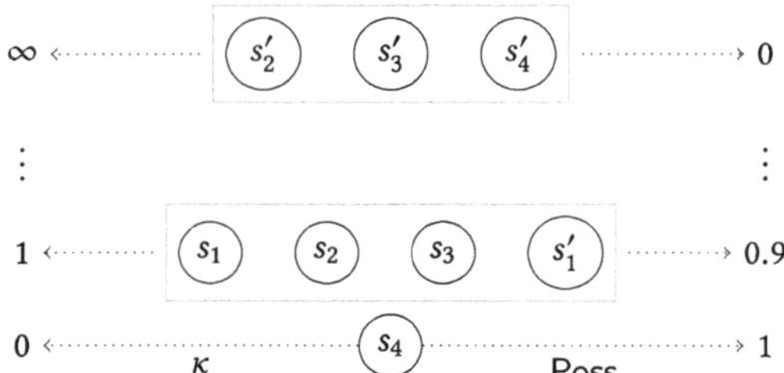

Figure 30 Example 56. (Left) The cardinal ranking κ. (Right) The possibility function Poss.

- $b \Rightarrow_{M_\kappa} f \wedge w$ since $\kappa([\![b \wedge (f \wedge w)]\!]) = \kappa(\{s_4\}) = 0 < 1 = \min_{s \in \{s_1, s_2, s_3\}}(\kappa(\{s\})) = \kappa([\![b \wedge \neg(f \wedge w)]\!])$
- $b \Rightarrow_{M_{\mathrm{Poss}}} f \wedge w$ since $\mathrm{Poss}([\![b \wedge (f \wedge w)]\!]) = \mathrm{Poss}(\{s_4\}) = 1 > .9 = \max_{s \in \{s_1, s_2, s_3\}}(\mathrm{Poss}(\{s\})) = \kappa([\![b \wedge \neg(f \wedge w)]\!])$
- $\neg w \not\Rightarrow_{M_\kappa} \neg f$ since $\kappa([\![\neg w \wedge \neg f]\!]) = \min_{s \in \{s_1, s_1'\}} = 1 \ / < 1 = \min_{s \in \{s_3, s_3'\}} = \kappa([\![\neg w \wedge f]\!])$, and
- $\neg w \not\Rightarrow_{M_{\mathrm{Poss}}} \neg f$ since $\mathrm{Poss}([\![\neg w \wedge \neg f]\!]) = \max_{s \in \{s_1, s_1'\}} = .9 \not< .9 = \max_{s \in \{s_3, s_3'\}} = \mathrm{Poss}([\![\neg w \wedge f]\!])$.

Entailment relations are induced in the usual way. Given a set of defaults $\mathcal{D}$, we let

- $A \Rightarrow B \in \mathsf{Cn}_{\mathrm{poss}}(\mathcal{D})$ iff for all possibilistic models $M = \langle \mathcal{S}, \mathrm{Poss}, v \rangle$ of $\mathcal{D}$, $A \Rightarrow_M B$,
- $A \Rightarrow B \in \mathsf{Cn}_{\mathrm{rank}}(\mathcal{D})$ iff for all ordinal ranking models $M = \langle \mathcal{S}, \kappa, v \rangle$ of $\mathcal{D}$, $A \Rightarrow_M B$.

It is a most astonishing result in NML that all these different perspectives lead exactly to a characterization of P-entailment, a result that strongly underlines the central character of its underlying reasoning principles.

Theorem 14.1 (Dubois and Prade, 1991; Geffner, 1992; Lehmann and Magidor, 1992). *Let $\mathcal{D}$ be a finite set of defaults. We have: $A \Rightarrow B \in \mathsf{Cn}_{\mathsf{P}}(\mathcal{D})$ iff $A \Rightarrow B \in \mathsf{Cn}_\epsilon(\mathcal{D})$ iff $A \Rightarrow B \in \mathsf{Cn}_{\mathrm{poss}}(\mathcal{D})$ iff $A \Rightarrow B \in \mathsf{Cn}_{\mathrm{rank}}(\mathcal{D})$ iff $A \Rightarrow B \in \mathsf{Cn}_{\mathsf{R}}(\mathcal{D})$.*

15 A Preferential Semantics for Some NMLs

In this section we present a preferential semantics for logics based on temperate accumulation and knowledge bases of the type $\langle \mathcal{A}_s, \mathcal{A}_d, \mathcal{R}_\mathsf{L} \rangle$,[63] such as Rescher

---

[63] In Section 11.3.1 we have denoted this class of knowledge bases by $\mathbf{K}_{\mathrm{mcon}}$.

and Manor's logics based on maxicon sets and Makinson's default assumptions (see Section 11.3.1).

In fact, this is exactly the semantics we introduced in Section 5.3, so our main aim in this section is to show its adequacy for temperate accumulation. We refer to Examples 21 and 22 in Section 5.3 for an illustration of this idea.

Let us briefly recall the general setup. We work in the context of a Tarski logic L (such as classical logic) which has an adequate model-theoretic semantic representation: for any set of L-sentences $\mathcal{S} \cup \{A\}$ it holds: $\mathcal{S} \vdash A$ iff for all L-models M of $\mathcal{S}$ (i.e., for all $B \in \mathcal{S}$, $M \models B$) it is the case that $M \models A$. In particular, we assume that the consistency of a set of sentences $\mathcal{S}$ can be expressed by $\mathcal{M}_\mathsf{L}(\mathcal{S}) \neq \emptyset$.

In order to determine whether A defeasibly follows from $\mathcal{K}$, we compare the L-models of the strict assumptions $\mathcal{A}_s$ in terms of how normal they interpret the defeasible assumptions in $\mathcal{A}_d$. For this, we consider the *normal part* of a given model M, which is simply the subset of defeasible assumptions it validates: $\mathcal{N}_\mathcal{K}(M) =_{\mathsf{df}} \{A \in \mathcal{A}_d \mid M \models A\}$. Now we define an order on the L-models of $\mathcal{A}_s$ by:

$$M \leq_\mathcal{K} M' \text{ iff } \mathcal{N}_\mathcal{K}(M') \subseteq \mathcal{N}_\mathcal{K}(M).$$

We select the most normal models of $\mathcal{K}$ and define a consequence relation $\vdash_\leq$ by:

$$\mathcal{K} \vdash_\leq A \text{ iff for all } M \in \min_{\leq_\mathcal{K}}(\mathcal{M}(\mathcal{A}_s)), M \models A.$$

In the following we show how $\vdash^{\mathsf{tem}}_{\cap\mathsf{PExt}}$ and $\vdash^{\mathsf{tem}}_{\cap\mathsf{AExt}}$ can be characterized by a semantics based on $\leq$.[64] For this we make use of the characterization of temperate accumulation in terms of maxicon sets (see Lemma 10.1 and Theorem 10.1).

Theorem 15.1. *Let* $\mathcal{K} = \langle \mathcal{A}_s, \mathcal{A}_d, \mathcal{R}_\mathsf{L} \rangle$ *be a knowledge base. Then,* $\mathcal{K} \vdash^{\mathsf{tem}}_{\cap\mathsf{PExt}} A$ *iff* $\mathcal{K} \vdash_\leq A$.

The theorem follows in view of the following lemmas.

Lemma 15.1. *For every* $M \in \min_\leq(\mathcal{M}(\mathcal{A}_s))$, $\mathcal{N}_\mathcal{K}(M) \in \mathsf{maxcon}(\mathcal{K})$.

Proof. Suppose that $M \in \min_\leq(\mathcal{M}(\mathcal{A}_s))$ and let $\mathcal{D} = \mathcal{N}(M)$. Thus, $\mathcal{D} \cup \mathcal{A}_s$ is consistent. Consider some $\mathcal{D}' \subseteq \mathcal{A}_d$ for which $\mathcal{D}' \cup \mathcal{A}_s$ is consistent and

---

64 Also $\vdash^{\mathsf{tem}}_{\cup\mathsf{ext}}$ can be characterized by a similar semantics; for details, see how this is achieved in adaptive logics in, e.g., Batens (2007), and Straßer (2014). In adaptive logics the semantic selection for $\vdash^{\mathsf{tem}}_{\cap\mathsf{PExt}}$ corresponds to the so-called minimal abnormality strategy, while the semantic selection for $\vdash^{\mathsf{tem}}_{\cap\mathsf{AExt}}$ corresponds to the reliability strategy. Adaptive logics offer adequate dynamic proof theories for each of these semantic methods.

$\mathcal{D} \subseteq \mathcal{D}'$. Thus, there is a $M' \in \mathcal{M}(\mathcal{A}_s \cup \mathcal{D}')$. Since $\mathcal{D}' \subseteq \mathcal{N}(M')$, $\mathcal{N}(M) \subseteq \mathcal{N}(M')$ and by the $\preceq$-minimality of M, $\mathcal{N}(M') = \mathcal{D} = \mathcal{D}'$. Thus, $\mathcal{D} \in \mathsf{maxcon}(\mathcal{K})$. $\qquad\square$

Lemma 15.2. *For every $\mathcal{D} \in \mathsf{maxcon}(\mathcal{K})$ there is an $M \in \min_{\preceq}(\mathcal{M}(\mathcal{A}_s))$ for which $\mathcal{N}_{\mathcal{K}}(M) = \mathcal{D}$.*

Proof. Suppose $\mathcal{D} \in \mathsf{maxcon}(\mathcal{K})$. By the consistency of $\mathcal{D} \cup \mathcal{A}_s$, there is an $M \in \mathcal{M}(\mathcal{A}_s \cup \mathcal{D})$. Consider a $M' \in \mathcal{M}(\mathcal{A}_s)$ for which $\mathcal{N}(M) \subseteq \mathcal{N}(M')$. Then $\mathcal{N}(M') \cup \mathcal{A}_s$ is consistent. Since $\mathcal{D} \subseteq \mathcal{N}(M)$ and the maximality of $\mathcal{D}$, $\mathcal{N}(M') = \mathcal{D}$. So, $\mathcal{N}(M') = \mathcal{N}(M)$ and thus, $M \in \min_{\preceq}(\mathcal{M}(\mathcal{A}_s))$. $\qquad\square$

Proof of Theorem 15.1. $\mathcal{K} \vdash^{\mathsf{tem}}_{\cap \mathsf{PExt}} A$, iff [by Proposition 11.3], for all $\mathcal{D} \in \mathsf{maxcon}(\mathcal{K})$, $A \in \mathsf{Cn}_{\mathsf{L}}(\mathcal{A}_s \cup \mathcal{D})$, iff [by Lemmas 15.1 and 15.2], for all $M \in \min_{\preceq}(\mathcal{M}(\mathcal{A}_s))$, $M \models A$, iff, $\mathcal{K} \vdash_{\preceq} A$. $\qquad\square$

We now move on to characterize $\vdash^{\mathsf{tem}}_{\cap \mathsf{AExt}}$ semantically. We can capture this consequence relation by defining a threshold function τ on the degree of normality a selected model is allowed to have.

$$\tau : \mathcal{K} \mapsto \bigcap \{ \mathcal{N}_{\mathcal{K}}(M') \mid M' \in \min_{\preceq}(\mathcal{M}) \}$$

$$\mathsf{core}_{\preceq}(\mathcal{K}) =_{\mathsf{df}} \{ M \in \mathcal{M}(\mathcal{A}_s) \mid \mathcal{N}_{\mathcal{K}}(M) \supseteq \tau(\mathcal{K}) \} .$$

So the core of $\mathcal{K}$ consists of those models whose normal part contains at least all those sentences that are part of the normal parts of every $\preceq$-minimal model. Clearly, each $\preceq$-minimal model belongs to the core, but possibly also other models. Let, moreover,

$$\mathcal{K} \vdash^{\mathsf{core}}_{\preceq} A \text{ iff for all } M \in \mathsf{core}_{\preceq}(\mathcal{K}), M \models A.$$

Given that $\mathsf{core}_{\preceq}(\mathcal{K}) \supseteq \min_{\preceq}(\mathcal{M}(\mathcal{A}_s))$, the consequence relation $\vdash^{\mathsf{core}}_{\preceq}$ will typically give rise to a more cautious reasoning style than $\vdash_{\preceq}$.

Example 57 (Example 21 cont.). For our $\mathcal{K}' = \langle \mathcal{A}'_s, \mathcal{A}'_d, \mathcal{R}_{\mathsf{CL}} \rangle$ with

$$\mathcal{A}'_s = \{ p, p \wedge \neg \mathsf{ab}_1 \supset q, p \wedge \neg \mathsf{ab}_2 \supset r, q \wedge \neg \mathsf{ab}_3 \supset \neg r, r \supset s, \neg r \supset s \},$$

and $\mathcal{A}'_d = \{ \neg \mathsf{ab}_1, \neg \mathsf{ab}_2, \neg \mathsf{ab}_3 \}$ we have three minimal models: M_1 with $\mathcal{N}_{\mathcal{K}'}(M_1) = \{ \neg \mathsf{ab}_1, \neg \mathsf{ab}_2 \}$, M_2 with $\mathcal{N}_{\mathcal{K}'}(M_2) = \{ \neg \mathsf{ab}_1, \neg \mathsf{ab}_3 \}$, and M_3 with $\mathcal{N}_{\mathcal{K}'}(M_3) = \{ \neg \mathsf{ab}_2, \neg \mathsf{ab}_3 \}$ (see Fig. 12). So, $\tau(\mathcal{K}') = \emptyset$ and therefore $\mathsf{core}_{\preceq}(\mathcal{K}') = \mathcal{M}(\mathcal{A}_s)$, and $\mathcal{K}' \vdash^{\mathsf{core}}_{\preceq} A$ iff $\mathcal{A}_s \vdash_{\mathsf{CL}} A$. This highlights the fact that $\vdash^{\mathsf{core}}_{\preceq}$ leads to a more cautious reasoning style than $\vdash_{\preceq}$.

We now consider $\mathcal{K}_2 = \mathcal{K}' \oplus_s q = \langle \mathcal{A}^2_s, \mathcal{A}_d, \mathcal{R}_{\mathsf{CL}} \rangle$, where $\mathcal{A}^2_s = \mathcal{A}'_s \cup \{q\}$. In Fig. 31 we highlight the models in $\mathsf{core}_{\preceq}(\mathcal{K}_2)$. In this case $\min_{\preceq}(\mathcal{M}(\mathcal{A}^2_s)) \subsetneq$

	r	ab_1	ab_2	ab_3
M_1	1	0	0	1
M_2	0	0	1	0
M_4	0	1	1	0
$M_5^i \ (i \in \{0,1\})$	i	0	1	1
M_6	1	1	0	1
$M_7^i \ (i \in \{0,1\})$	i	1	1	1

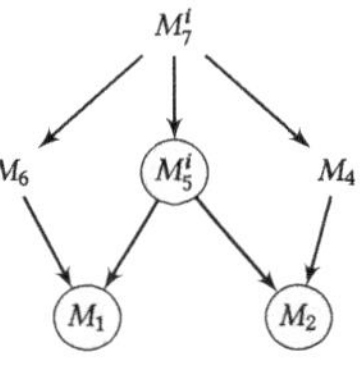

Figure 31 The order $\leq$ on the models of $\mathcal{K}_2$ in Example 57. Highlighted are the models in $\mathrm{core}_{\leq}(\mathcal{K}_2)$. The atoms p, q, and s are true in every model of $\mathcal{A}_s^2$.

$\mathrm{core}_{\leq}(\mathcal{K}_2) \subsetneq \mathcal{M}(\mathcal{A}_s^2)$. This is reflected, for instance, in the consequences $\mathcal{K}_2 \vdash_{\leq}^{\mathrm{core}} \neg\mathsf{ab}_1$ while $\mathcal{A}_s \not\vdash_{\mathrm{CL}} \neg\mathsf{ab}_1$, and $\mathcal{K}_2 \vdash_{\leq} \neg(\mathsf{ab}_2 \wedge \mathsf{ab}_3)$ while $\mathcal{K}_2 \not\vdash_{\leq}^{\mathrm{core}} \neg(\mathsf{ab}_2 \wedge \mathsf{ab}_3)$.

With Lemmas 15.1 and 15.2 we immediately get:

Corollary 15.1. *Let $\mathcal{K} = \langle \mathcal{A}_s, \mathcal{A}_d, \mathcal{R}_{\mathsf{L}} \rangle$ be a knowledge base and $M \in \mathcal{M}(\mathcal{A}_s)$. Then, $M \in \mathrm{core}_{\leq}(\mathcal{K})$ iff $\mathcal{N}_{\mathcal{K}}(M) \supseteq \bigcap \mathrm{maxcon}(\mathcal{K})$.*

Theorem 15.2. *Let $\mathcal{K} = \langle \mathcal{A}_s, \mathcal{A}_d, \mathcal{R}_{\mathsf{L}} \rangle$ be a knowledge base. Then, $\mathcal{K} \vdash_{\leq}^{\mathrm{core}} A$ iff $\mathcal{K} \vdash_{\cap \mathsf{AExt}}^{\mathrm{tem}} A$.*

Proof. Suppose $\mathcal{K} \vdash_{\cap \mathsf{AExt}}^{\mathrm{tem}} A$. Thus, by Proposition 11.3, $\bigcap \mathrm{maxcon}(\mathcal{K}) \cup \mathcal{A}_s \vdash_{\mathsf{L}} A$. Let $M \in \mathrm{core}_{\leq}(\mathcal{K})$. By Corollary 15.1, $\mathcal{N}(M) \supseteq \bigcap \mathrm{maxcon}(\mathcal{K})$ and so $M \in \mathcal{M}(\bigcap \mathrm{maxcon}(\mathcal{K}) \cup \mathcal{A}_s)$. Thus, $M \models A$. So, $\mathcal{K} \vdash_{\leq}^{\mathrm{core}} A$.

Suppose $\mathcal{K} \not\vdash_{\cap \mathsf{AExt}}^{\mathrm{tem}} A$. Thus, by Proposition 11.3, $\bigcap \mathrm{maxcon}(\mathcal{K}) \cup \mathcal{A}_s \not\vdash_{\mathsf{L}} A$. So, there is a $M \in \mathcal{M}(\mathcal{A}_s \cup \bigcap \mathrm{maxcon}(\mathcal{K}))$ such that $M \not\models A$. So, $\mathcal{N}(M) \supseteq \bigcap \mathrm{maxcon}(\mathcal{K})$. By Corollary 15.1, $M \in \mathrm{core}_{\leq}(\mathcal{K})$. So, $\mathcal{K} \not\vdash_{\leq}^{\mathrm{core}} A$. $\qquad\square$

Combining our previous results with the result in Proposition 11.3, we get:

Corollary 15.2. *Let $\mathcal{K} = \langle \mathcal{A}_s, \mathcal{A}_d, \mathcal{R}_{\mathsf{L}} \rangle$ be a knowledge base. Then,*

1. $\mathcal{K} \vdash_{\cap \mathsf{PExt}}^{\mathrm{tem}} A$ *iff* $\mathcal{K} \vdash_{\cap \mathsf{Pext}}^{\mathrm{mcon}} A$ *iff* $\mathcal{K} \vdash_{\leq} A$.
2. $\mathcal{K} \vdash_{\cap \mathsf{AExt}}^{\mathrm{tem}} A$ *iff* $\mathcal{K} \vdash_{\cap \mathsf{Aext}}^{\mathrm{mcon}} A$ *iff* $\mathcal{K} \vdash_{\leq}^{\mathrm{core}} A$.

16 Logic Programming

Logic programming is a declarative approach to problem solving. The idea is that a user describes a given reasoning problem by means of a so-called logic program in a simple syntax, without the need of encoding an algorithm to solve the problem. Automated proof procedures or semantic methods are then used to provide answers to queries. With the addition of negation-as-failure(-to-prove) (Section 16.1) or default negation, logic programming became a key paradigm in NML. It gave rise to a rich variety of applications, from legal reasoning (Sergot et al., 1986), to planning (including applications for the Space Shuttle program in Nogueira et al. (2001)), to cognitive science (Stenning & Van Lambalgen, 2008), and others. In this section we will introduce one of the central semantical approaches based on stable models (Section 16.2), which under the addition of classical negation became known as answer set programming (in short: ASP, Section 16.3). In Section 16.4 we note that ASP and default logic coincide under a translation and that ASP can be considered a form of formal argumentation.

16.1 Normal Logic Programs and Default Negation

A *logic program* in its simplest form is a collection of strict inference rules of the form

$$B_1, \ldots, B_n \rightarrow A \tag{16.1.1}$$

where $A, B_1, \ldots, B_n$ are atomic formulas (incl. $\top$ or $\bot$).[65] These rules are called the clauses of the program. Factual information is represented by rules with empty bodies, such as $\rightarrow A$. We reason with such programs as one would expect: C follows from a program $\Pi = \{R_1, \ldots, R_n\}$ just in case there is an argument based on $R_1, \ldots, R_n$ with the conclusion C (recall Definition 5.1).

Similar to default logic, logic programming also accommodates defeasible assumptions in the body of rules such as:

On Sunday mornings Jane goes jogging, except it is stormy.

In logic programming the "except ..." part is expressed with a dedicated negation $\sim$ whose exact interpretation we discuss as follows:

```
sundayMorning, ~stormy  →  jogging
```
(16.1.2)

More generally, we are now dealing with rules of the form

$$B_1, \ldots, B_n, \sim C_1 \ldots, \sim C_m \rightarrow A \tag{16.1.3}$$

where $A, B_1, \ldots, B_n, C_1, \ldots, C_m$ are atomic formulas. Sets of rules Π of the form (16.1.3) are called *normal logic programs*. The technical term for $\sim$ is

---

[65] These rules are often written "$A \leftarrow B_1, \ldots, B_n$", but in order to keep our presentation coherent, we write them in the same way as the strict rules in previous sections. Since we don't consider rules with empty conclusions in this Element, we added $\bot$ to express (somewhat unorthodoxically) clauses such as $B_1, \ldots, B_n \rightarrow$ equivalently by $B_1, \ldots, B_n \rightarrow \bot$. This is an inconsequential for what follows.

"negation-as-failure(-to-prove)" or simply "default negation." The basic idea is that $\sim\!A$ is considered true in the context of Π unless there is an argument for A (based on Π). So, `jogging` is entailed by the program only consisting of the rule (16.1.2), but if we add $\rightarrow$ `stormy` it should not be entailed.

How to define a nonmonotonic consequence relation for negation-as-failure? Prima facie, the following simple (but ultimately flawed) idea seems to be in its spirit. We consider arguments that can be built with the rules in the given program Π and that are based on defeasible assumptions of the type $\sim\!A$. Let for this $\Pi^{\sim}$ be all formulas of the type $\sim\!A$, where A occurs in some rule in Π and let $\mathcal{K}_\Pi$ be the knowledge base consisting of the defeasible assumptions $\Pi^{\sim}$ and the strict rules in Π. So $\mathcal{K}_\Pi$ is of the form $\langle \mathcal{A}_s : \emptyset, \mathcal{A}_d : \Pi^{\sim}, \mathcal{R}_s : \Pi, \mathcal{R}_d : \emptyset \rangle$, or in shorter notation $\langle \Pi^{\sim}, \Pi \rangle$. We then let an atom A be entailed by Π just in case the following two criteria are fulfilled:

1. there is an argument a for A in $\mathsf{Arg}_{\mathcal{K}_\Pi}$ (recall Definition 5.1), and
2. there is no argument for C in $\mathsf{Arg}_{\mathcal{K}_\Pi}$ for any $\sim\!C$ occurring in a.

This would allow us to conclude `jogging` from

$$\Pi_1 = \{\ \rightarrow\ \texttt{sundayMorning},\ \texttt{sundayMorning}, \sim\!\texttt{stormy}\ \rightarrow\ \texttt{jogging}\}.$$

The reason is that, where $\mathcal{K}_1 = \mathcal{K}_{\Pi_1} = \langle \Pi_1^{\sim}, \Pi_1 \rangle$, there is an argument a in $\mathsf{Arg}_{\mathcal{K}_1}$ for `jogging`, namely $a = \langle\langle\ \rightarrow \texttt{sundayMorning}\rangle, \langle\sim\!\texttt{stormy}\rangle\ \rightarrow \texttt{jogging}\rangle$, and there is no argument for `stormy` in $\mathsf{Arg}_{\mathcal{K}_1}$. At the same time, this approach blocks the conclusion `jogging` from $\Pi_1' = \Pi_1 \cup \{\ \rightarrow\ \texttt{stormy}\}$ since now there is an argument $b = \langle\ \rightarrow \texttt{stormy}\rangle$ for `stormy` in $\mathsf{Arg}_{\mathcal{K}_1'}$, where $\mathcal{K}_1' = \mathcal{K}_{\Pi_1'}$.

However, we run quickly into problems with our naive approach once the logic programs are slightly more involved.

Example 58. Consider, for instance, the following logic program:

$$\Pi_2 = \{\rightarrow\ s,\ \sim\!s\ \rightarrow\ q,\ \sim\!q\ \rightarrow\ r\}$$

In this case, although it seems reasonable to infer r, our naive approach doesn't permit it. To see this, we observe that the argument $a_r = \langle\langle\sim\!q\rangle\ \rightarrow\ r\rangle$ for r relies on the assumption $\sim\!q$. Although q can be concluded in view of a (counter-)argument $a_q = \langle\langle\sim\!s\rangle\ \rightarrow\ q\rangle$ based on the assumption $\sim\!s$, the latter is problematic since s follows strictly in Π_2 by the argument $a_s = \langle\ \rightarrow\ s\rangle$. This kind of reinstatement, in which an attacked argument is successfully defended by a nonattacked argument, cannot be handled by our naive approach.[66]

---

[66] We give an adequate argumentative characterization in Section 16.4.

Several ways that deal with such and similar problems have been proposed in various semantics for logic programming (see e.g., Eiter et al. (2009)). In the following we will focus paradigmatically on one of the central approaches based on so-called stable models (Gelfond & Lifschitz, 1988).

16.2 Stable Models

A way to tackle the problem of reasoning with logic programs that contain default negation is by considering interpretations of programs. Let us start with the simple case of a $\sim$-free logic program Π consisting of rules of the form (16.1.1). A model M of Π is a function that associates each atom C occurring in a rule in Π with true (written $M \models C$) or false (written $M \not\models C$). As usual, we let $M \models \top$ and $M \not\models \bot$. Where $r = B_1, \ldots, B_n \rightarrow A$, we write $M \models r$ ("M validates r") in case $M \models B_1$, ..., $M \models B_n$ implies $M \models A$. A compact representation is by letting M be the set of those atoms in Π that it interprets as true (and so $C \in M$ iff $M \models C$).[67]

Example 59. Let $\Pi = \{ \ \rightarrow p, \ p \ \rightarrow \ q\}$ and consider $M_1 = \emptyset$, $M_2 = \{p\}$, $M_3 = \{q\}$, and $M_4 = \{p, q\}$. Then, M_1, M_2, and M_3 are not models of Π: M_1 and M_3 violate the first rule (since $p \notin M_1$ and $p \notin M_3$) and M_2 violates the second rule (since $q \notin M_2$ although $p \in M_2$). The only model of Π is M_4.

It is easy to see that a $\sim$-free program Π has a *minimal model*, that is, a model M of Π such that for all other models M' of Π, $M' \not\subset M$. In fact, as the reader can easily verify, the minimal program will consist exactly of the conclusions of arguments based on the rules in Π.

Fact 16.1. *Let Π be a $\sim$-free program. Then,* $\mathsf{Con}[\mathsf{Arg}_{\mathcal{K}_\Pi}]$ *is the minimal model of* Π.

As we have seen in the previous section, things get more interesting when we also consider default negation $\sim$. For this we adjust the notion of validity in a model.

Definition 16.1. Let $M \cup \{C\}$ be a set of atoms. We let

- $M \models C$, iff, $C \in M$ or $C = \top$ and
- $M \models \sim C$, iff, $M \not\models C$.

Where r is a rule of type (16.1.3),

---

[67] The set of atoms that occur in a program Π is called its *Herbrand base* and sets of atoms in the Herbrand base of Π are called *Herbrand interpretations* of Π.

- $M \models r$, iff, $M \models B_1, \ldots, M \models B_n, M \models {\sim}C_1, \ldots, M \models {\sim}C_m$ implies $M \models A$.

We write $M_{\Pi}^{\sim}$ for the set $\{{\sim}C \in \Pi^{\sim} \mid M \models {\sim}C\}$ and $\mathrm{Atoms}(\Pi)$ for the set of atoms occurring in Π.

Let Π be a normal logic program and $M \subseteq \mathrm{Atoms}(\Pi)$. We say that M is a *model of* Π in case $M \models r$ for all $r \in \Pi$. We write $\mathcal{M}(\Pi)$ for the set of all models of Π.

By having another look at Π_2 we note that not all models of a given program are equally representative of a rational reasoner.

Example 60 (Example 58 cont.). We consider the following candidates for models of Π_2:

$$M_1 = \{s,r\} \qquad M_2 = \{s,q,r\} \qquad M_3 = \{s\}$$

We have $M_i \models {\sim}q$ for $i \in \{1,3\}$ and $M_2 \not\models {\sim}q$. M_3 is not a model of Π_2 since $M_3 \not\models {\sim}q \rightarrow r$. M_1 and M_2 are models of Π_2.

However, we also notice problems with M_2. In particular we have $M_2 \models q$, although the only argument for q based on Π_2 is $\langle {\sim}s \rangle \rightarrow q$ while $M_2 \not\models {\sim}s$. So, q is "unfounded" in M_2: it is valid but not supported by an argument in M_2. A desideratum for us will thus be that models M of a program Π are founded in these programs in the sense that every atom contained in M can be inferred by means of Π and the defeasible assumptions $M_{\Pi}^{\sim}$ in M. Let us make this precise.

Definition 16.2. Let Π be a normal logic program and $M \subseteq \mathrm{Atoms}$ be a model. We let $\mathcal{K}_{\Pi}^{M} =_{\mathrm{df}} \langle M_{\Pi}^{\sim}, \Pi \rangle$ be the knowledge base consisting of the defeasible assumptions in $M_{\Pi}^{\sim}$ and the rules in Π. A model M of Π is *founded (in Π)* if for each $A \in M$ there is an argument $a \in \mathrm{Arg}_{\mathcal{K}_{\Pi}^{M}}$ with conclusion A (so, $M = \mathrm{Con}[\mathrm{Arg}_{\mathcal{K}_{\Pi}^{M}}] \cap \mathrm{Atoms}(\Pi)$).

In order to filter out unfounded models, Gelfond and Lifschitz (1988) have proposed the concept of a *reduction program*.

Definition 16.3. Given a model M of Π, we let *the reduction of Π by M*, written Π^{M}, be the result of (i) replacing each occurrence of a ${\sim}$-negated formula ${\sim}C$ in Π by $\top$ in case $M \models {\sim}C$ and by $\bot$ else, and of (ii) adding the rule $r_{\top} = \rightarrow \top$.

Definition 16.4. Let Π be a normal logic program. M is a *stable model* of Π in case it is identical to the minimal model of Π^{M}. We write $\mathrm{stable}(\Pi)$ for the set of stable models of Π.

It is reassuring to note that (a) Π^M is a $\sim$-free program and therefore has a minimal model (see Fact 16.1), and (b) if M is a model of Π^M, then it is also a model of Π.

Lemma 16.1. *Let $M \subseteq \mathrm{Atoms}(\Pi)$ and $M \in \mathcal{M}(\Pi^M)$. Then, $M \in \mathcal{M}(\Pi)$.*

Proof. Let $A_1, \ldots, A_n, \sim C_1', \ldots, \sim C_m' \rightarrow B \in \Pi$ such that $A_1, \ldots, A_n \in M$ and $M \models \sim C_i'$ for each $i \in \{1, \ldots, m\}$. Thus, $A_1, \ldots, A_n, \top, \ldots, \top \rightarrow B \in \Pi^M$. Since $M \in \mathcal{M}(\Pi^M)$, $B \in M$. $\qquad\qquad\square$

Example 61 (Example 60 cont.). Let us put this idea to a test with Π_2 and the two models $M_1 = \{s, r\}$ and $M_2 = \{s, q, r\}$.

Π_2	$\Pi_2^{M_1}$	$\Pi_2^{M_2}$
$\sim q \rightarrow r$	$\top \rightarrow r$	$\bot \rightarrow r$
$\sim s \rightarrow q$	$\bot \rightarrow q$	$\bot \rightarrow q$
$\rightarrow s$	$\rightarrow s$	$\rightarrow s$
	$\rightarrow \top$	$\rightarrow \top$

The minimal model of $\Pi_2^{M_1}$ is M_1, the minimal model of $\Pi_2^{M_2}$ is $M_2' = \{s\} \subsetneq M_2$. So, as expected, while M_1 is a stable model of Π_2, M_2 is not.

Stable models do not exist for every program. Indeed, for some logic programs the only existing models are unfounded ones.

Example 62. A case in point is $\Pi_\bot = \{\sim p \rightarrow p\}$. Note that $M_0 = \emptyset$ is not a model of $\Pi_\bot$ since $M_0 \models \sim p$ and so p would have to be true in M_0 to be a model of $\Pi_\bot$. So we are left with $M_1 = \{p\}$. But this model is not founded.[68]

Programs containing conflicts may give rise to several stable models.

Example 63. As a simple example, consider $\Pi_{\mathrm{conf}} = \{\sim q \rightarrow p, \sim p \rightarrow q\}$. $M_0 = \emptyset$ is not a model of Π_{conf}, since both rules are applicable in M_0, but $p, q \notin M_0$. On the other hand, $M_{pq} = \{p, q\}$ is not minimal (and hence unfounded), since neither rule is applicable in M_{pq}. We are left with $M_p = \{p\}$ and $M_q = \{q\}$. As the reader can easily verify, these two models are stable.

---

[68] There are three-valued semantics for stable models in which a stable model exists that assigns to p a third truth value, *undecided* (Przymusinski, 1990).

16.3 Extended Logic Programs and Answer Sets

So far we have limited our attention to a rather weak language, only consisting of atoms and their default negations. We now will add another negation $\neg$ to the mix which will behave more similar to classical negation. This puts us in the realm of *extended logic programs*, which are sets of rules of the form

$$\ell_1, \ldots, \ell_n, {\sim}\ell_1', \ldots, {\sim}\ell_m' \;\rightarrow\; \ell \tag{16.3.1}$$

where $\ell, \ell_1, \ldots, \ell_n, \ell_1', \ldots, \ell_m'$ are $\neg$-literals, that is, atoms or $\neg$-negated atoms. $\mathrm{Lit}^\neg(\Pi)$ denotes the set of all $\neg$-literals occurring in an extended program Π.

It is our task now to enhance the notion of a model to extended programs. A simple way is by means of a translation τ of a given extended program Π to a normal program Π' (Gelfond & Lifschitz, 1991) in which each occurrence of some $\ell = \neg p$ is replaced by a new atom p' (not occurring in Π). We then consider only those models M of $\tau(\Pi)$ for which

- $p \notin M$ or $p' \notin M$ for all atoms p or
- M contains all p and p' for all atoms p in Π.[69]

We then translate M back by considering $\tau^{-1}(M) = \{A \in M \mid A \in \mathrm{Atoms}\} \cup \{\neg A \mid A' \in M\}$, replacing atoms of the form p' by $\neg p$. If M is a stable model of Π' then we define $\tau^{-1}(M)$ to be a *stable model of* Π. The latter are also known as *answer sets* of Π.

Of course, we can also define a nonmonotonic consequence relation based on answer sets: where A is a $\neg$-literal, or a $\sim$-negated $\neg$-literal and Π is an extended logic program we let:

$$\Pi \vdash_{\mathsf{asp}} A \text{ iff for all answer sets } M \text{ of } \Pi, M \models A.$$

Example 64. We consider the extended logic program Π_3 consisting of:

$$
\begin{aligned}
r_1 &= \quad \texttt{sundayMorning, {\sim}stormy, {\sim}{\neg}jogging} \;\rightarrow\; \texttt{jogging}\\
r_2 &= \quad \texttt{working, {\sim}jogging} \;\rightarrow\; \texttt{{\neg}jogging}\\
r_3 &= \quad \rightarrow\; \texttt{sundayMorning}\\
r_4 &= \quad \rightarrow\; \texttt{working}
\end{aligned}
$$

In the translated program $\tau(\Pi_3)$, rules 1 and 2 are replaced by:

$$
\begin{aligned}
r_1' &= \quad \texttt{sundayMorning, {\sim}stormy, {\sim}jogging'} \;\rightarrow\; \texttt{jogging}\\
r_2' &= \quad \texttt{working, {\sim}jogging} \;\rightarrow\; \texttt{jogging'}
\end{aligned}
$$

---

[69] This condition makes sure that from an inconsistent program anything is derivable (see Example 65).

Table 12 Models of $\tau(\Pi_3)$ (Example 64)

	M_1	M_2	M_3	M_4	M_5
`working`	✓	✓	✓	✓	✓
`sundayMorning`	✓	✓	✓	✓	✓
`jogging`	✓			✓	✓
`jogging'`		✓	✓		✓
`stormy`			✓	✓	✓
r'_1	✓	✓	✓	✓	✓
r'_2	✓	✓	✓	✓	✓

We have two stable models of $\tau(\Pi_3)$, as the reader can easily verify by inspecting Table 12.

$M_1 = \{$`sundayMorning, working, jogging`$\}$ and

$M_2 = \{$`sundayMorning, working, jogging'`$\}$.

So, the answer sets of Π_3 are M_1 and

$M'_2 = \{$`sundayMorning, working, ¬jogging`$\}$.

We note that $\neg$`stormy` $\notin M_1 \cup M'_2$, but $M_1 \models\, {\sim}$`stormy` and $M_2 \models\, {\sim}$`stormy`. This shows that negation-as-failure as interpreted in answer set programming does not realize a closed-world assumption in the strong sense that every atom A that is not derivable is interpreted as strongly negated, $\neg A$.[70]

If we add the additional rule $\rightarrow$ `stormy` to Π_3, resulting in Π'_3, we end up with one answer set, namely

$M_3 = \{$`sundayMorning, working, stormy, ¬jogging`$\}$.

In terms of nonmonotonic consequence we have

- $\Pi_3 \vdash_{\mathsf{asp}} {\sim}$`stormy`, while $\Pi'_3 \vdash_{\mathsf{asp}}$ `stormy`, and
- $\Pi'_3 \vdash_{\mathsf{asp}} \neg$`jogging`, while $\Pi_3 \nvdash_{\mathsf{asp}}$ `jogging` and $\Pi_3 \nvdash_{\mathsf{asp}} \neg$`jogging`.

Example 65. There are extended programs with only inconsistent (stable) models, for example, $\Pi_\perp = \{\ \rightarrow p,\ \rightarrow \neg p\}$. The only model of $\tau(\Pi_\perp) = \{\rightarrow p,\ \rightarrow p'\}$ is $M_\perp = \{p, p'\}$. So the only model of $\Pi_\perp$ is $\tau^{-1}(M_\perp) = \{p, \neg p\}$.

---

[70] Alternative interpretations of $\sim$ are offered, e.g., by the completion semantics (Clark, 1977) and its weak variant that led to applications in the psychology of reasoning (Stenning & Van Lambalgen, 2008).

16.4 Answer Sets, Defaults, and Argumentation

Answer sets are closely related to the extensions of Reiter's default logic (Section 12.2).[71] We can translate a clause of the form (16.3.1) to a (possibly) nonnormal default by

$$\tau_{\text{rei}}\big(\ell_1,\ldots,\ell_n,{\sim}\ell'_1,\ldots,{\sim}\ell'_m \to \ell\big) \;=\; \frac{\ell_1,\ldots,\ell_n \quad -\ell'_1,\ldots,-\ell'_m}{\ell},$$

where for an atom A, $-A =_{\text{df}} \neg A$ and $-\neg A =_{\text{df}} A$. Let the resulting translation of an extended program Π be

$$\mathcal{K}_{\text{rei}}(\Pi) = \big\langle \mathcal{A}_s : \emptyset, \mathcal{R}_{\text{CL}}, \mathcal{R}_d : \{\tau_{\text{rei}}(r) \mid r \in \Pi\}\big\rangle.$$

Example 66. We have $\mathcal{K}_{\text{rei}}(\Pi_3) = \langle \emptyset, \mathcal{R}_{\text{CL}}, \mathcal{R}_d\rangle$, where $\mathcal{R}_d$ consists of the following general default rules:

$$d_1 = \frac{\texttt{sundayMorning} \quad \neg\texttt{stormy},\texttt{jogging}}{\texttt{jogging}} \qquad d_2 = \frac{\texttt{working} \quad \neg\texttt{jogging}}{\neg\texttt{jogging}}$$

$$d_3 = \frac{}{\texttt{sundayMorning}} \qquad\qquad d_4 = \frac{}{\texttt{working}}$$

Theorem 16.1 (Gelfond and Lifschitz, 1991). *Let Π be an extended program and $M \subseteq \text{Lit}^{\neg}(\Pi)$. Then,*

1. *if $M \in \text{stable}(\Pi)$, then $\text{Cn}_{\text{CL}}(M) \in \text{PExt}_{\text{gr}}(\Pi_{\text{rei}})$, and*
2. *for every $\mathcal{E} \in \text{PExt}_{\text{gr}}(\Pi_{\text{rei}})$ there is exactly one $M \in \text{stable}(\Pi)$ for which $\mathcal{E} = \text{Cn}_{\text{CL}}(M)$.*

Given this result the metatheoretic results for Reiter's greedy approach immediately apply (see Section 12.1), such as cautious transitivity for $\vdash_{\text{asp}}$.[72]

In the following we show that answer sets can also be expressed in logical argumentation.[73] We will improve our previous naive attempt (see Section 16.1 and recall the problematic Example 58) by allowing for reinstatement.

Definition 16.5. Let Π be an extended logic program. We let $\mathcal{AF}_\Pi = \langle \text{Arg}_{\mathcal{K}_\Pi}, \leadsto\rangle$, where $\mathcal{K}_\Pi = \langle \Pi^{\sim}, \Pi\rangle$ and for $a, b \in \text{Arg}_{\mathcal{K}_\Pi}$, we let a attack b (in signs $a \leadsto b$) if there is a sub-argument $\langle{\sim}\ell\rangle$ of b such that $\text{Con}(a) = \ell$.

---

[71] There are also close relations to temperate accumulation. E.g., in Besold et al. (2017) we find a characterization of input-ouput logic in logic programming.

[72] For this one has to define $\Pi \oplus_s A$ by $\Pi \cup \{\to A\}$.

[73] Close connections between various semantics of logic programming and structured argumentation have been observed in Caminada and Schulz (2017).

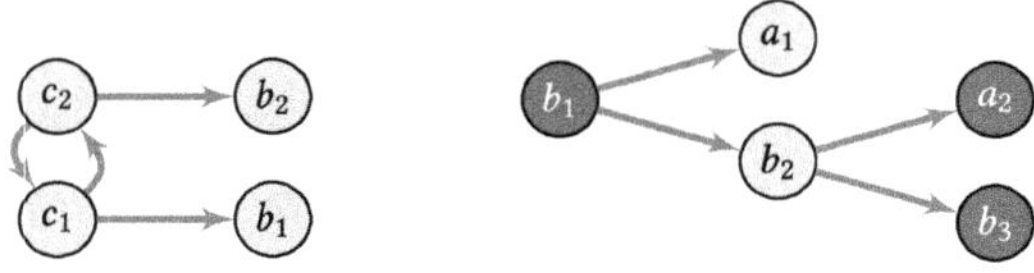

Figure 32 Argumentation framework for Examples 67 (left) and 68 (right). We omit nonattacked arguments.

Example 67 (Example 64 cont.). We consider Π_3 and list arguments in $\mathrm{Arg}_{\mathcal{K}_{\Pi_3}}$ that give rise to the argumentation framework in Fig. 32 (left).

$a_0 =$	$\langle\ \rightarrow \texttt{working}\rangle$	$b_3 =$	$\langle\sim\texttt{stormy}\rangle$
$a_1 =$	$\langle\ \rightarrow \texttt{sundayMorning}\rangle$	$c_1 =$	$\langle a_1, b_2, b_3 \rightarrow \texttt{jogging}\rangle$
$b_1 =$	$\langle\sim\texttt{jogging}\rangle$	$c_2 =$	$\langle a_0, b_1 \rightarrow \neg\texttt{jogging}\rangle$
$b_2 =$	$\langle\sim\neg\texttt{jogging}\rangle$		

We obtain two stable extensions of $\mathcal{AF}_{\Pi_3}$:

$$\mathcal{E}_1 = \{a_0, a_1, b_2, b_3, c_1\} \text{ and } \mathcal{E}_2 = \{a_0, a_1, b_1, b_3, c_2\}.$$

The set of conclusions (in $\mathrm{Lit}^-(\Pi_3)$) of arguments in the two stable models correspond to the two answer sets of Π_3, namely:

$M_1 = \{\texttt{working}, \texttt{sundayMorning}, \texttt{jogging}\}$ and

$M_2 = \{\texttt{working}, \texttt{sundayMorning}, \neg\texttt{jogging}\}$

Example 68 (Example 58 cont.). We consider the problematic example for our naive argumentation-based account, Π_2. We have the following arguments in $\mathrm{Arg}_{\mathcal{K}_{\Pi_2}}$, giving rise to the argumentation framework in Fig. 32 (right).

$a_1 =$	$\langle\sim s\rangle$	$b_1 =$	$\langle\ \rightarrow s\rangle$	$b_2 =$	$\langle a_1 \rightarrow q\rangle$
$a_2 =$	$\langle\sim q\rangle$			$b_3 =$	$\langle a_2 \rightarrow r\rangle$

The unique stable extension of $\mathcal{AF}_{\Pi_2}$ is $\mathcal{E} = \{b_1, a_2, b_3\}$ (highlighted). The set of atoms in $\mathrm{Con}[\mathcal{E}]$ is identical to the only stable model of Π_2, namely $\{s, r\}$.

The correspondence is not coincidental. For a given extended logic program Π let $\texttt{stable}_\top(\Pi)$ be the set of consistent answer sets of Π, that is, those stable models of Π that do not contain contradictory literals.[74]

Theorem* 16.2. *Let Π be an extended logic program.*

---

[74] Recall that $\mathrm{Arg}_{\mathcal{K}_{\Pi}}(M_{\Pi}^{\sim})$ denotes those arguments in $\mathrm{Arg}_{\mathcal{K}_{\Pi}}$ which only make use of defeasible assumptions in $M_{\Pi}^{\sim}$.

1. *If* $M \in \mathrm{stable}_\top(\Pi)$, *then* $\mathrm{Arg}_{\mathcal{K}_\Pi}(M_\Pi^\sim) \in \mathrm{stable}(\mathcal{K}_\Pi)$.
2. *If* $\mathcal{E} \in \mathrm{stable}(\mathcal{K}_\Pi)$ *and* $M = \mathrm{Con}[\mathcal{E}] \cap \mathrm{Lit}^\neg$, *then* $M \in \mathrm{stable}_\top(\Pi)$.

Selected Further Readings

Friedman and Halpern (1996) provided a unifying approach to default reasoning based on plausibility orders covering many of the previously mentioned NMLs, such as the preferential semantics of Kraus et al. (1990), the possibilistic approach by Benferhat et al. (1992), ordinal rankings by Spohn (1988), and ϵ-semantics (Adams, 1975; Pearl, 1989). Another generalization is provided in Arieli and Avron (2000), who go beyond a classical base logic. Preferential conditionals have been embedded in the scope of a full logical language (so that they are allowed to occur in the scope of logical connectives such as $\wedge, \vee, \neg$) in conditional logics (Asher & Morreau, 1991; Boutilier, 1994a; Friedman & Halpern, 1996). First-order versions of preferential consequence relations and conditional logics have been investigated, for example, in Delgrande (1998); Friedman et al. (2000) and Lehmann and Magidor (1990). Proof theories for conditional logics in the style of Kraus et al. (1990) can be found in Giordano et al. (2009), and for rational closure in Straßer (2009b) in terms of adaptive logics. Deep connections between preferential approaches and belief revision have been observed in many places, for example, Boutilier (1994b), Gärdenfors (1990), Rott et al. (2021).

Logics based on preferential semantics and logic programming have been characterized in terms of artificial neural nets; see for example Besold et al. (2017), Hölldobler and Kalinke (1994), and Leitgeb (2018).

An overview and introduction to logic programming with an emphasis on answer sets is, in book form, Lifschitz (2019), and more compactly, Eiter et al. (2009). As the reader will expect, many variants of logic programming exist, including disjunctions (Minker, 1994), preferences (Schaub & Wang, 2001), probabilities (Ng & Subrahmanian, 1992) with connections to deep learning (Manhaeve et al., 2021), and so on. Logic programming has been successfully applied in the psychology of reasoning (Saldanha, 2018; Stenning & Van Lambalgen, 2008).

Appendix A
Proofs for Part II

A.1 Proofs for Section 10

Proofs of Theorem 10.2 and Proposition 10.1

Let in this section $i \in \{s, d\}$, nmL be a NML with an associated class of knowledge bases $\mathbf{K}_{\mathsf{nmL}}$ and let $\mathcal{K} \in \mathbf{K}_{\mathsf{nmL}}$.

Lemma A.1. *If (arg) holds, we have: (i) If $\mathcal{D} \subseteq \mathrm{Def}(\mathcal{K} \oplus_i A)$ and $A \in \mathrm{Con}[\mathrm{Arg}_{\mathcal{K}}(\mathcal{D} \ominus_i^{\mathcal{K}} A)]$, $\mathrm{Con}[\mathrm{Arg}_{\mathcal{K}}(\mathcal{D} \ominus_i^{\mathcal{K}} A)] = \mathrm{Con}[\mathrm{Arg}_{\mathcal{K} \oplus_i A}(\mathcal{D})]$. (ii) If $\mathcal{D} \subseteq \mathrm{Def}(\mathcal{K})$ and $A \in \mathrm{Con}[\mathrm{Arg}_{\mathcal{K}}(\mathcal{D})]$, $\mathrm{Con}[\mathrm{Arg}_{\mathcal{K}}(\mathcal{D})] = \mathrm{Con}[\mathrm{Arg}_{\mathcal{K} \oplus_i A}(\mathcal{D} \oplus_i A)]$.*

Proof. Item (i). "$\subseteq$" follows by (arg-mono). For "$\supseteq$" we consider the two cases (a) $A \in \mathrm{Def}(\mathcal{K})$ and (b) $A \notin \mathrm{Def}(\mathcal{K})$. In case (a), $\mathcal{D} \ominus_i^{\mathcal{K}} A = \mathcal{D}$. By (arg-trans), $\mathrm{Con}[\mathrm{Arg}_{\mathcal{K} \oplus A}(\mathcal{D} \oplus A)] \subseteq \mathrm{Con}[\mathrm{Arg}_{\mathcal{K}}(\mathcal{D} \ominus_i^{\mathcal{K}} A)]$. Since $\mathrm{Con}[\mathrm{Arg}_{\mathcal{K} \oplus A}(\mathcal{D})] \subseteq \mathrm{Con}[\mathrm{Arg}_{\mathcal{K} \oplus A}(\mathcal{D} \oplus A)]$, "$\supseteq$" follows. Item (ii) is analogous. $\square$

Fact A.1. *Let $\mathbf{D} \subseteq \wp(\mathrm{Def}(\mathcal{K}))$. Then, $\bigcap\{\mathrm{Arg}_{\mathcal{K}}(\mathcal{D}) \mid \mathcal{D} \in \mathbf{D}\} = \mathrm{Arg}_{\mathcal{K}}(\bigcap \mathbf{D})$.*

Theorem* 10.2. *Given (arg), the logical dependencies of Fig. 23 hold for both accumulation methods.*

Proof. Items .1, .2, .3, and .4 are trivial.

For (i) suppose $\mathcal{K} \vdash_{\cap\mathsf{PExt}} A$. Ad (i.1). Suppose $\mathrm{CT}_i(\mathrm{DExt})$ and $\mathcal{E} \in \mathrm{PExt}(\mathcal{K})$. Thus, there is a $\mathcal{D} \in \mathrm{DExt}(\mathcal{K})$ for which $\mathcal{E} = \mathrm{Con}[\mathrm{Arg}_{\mathcal{K}}(\mathcal{D})]$. By $\mathrm{CT}_i(\mathrm{DExt})$, $\mathcal{D} \oplus_i A \in \mathrm{DExt}(\mathcal{K} \oplus_i A)$. Since $\mathcal{K} \vdash_{\cap\mathsf{PExt}} A$, $A \in \mathcal{E}$. By Lemma A.1 (ii), $\mathrm{Con}[\mathrm{Arg}_{\mathcal{K} \oplus_i A}(\mathcal{D} \oplus_i A)] = \mathcal{E} \in \mathrm{PExt}(\mathcal{K} \oplus_i A)$.

Ad (i.2). Suppose $\mathrm{CM}_i(\mathrm{DExt})$ and $\mathcal{E} \in \mathrm{PExt}(\mathcal{K} \oplus_i A)$. Thus, there is a $\mathcal{D} \in \mathrm{DExt}(\mathcal{K} \oplus_i A)$ for which $\mathcal{E} = \mathrm{Con}[\mathrm{Arg}_{\mathcal{K} \oplus_i A}(\mathcal{D})]$. By $\mathrm{CM}_i(\mathrm{DExt})$, $\mathcal{D} \ominus_i^{\mathcal{K}} A \in \mathrm{DExt}(\mathcal{K})$. Since $\mathcal{K} \vdash_{\cap\mathsf{PExt}} A$, $A \in \mathrm{Con}[\mathrm{Arg}_{\mathcal{K}}(\mathcal{D} \ominus_i A)]$. By Lemma A.1 (i), $\mathrm{Con}[\mathrm{Arg}_{\mathcal{K}}(\mathcal{D} \ominus_i^{\mathcal{K}} A)] = \mathcal{E} \in \mathrm{PExt}(\mathcal{K})$.

For (ii) suppose $\mathcal{K} \vdash_{\cap\mathsf{AExt}} A$. So, there is an $a \in \bigcap\{\mathrm{Arg}_{\mathcal{K}}(\mathcal{D}) \mid \mathcal{D} \in \mathrm{DExt}(\mathcal{K})\}$ with $\mathrm{Con}(a) = A$. By Fact A.1, where $\mathcal{D}^\star = \bigcap \mathrm{DExt}(\mathcal{K})$, $a \in \mathrm{Arg}_{\mathcal{K}}(\mathcal{D}^\star)$. Clearly, $\mathcal{K} \vdash_{\cap\mathsf{PExt}} A$. Ad (ii.1). Suppose $\mathrm{CT}_i(\mathrm{DExt})$ and $\mathcal{K} \oplus_i A \vdash_{\cap\mathsf{AExt}} B$. So, there is a $b \in \bigcap\{\mathrm{Arg}_{\mathcal{K} \oplus_i A}(\mathcal{D}) \mid \mathcal{D} \in \mathrm{DExt}(\mathcal{K} \oplus_i A)\}$ with $\mathrm{Con}(b) = B$. We have to show that there is a $c \in \bigcap\{\mathrm{Arg}_{\mathcal{K}}(\mathcal{D}) \mid \mathcal{D} \in \mathrm{DExt}(\mathcal{K})\}(= \mathrm{Arg}_{\mathcal{K}}(\mathcal{D}^\star))$ with $\mathrm{Con}(c) = B$.

By Fact A.1, where $\mathcal{D}^\dagger = \bigcap \mathrm{DExt}(\mathcal{K} \oplus_i A)$, $b \in \mathrm{Arg}_{\mathcal{K} \oplus_i A}(\mathcal{D}^\dagger)$. By $\mathrm{CT}_i(\mathrm{DExt})$, $\mathcal{D}^\dagger \subseteq \mathcal{D}^\star \oplus_i A$. So, $b \in \mathrm{Arg}_{\mathcal{K} \oplus_i A}(\mathcal{D}^\star \oplus_i A)$. By (arg-trans), there is a $c \in \mathrm{Arg}_{\mathcal{K}}(\mathcal{D}^\star)$ with $\mathrm{Con}(c) = \mathrm{Con}(b)$.

Ad (ii.2). Suppose $CM_i(DExt)$ and $\mathcal{K} \vdash_{\cap AExt} B$. So, there is a $b \in Arg_{\mathcal{K}}(\mathcal{D}^\star)$ with $Con(b) = B$. Let $\mathcal{D}^\ddagger = \bigcap DExt(\mathcal{K} \oplus_i A)$. By $CM_i(DExt)$, $\mathcal{D}^\ddagger \ominus_i^{\mathcal{K}} A \supseteq \mathcal{D}^\star$. By (arg-mono), $b \in Arg_{\mathcal{K} \oplus_i A}(\mathcal{D}^\ddagger)$ and hence $\mathcal{K} \oplus_i A \vdash_{\cap AExt} B$.

Ad (iii.1). Suppose $CT_i(PExt)$, $\mathcal{K} \vdash_{\cap PExt} A$, and $\mathcal{K} \oplus_i A \vdash_{\cap PExt} B$. Consider $\mathcal{E} \in PExt(\mathcal{K})$. By $CT_i(PExt)$, $\mathcal{E} \in PExt(\mathcal{K} \oplus_i A)$. By the supposition, $B \in \mathcal{E}$. So, for all $\mathcal{E} \in PExt(\mathcal{K})$, $B \in \mathcal{E}$ and hence $\mathcal{K} \vdash_{\cap PExt} B$. Ad (iii.2). Suppose $CM_i(PExt)$, $\mathcal{K} \vdash_{\cap PExt} A$, and $\mathcal{K} \vdash_{\cap PExt} B$. Consider $\mathcal{E} \in PExt(\mathcal{K} \oplus_i A)$. By $CM_i(PExt)$, $\mathcal{E} \in PExt(\mathcal{K})$. By the supposition, $B \in \mathcal{E}$. So, for all $\mathcal{E} \in PExt(\mathcal{K} \oplus_i A)$, $B \in \mathcal{E}$ and hence $\mathcal{K} \oplus_i A \vdash_{\cap PExt} B$. $\qquad\square$

Proposition* 10.1. *Let $i \in \{s, d\}$. Given (arg), $CT_i(DExt)$ holds for both accumulation methods.*

Proof. Let $\oplus = \oplus_i$ and $\tau \in \{\mathtt{tem}, \mathtt{gr}\}$. Suppose $\mathcal{K} \vdash_{\cap PExt}^{\tau} A$. Let $\mathcal{D} \in DExt_\tau(\mathcal{K})$ and so $A \in Con[Arg_{\mathcal{K}}(\mathcal{D})]$. We have to show that $\mathcal{D} \oplus A \in DExt_\tau(\mathcal{D} \oplus A)$. By Lemma A.1, $Con[Arg_{\mathcal{K}}(\mathcal{D}')] = Con[Arg_{\mathcal{K} \oplus A}(\mathcal{D}' \oplus A)]$ for any $\mathcal{D} \subseteq \mathcal{D}' \subseteq Def(\mathcal{K})$. Thus, ($\star$), $Cons_{\mathcal{K}}(\mathcal{D}) \oplus A = Cons_{\mathcal{K} \oplus A}(\mathcal{D} \oplus A)$ and $Trig_{\mathcal{K}}(\mathcal{D}) \oplus A = Trig_{\mathcal{K} \oplus A}(\mathcal{D} \oplus A)$.

By Theorem 10.1, $\mathcal{D} = Cons_{\mathcal{K}}(\mathcal{D})$ ($\tau = \mathtt{tem}$) resp. $\mathcal{D} = Trig_{\mathcal{K}}^{\top}(\mathcal{D})$ ($\tau = \mathtt{gr}$). With ($\star$), $\mathcal{D} \oplus A = Cons_{\mathcal{K}}(\mathcal{D} \oplus A)$ resp. $\mathcal{D} \oplus A = Trig_{\mathcal{K}}^{\top}(\mathcal{D} \oplus A)$, and so $\mathcal{D} \oplus A \in DExt_\tau(\mathcal{D} \oplus A)$. $\qquad\square$

Proof of Propositions 10.2 and 10.3

Throughout the section we consider a given nmL with (a nonprioritized) $\mathcal{K} \in \mathbf{K}_{\mathsf{nmL}}$ and let $i \in \{s, d\}$ and $\tau \in \{\mathtt{tem}, \mathtt{gr}\}$. We suppose that (arg-re) holds, $A \in Cn_{\mathcal{R}_s}(\{B\})$, and $B \in Cn_{\mathcal{R}_s}(\{A\})$.

Lemma A.2. *Let $\mathcal{D} \subseteq Def(\mathcal{K})$. Then*

(i) $Con[Arg_{\mathcal{K} \oplus_s A}(\mathcal{D})] = Con[Arg_{\mathcal{K} \oplus_s B}(\mathcal{D})]$,
(ii) $Cons_{\mathcal{K} \oplus_s A}(\mathcal{D}) = Cons_{\mathcal{K} \oplus_s B}(\mathcal{D})$, *and*
(iii) $Trig_{\mathcal{K} \oplus_s A}^{\top}(\mathcal{D}) = Trig_{\mathcal{K} \oplus_s B}^{\top}(\mathcal{D})$.

Proof. For (i) let $a \in Arg_{\mathcal{K} \oplus_s A}(\mathcal{D})$. By (arg-re), there is a $b \in Arg_{\mathcal{K} \oplus_s B}(\mathcal{D})$ with $Con(a) = Con(b)$. Analogously for the other direction and thus (i) holds. Ad (ii). By (i), for every $C \in Def(\mathcal{K})$,

$$Con[Arg_{\mathcal{K} \oplus_s A}(\mathcal{D} \oplus_d C)] = Con[Arg_{\mathcal{K} \oplus_s B}(\mathcal{D} \oplus_d C)].$$

Thus, $Cons_{\mathcal{K} \oplus_s A}(\mathcal{D}) = Cons_{\mathcal{K} \oplus_s B}(\mathcal{D})$. (iii) follows by (i–ii). $\qquad\square$

Lemma A.3. *Let $\mathcal{D} \subseteq Def(\mathcal{K} \oplus_d A)$ and $A \in \mathcal{D}$. Then* *(i)* $\mathsf{Con}[\mathsf{Arg}_{\mathcal{K}\oplus_d A}(\mathcal{D})] = \mathsf{Con}[\mathsf{Arg}_{\mathcal{K}\oplus_d B}((\mathcal{D}\ominus_d^{\mathcal{K}} A)\oplus_d B)]$,

(ii) $(\mathsf{Cons}_{\mathcal{K}\oplus_d A}(\mathcal{D})\ominus_d^{\mathcal{K}} A)\oplus_d B = \mathsf{Cons}_{\mathcal{K}\oplus_d B}((\mathcal{D}\ominus_d^{\mathcal{K}} A)\oplus_d B)$, *if* $\mathcal{D}\subseteq$ $\mathsf{Cons}_{\mathcal{K}\oplus_d A}(\mathcal{D})$, *and*

(iii) $(\mathsf{Trig}_{\mathcal{K}\oplus_d A}^{\top}(\mathcal{D})\ominus_d^{\mathcal{K}} A)\oplus_d B = \mathsf{Trig}_{\mathcal{K}\oplus_d B}^{\top}((\mathcal{D}\ominus_d^{\mathcal{K}} A)\oplus_d B)$.

Proof. Ad (i). "$\subseteq$". Consider $a\in\mathsf{Arg}_{\mathcal{K}\oplus_d A}(\mathcal{D})$. By (arg-re), there is a $b\in\mathsf{Arg}_{\mathcal{K}\oplus_d B}((\mathcal{D}\ominus_d^{\mathcal{K}} A)\oplus_d B)$ with $\mathsf{Con}(a) = \mathsf{Con}(b)$.

"$\supseteq$". Consider $b\in\mathsf{Arg}_{\mathcal{K}\oplus_d B}((\mathcal{D}\ominus_d^{\mathcal{K}} A)\oplus_d B)$. If $B\notin\mathsf{Def}(b)$, $b\in\mathsf{Arg}_{\mathcal{K}\oplus_d A}(\mathcal{D})$. Else, by (arg-re), there is an $a\in\mathsf{Arg}_{\mathcal{K}\oplus_d A}(\mathcal{D})$ with $\mathsf{Con}(a) = \mathsf{Con}(b)$. Altogether this proves (i).

Ad (ii). Suppose $\mathcal{D}\subseteq\mathsf{Cons}_{\mathcal{K}\oplus_d A}(\mathcal{D})$. Since by (i), for all $C\in\mathsf{Def}(\mathcal{K})$, $\mathsf{Con}[\mathsf{Arg}_{\mathcal{K}\oplus_d A}(\mathcal{D}\oplus_d C)] = \mathsf{Con}[\mathsf{Arg}_{\mathcal{K}\oplus_d B}(((\mathcal{D}\ominus_d^{\mathcal{K}} A)\oplus_d B)\oplus_d C)]$, we have: $C\in\mathsf{Cons}_{\mathcal{K}\oplus_d A}(\mathcal{D})$ iff $C\in\mathsf{Cons}_{\mathcal{K}\oplus_d B}((\mathcal{D}\ominus_d^{\mathcal{K}} A)\oplus_d B)$. Since $\mathsf{Con}[\mathsf{Arg}_{\mathcal{K}\oplus_d A}(\mathcal{D})]$ is consistent and by (i), so is $\mathsf{Con}[\mathsf{Arg}_{\mathcal{K}\oplus_d B}((\mathcal{D}\ominus_d^{\mathcal{K}} A)\oplus_d B)]$. So, $B\in\mathsf{Cons}_{\mathcal{K}\oplus_d B}((\mathcal{D}\ominus_d^{\mathcal{K}} A)\oplus_d B)$. Altogether this proves (ii).

(iii) follows with (i) and (ii). $\qquad\qquad\square$

Lemma A.4. *Let* $\mathcal{D}\subseteq\mathsf{Def}(\mathcal{K})$ *and* $A, B\notin\mathcal{D}$. *Then*

(i) $\mathsf{Con}[\mathsf{Arg}_{\mathcal{K}\oplus_d A}(\mathcal{D})] = \mathsf{Con}[\mathsf{Arg}_{\mathcal{K}\oplus_d B}(\mathcal{D})]$,

(ii) $\mathsf{Cons}_{\mathcal{K}\oplus_d A}(\mathcal{D}) = \mathsf{Cons}_{\mathcal{K}\oplus_d B}(\mathcal{D})$ *if* $A\notin\mathsf{Cons}_{\mathcal{K}\oplus_d A}(\mathcal{D})$, *and*

(iii) $\mathsf{Trig}_{\mathcal{K}\oplus_d A}^{\top}(\mathcal{D}) = \mathsf{Trig}_{\mathcal{K}\oplus_d B}^{\top}(\mathcal{D})$.

Proof. Suppose $A\neq B$, otherwise the lemma is trivial. Ad (i). This holds trivially since $A, B\notin\mathcal{D}$.

Ad (ii). We first note that ($\star$) $\mathsf{Con}[\mathsf{Arg}_{\mathcal{K}\oplus_d A}(\mathcal{D}\oplus_d A)]$ is inconsistent since $A\notin\mathsf{Cons}_{\mathcal{K}\oplus_d A}(\mathcal{D})$.

Consider $C\in\mathsf{Def}(\mathcal{K})\setminus\{A, B\}$. Since by (i) $\mathsf{Con}[\mathsf{Arg}_{\mathcal{K}\oplus_d A}(\mathcal{D}\oplus_d C)] = \mathsf{Con}[\mathsf{Arg}_{\mathcal{K}\oplus_d B}(\mathcal{D}\oplus_d C)]$, $C\in\mathsf{Cons}_{\mathcal{K}\oplus_d A}(\mathcal{D})$ iff $C\in\mathsf{Cons}_{\mathcal{K}\oplus_d B}(\mathcal{D})$.

So, $\mathsf{Cons}_{\mathcal{K}\oplus_d A}(\mathcal{D})\setminus\{A, B\} = \mathsf{Cons}_{\mathcal{K}\oplus_d B}(\mathcal{D})\setminus\{A, B\}$. We now show $A, B\notin\mathsf{Cons}_{\mathcal{K}\oplus_d A}(\mathcal{D})\cup\mathsf{Cons}_{\mathcal{K}\oplus_d B}(\mathcal{D})$ which completes the proof of (ii).

Suppose $A\in\mathsf{Def}(\mathcal{K})$. Trivially,

$$\mathsf{Con}[\mathsf{Arg}_{\mathcal{K}\oplus_d A}(\mathcal{D}\oplus_d A)] = \mathsf{Con}[\mathsf{Arg}_{\mathcal{K}\oplus_d B}(\mathcal{D}\oplus_d A)].$$

By ($\star$), $A\notin\mathsf{Cons}_{\mathcal{K}\oplus_d B}(\mathcal{D})$. Moreover, by Lemma A.3, $\mathsf{Con}[\mathsf{Arg}_{\mathcal{K}\oplus_d B}(\mathcal{D}\oplus_d B)] = \mathsf{Con}[\mathsf{Arg}_{\mathcal{K}\oplus_d A}(\mathcal{D}\oplus_d A)]$ and so by ($\star$), $B\notin\mathsf{Cons}_{\mathcal{K}\oplus_d B}(\mathcal{D})$.

Suppose $A\notin\mathsf{Def}(\mathcal{K})$. Then, $A\notin\mathsf{Cons}_{\mathcal{K}\oplus_d B}(\mathcal{D})$ since $\mathsf{Cons}_{\mathcal{K}\oplus_d B}(\mathcal{D})\subseteq\mathsf{Def}(\mathcal{K}\oplus_d B)$ and $A\notin\mathsf{Def}(\mathcal{K}\oplus_d B)$. By Lemma A.3, $\mathsf{Con}[\mathsf{Arg}_{\mathcal{K}\oplus_d B}(\mathcal{D}\oplus_d B)] = \mathsf{Con}[\mathsf{Arg}_{\mathcal{K}\oplus_d A}(\mathcal{D}\oplus_d A)]$ and by ($\star$), $B\notin\mathsf{Cons}_{\mathcal{K}\oplus_d B}(\mathcal{D})$.

If $B\notin\mathsf{Def}(\mathcal{K})$, $B\notin\mathsf{Cons}_{\mathcal{K}\oplus_d A}(\mathcal{D})$ since $\mathsf{Cons}_{\mathcal{K}\oplus_d A}(\mathcal{D})\subseteq\mathsf{Def}(\mathcal{K}\oplus_d A)$ and $B\notin\mathsf{Def}(\mathcal{K}\oplus_d A)$.

If $B \in \mathrm{Def}(\mathcal{K})$, and where † follows by Lemma A.3,

$$\mathrm{Con}[\mathrm{Arg}_{\mathcal{K} \oplus_d A}(\mathcal{D} \oplus_d B)] = \mathrm{Con}[\mathrm{Arg}_{\mathcal{K} \oplus_d A \oplus_d B}(\mathcal{D} \oplus_d B)] =^{\dagger}$$
$$\mathrm{Con}[\mathrm{Arg}_{\mathcal{K} \oplus_d A \oplus_d A}(\mathcal{D} \oplus_d A)] = \mathrm{Con}[\mathrm{Arg}_{\mathcal{K} \oplus_d A}(\mathcal{D} \oplus_d A)].$$

By $(\star)$, $B \notin \mathrm{Cons}_{\mathcal{K} \oplus_d A}(\mathcal{D})$.

(iii) follows immediately with (i) and (ii). $\qquad\square$

Lemma A.5. *Let* $\oplus = \oplus_i$, $\mathcal{D} \in \mathrm{DExt}(\mathcal{K} \oplus A)$, *and*

$$\pi_i(\mathcal{D}) = \begin{cases} \mathcal{D} & i = s \\ \mathcal{D} \setminus \{B\} & i = d, A \notin \mathcal{D} \\ (\mathcal{D} \ominus_d^{\mathcal{K}} A) \oplus_d B & i = d, A \in \mathcal{D} \end{cases}$$

Then,

(i) $\pi_i(\mathcal{D}) \in \mathrm{DExt}(\mathcal{K} \oplus B)$ *and*

(ii) $\mathrm{Con}[\mathrm{Arg}_{\mathcal{K} \oplus A}](\mathcal{D}) = \mathrm{Con}[\mathrm{Arg}_{\mathcal{K} \oplus B}(\pi_i(\mathcal{D}))].$

Proof. By Theorem 10.1,

$$\mathcal{D} = \mathrm{Cons}_{\mathcal{K} \oplus A}(\mathcal{D}) \ (\tau = \mathtt{tem}) \ \text{resp.} \ \mathcal{D} = \mathrm{Trig}_{\mathcal{K} \oplus A}^{\top}(\mathcal{D}) \ (\tau = \mathtt{gr}). \qquad (\dagger)$$

Consider $i = s$. So $\mathcal{D} \subseteq \mathrm{Def}(\mathcal{K})$. By (†) and Lemma A.2, (ii) and $\mathcal{D} = \mathrm{Cons}_{\mathcal{K} \oplus B}(\mathcal{D})$ resp. $\mathcal{D} = \mathrm{Trig}_{\mathcal{K} \oplus B}^{\top}(\mathcal{D})$ and so (i).

Consider $i = d$. If $A \in \mathcal{D}$, by (†) and Lemma A.3, (ii) $\mathrm{Con}[\mathrm{Arg}_{\mathcal{K} \oplus A}(\mathcal{D})] = \mathrm{Con}[\mathrm{Arg}_{\mathcal{K} \oplus B}((\mathcal{D} \ominus_d^{\mathcal{K}} A) \oplus B)]$ and $(\mathcal{D} \ominus_d^{\mathcal{K}} A) \oplus B = \mathrm{Cons}_{\mathcal{K} \oplus B}((\mathcal{D} \ominus_d^{\mathcal{K}} A) \oplus B)$ $(\tau = \mathtt{tem})$ resp. $(\mathcal{D} \ominus_d^{\mathcal{K}} A) \oplus B = \mathrm{Trig}_{\mathcal{K} \oplus B}^{\top}((\mathcal{D} \ominus_d^{\mathcal{K}} A) \oplus B)$ $(\tau = \mathtt{gr})$ and so (i) $\pi_d(\mathcal{D}) \in \mathrm{DExt}_{\tau}(\mathcal{K} \oplus B)$.

If $A \notin \mathcal{D}$, assume first for a contradiction that $B \in \mathcal{D}$. Then $\mathcal{D} \subseteq \mathrm{Def}(\mathcal{K})$ and $\mathcal{K} \oplus B = \mathcal{K}$. By (arg-re), $\mathrm{Con}[\mathrm{Arg}_{\mathcal{K} \oplus A}(\mathcal{D} \oplus A)] \subseteq \mathrm{Con}[\mathrm{Arg}_{\mathcal{K} \oplus A}(\mathcal{D})]$ (since for every argument a in $\mathrm{Arg}_{\mathcal{K} \oplus A}(\mathcal{D} \oplus A)$ there is a $b \in \mathrm{Arg}_{\mathcal{K} \oplus A}(\mathcal{D} \oplus B(= \mathcal{D}))$ with $\mathrm{Con}(a) = \mathrm{Con}(b)$). Since $\mathrm{Con}[\mathrm{Arg}_{\mathcal{K} \oplus A}(\mathcal{D})]$ is consistent, so is $\mathrm{Arg}_{\mathcal{K} \oplus A}(\mathcal{D} \oplus A)$. But then $A \in \mathrm{Cons}_{\mathcal{K} \oplus A}(\mathcal{D})$ resp. $A \in \mathrm{Trig}_{\mathcal{K} \oplus A}^{\top}(\mathcal{D})$ in contradiction to (†). So, $B \notin \mathcal{D}$. By (†) and Lemma A.4, (ii) $\mathrm{Con}[\mathrm{Arg}_{\mathcal{K} \oplus A}(\mathcal{D})] = \mathrm{Con}[\mathrm{Arg}_{\mathcal{K} \oplus B}(\mathcal{D})]$ and $\mathcal{D} = \mathrm{Cons}_{\mathcal{K} \oplus B}(\mathcal{D})$ $(\tau = \mathtt{tem})$ resp. $\mathcal{D} = \mathrm{Trig}_{\mathcal{K} \oplus B}^{\top}(\mathcal{D})$ $(\tau = \mathtt{gr})$ and so (i) $\mathcal{D} \in \mathrm{DExt}_{\tau}(\mathcal{K} \oplus B)$. $\qquad\square$

Proposition* 10.2. *Let* $i \in \{s, d\}$, $\tau \in \{\mathtt{tem}, \mathtt{gr}\}$ *and* $\vdash \in \{\vdash_{\cap\mathrm{AExt}}^{\tau}, \vdash_{\cap\mathrm{PExt}}^{\tau}\}$. *If (arg-re),* $LLE_i(\vdash)$ *holds.*

Proof. Suppose $\mathcal{K} \oplus_i B \vdash_{\cap\mathrm{AExt}}^{\tau} C$. By Fact A.1, there is an argument $a \in \mathrm{Arg}_{\mathcal{K} \oplus_i B}(\bigcap \mathrm{DExt}_{\tau}(\mathcal{K} \oplus_i B))$ with $\mathrm{Con}(a) = C$. Since, by Lemma A.5, $\{\pi_i(\mathcal{D}) \mid$

$\mathcal{D} \in \mathsf{DExt}_\tau(\mathcal{K} \oplus_i A)\} \subseteq \mathsf{DExt}_\tau(\mathcal{K} \oplus_i B)$, $a \in \mathsf{Arg}_{\mathcal{K} \oplus_i B}(\bigcap \{\pi_i(\mathcal{D}) \mid \mathcal{D} \in \mathsf{DExt}_\tau(\mathcal{K} \oplus_i A)\})$. Let $b \in \mathsf{Arg}_{\mathcal{K} \oplus_i A}$ with $\mathsf{Con}(b) = \mathsf{Con}(a)$ as in (arg-re). We show that (†) $b \in \mathsf{Arg}_{\mathcal{K} \oplus_i A}(\bigcap \mathsf{DExt}_\tau(\mathcal{K} \oplus_i A))$ which implies $\mathcal{K} \oplus_i A \vdash^\tau_{\cap\mathsf{AExt}} C$.

For (†), first consider the case $i = s$. Then $\mathsf{Def}(a) = \mathsf{Def}(b)$ and $\pi_s(\mathcal{D}) = \mathcal{D}$. Therefore $\bigcap \{\pi_s(\mathcal{D}) \mid \mathcal{D} \in \mathsf{DExt}_\tau(\mathcal{K} \oplus_s A)\} = \bigcap \mathsf{DExt}_\tau(\mathcal{K} \oplus_s A)$ and therefore (†).

Consider now the case $i = d$ and let $\mathcal{D} \in \mathsf{DExt}_\tau(\mathcal{K} \oplus_d A)$.

Suppose first that $B \notin \mathsf{Def}(a)$. Then by (arg-re) $\mathsf{Def}(a) = \mathsf{Def}(b)$. Since $\mathsf{Def}(a) \subseteq \pi_d(\mathcal{D})$, $\mathsf{Def}(b) \subseteq \pi_d(\mathcal{D})$. Either $\mathcal{D} \setminus \{B\} = \pi_d(\mathcal{D})$ or $(\mathcal{D} \ominus_d^\mathcal{K} A) \oplus_d B = \pi_d(\mathcal{D})$. In the first case $\mathsf{Def}(b) \subseteq \mathcal{D} \setminus \{B\} \subseteq \mathcal{D}$ and in the second case, since $B \notin \mathsf{Def}(b)$, $\mathsf{Def}(b) \subseteq \mathcal{D} \ominus_d^\mathcal{K} B \subseteq \mathcal{D}$. Altogether $\mathsf{Def}(b) \subseteq \mathcal{D}$ for any $\mathcal{D} \in \mathsf{DExt}_\tau(\mathcal{K} \oplus_d A)$ and so (†).

Suppose now that $B \in \mathsf{Def}(a)$. Then by (arg-re), $\mathsf{Def}(b) = (\mathsf{Def}(a) \setminus \{B\}) \cup \{A\}$. Either $\mathcal{D} \setminus \{B\} = \pi_d(\mathcal{D})$ or $(\mathcal{D} \ominus_d^\mathcal{K} A) \oplus_d B = \pi_d(\mathcal{D})$. The former case is impossible since $\mathsf{Def}(a) \subseteq \pi_d(\mathcal{D})$ and $B \in \mathsf{Def}(a)$. Since $\mathcal{D}$ is an arbitrary member of $\mathsf{DExt}_\tau(\mathcal{K} \oplus_d A)$, $\pi_d(\mathcal{D}') = (\mathcal{D}' \ominus_d^\mathcal{K} A) \oplus_d B$ for all $\mathcal{D}' \in \mathsf{DExt}_\tau(\mathcal{K} \oplus_d A)$. This means that $A \in \mathcal{D}'$ for every $\mathcal{D}' \in \mathsf{DExt}_\tau(\mathcal{K} \oplus_d A)$. Since $\mathsf{Def}(b) \setminus \{A\} \subseteq \mathsf{Def}(a) \subseteq (\mathcal{D} \ominus_d^\mathcal{K} A) \oplus_d B$ and $B \notin \mathsf{Def}(b)$, $\mathsf{Def}(b) \subseteq \mathcal{D}$. Altogether, this proves (†).

Suppose $\mathcal{K} \oplus_i B \vdash^\tau_{\cap\mathsf{PExt}} C$. Let $\mathcal{D} \in \mathsf{DExt}_\tau(\mathcal{K} \oplus_i A)$. By Lemma A.5, $\pi_i(\mathcal{D}) \in \mathsf{DExt}(\mathcal{K} \oplus_i B)$ and $\mathsf{Con}[\mathsf{Arg}_{\mathcal{K} \oplus_i A}(\mathcal{D})] = \mathsf{Con}[\mathsf{Arg}_{\mathcal{K} \oplus_i B}(\pi_i(\mathcal{D}))]$. Since $C \in \mathsf{Con}[\mathsf{Arg}_{\mathcal{K} \oplus_i B}(\pi_i(\mathcal{D}))]$, also $C \in \mathsf{Con}[\mathsf{Arg}_{\mathcal{K} \oplus_i A}(\mathcal{D})]$. So, $\mathcal{K} \oplus_i A \vdash^\tau_{\cap\mathsf{PExt}} C$. $\square$

Proposition* 10.3. *Let* $\tau \in \{\texttt{tem}, \texttt{gr}\}$ *and* $\vdash \in \{\vdash^\tau_{\cap\mathsf{AExt}}, \vdash^\tau_{\cap\mathsf{PExt}}, \vdash^\tau_{\cup\mathsf{Ext}}\}$. *If (arg-strict), Ref($\vdash$) and RW($\vdash$) hold.*

Proof. For (Ref($\vdash$)) we have to show that $\mathcal{K} \oplus_s A \vdash A$. By (arg-strict) $a = \langle A \rangle \in \mathsf{Arg}_{\mathcal{K} \oplus_s A}(\emptyset)$ and so $a \in \bigcap_{\mathcal{D} \in \mathsf{DExt}(\mathcal{K} \oplus_s A)} \mathsf{Arg}_{\mathcal{K} \oplus_i A}(\mathcal{D})$. This implies, $\mathcal{K} \oplus_s A \vdash A$. The proof of (RW($\vdash$)) is similar and left to the reader as an easy exercise. $\square$

A.2 Proofs for Section 11

Proof of Proposition 11.1

Proposition* 11.1. *Let* $i \in \{s, d\}$. *Given (arg), C_i(DExt) holds for* $\mathbf{K}_\Omega$.

Proof. Suppose (arg) and $\mathcal{K} \vdash^{\texttt{tem}}_{\cap\mathsf{PExt}} A$. In view of Proposition 10.1 we only have to show $\mathsf{CM}_i(\mathsf{DExt})$. Let $\mathcal{D} \in \mathsf{DExt}(\mathcal{K} \oplus_i A)$. By Theorem 10.1, $\mathcal{D} = \mathsf{Cons}_{\mathcal{K} \oplus_i A}(\mathcal{D})$. We have to show that $\mathcal{D} \ominus_i^\mathcal{K} A = \mathsf{Cons}_\mathcal{K}(\mathcal{D} \ominus_i^\mathcal{K} A)$. By (arg-mono), $\mathsf{Con}[\mathsf{Arg}_\mathcal{K}(\mathcal{D} \ominus_i^\mathcal{K} A)] \subseteq \mathsf{Con}[\mathsf{Arg}_{\mathcal{K} \oplus_i A}(\mathcal{D})]$ and by the consistency of $\mathcal{D}$ in $\mathcal{K} \oplus_i A$, $\mathcal{D} \ominus_i^\mathcal{K} A$ is consistent in $\mathcal{K}$. Thus, there is a $\mathcal{D}' \in \mathsf{DExt}(\mathcal{K})$ such that

$\mathcal{D} \ominus_i^{\mathcal{K}} A \subseteq \mathcal{D}'$. By the supposition, $A \in \mathsf{Con}[\mathsf{Arg}_{\mathcal{K}}(\mathcal{D}')]$ and by Lemma A.1, $\mathsf{Con}[\mathsf{Arg}_{\mathcal{K}}(\mathcal{D}')] = \mathsf{Con}[\mathsf{Arg}_{\mathcal{K} \oplus_i A}(\mathcal{D}' \oplus_i A)]$. Also, we have, $\mathsf{Con}[\mathsf{Arg}_{\mathcal{K} \oplus_i A}(\mathcal{D})] \subseteq \mathsf{Con}[\mathsf{Arg}_{\mathcal{K} \oplus_i A}(\mathcal{D} \oplus_i A)]$. Since $\mathsf{Con}[\mathsf{Arg}_{\mathcal{K} \oplus_i A}(\mathcal{D} \oplus_i A)] \subseteq \mathsf{Con}[\mathsf{Arg}_{\mathcal{K} \oplus_i A}(\mathcal{D}' \oplus_i A)]$ and the latter set is consistent, $\mathcal{D} \oplus_i A$ is consistent in $\mathcal{K} \oplus_i A$. So, $\mathcal{D} \oplus_i A = \mathcal{D}' \oplus_i A$ and therefore $\mathcal{D} \ominus_i^{\mathcal{K}} A = \mathcal{D}'$. Thus, $\mathcal{D} \ominus_i^{\mathcal{K}} A \in \mathsf{DExt}(\mathcal{K})$. $\qquad\square$

Proof of Theorem 11.2

Theorem⋆ 11.2. *Let* nmL *be based on temperate accumulation, let* $\mathcal{K} \in \mathbf{K}_{\mathsf{nmL}}$ *be of the form* $\langle \mathcal{A}_s, \mathcal{A}_d, \mathcal{R}_s, \mathcal{R}_d \rangle$, *and let* $\mathcal{K}^{\star}$ *be the translation defined in Definition 11.1. Then,* $\mathsf{DExt}(\mathcal{K}) = \mathsf{DExt}(\mathcal{K}^{\star})$ *and* $\mathsf{PExt}(\mathcal{K}) = \mathsf{PExt}(\mathcal{K}^{\star})$.

In the proof of Theorem 11.2 we make use of the following lemma.

Lemma A.6. 1. *For every* $a \in \mathsf{Arg}_{\mathcal{K}}$ *there is an* $a^{\star} \in \mathsf{Arg}_{\mathcal{K}^{\star}}$ *with* $\mathsf{Con}(a) = \mathsf{Con}(a^{\star})$ *and* $\mathsf{Def}_{\mathcal{K}}(a) = \mathsf{Def}_{\mathcal{K}^{\star}}(a^{\star})$.
  2. *For every* $a^{\star} \in \mathsf{Arg}_{\mathcal{K}^{\star}}$ *for which* $\mathcal{R}_s^{\star}(a) \subseteq \mathcal{R}_s^{\mathsf{mp}} \cup \mathcal{R}_s$ *there is an* $a \in \mathsf{Arg}_{\mathcal{K}}$ *for which* $\mathsf{Con}(a) = \mathsf{Con}(a^{\star})$ *and* $\mathsf{Def}_{\mathcal{K}}(a) = \mathsf{Def}_{\mathcal{K}^{\star}}(a^{\star})$.
  3. *Let* $\mathcal{D} \subseteq \mathsf{Def}(\mathcal{K})$. *Then (i)* $\mathsf{Con}[\mathsf{Arg}_{\mathcal{K}}(\mathcal{D})] = \mathsf{Con}[\mathsf{Arg}_{\mathcal{K}^{\star}}(\mathcal{D})] \cap \mathsf{sent}_{\mathcal{L}}$ *and (ii)* $\mathsf{Cons}_{\mathcal{K}}(\mathcal{D}) = \mathsf{Cons}_{\mathcal{K}^{\star}}(\mathcal{D})$.

Proof. We show item 1. Item 2 is shown analogously. It is shown inductively over the length of a. In the base case, $a = \langle A \rangle \in \mathsf{Arg}_{\mathcal{K}}$ for some $A \in \mathcal{A}_d \cup \mathcal{A}_s$. Then let $a^{\star} = a$.

For the inductive step, suppose that $a = a_1, \ldots, a_n \Rightarrow A \in \mathsf{Arg}_{\mathcal{K}}$, where $r = (A_1, \ldots, A_n \Rightarrow A) \in \mathcal{R}_d$ and $\mathsf{Con}(a_i) = A_i$ for each $i = 1, \ldots, n$. By the inductive hypothesis, for each $i \in \{1, \ldots, n\}$, there is an $a_i^{\star} \in \mathsf{Arg}_{\mathcal{K}^{\star}}$ with $\mathsf{Con}(a_i) = \mathsf{Con}(a_i^{\star})$ and $\mathsf{Def}_{\mathcal{K}}(a_i) = \mathsf{Def}_{\mathcal{K}^{\star}}(a_i^{\star})$. Let $a^{\star} = a_1^{\star}, \ldots, a_n^{\star}, \langle r \rangle \rightarrow A$. Clearly, $\mathsf{Con}(a) = \mathsf{Con}(a^{\star}) = A$ and $\mathsf{Def}_{\mathcal{K}}(a) = \bigcup_{i=1}^{n} \mathsf{Def}_{\mathcal{K}}(a_i) \cup \{r\} = \mathsf{Def}_{\mathcal{K}^{\star}}(a^{\star})$. The case $a = a_1, \ldots, a_n \rightarrow A \in \mathsf{Arg}_{\mathcal{K}}$ is analogous.

Item 3. (i) follows immediately with Items 1 and 2. (Note that for all $a \in \mathsf{Arg}_{\mathcal{K}^{\star}}(\mathcal{D})$ for which $\mathcal{R}_s^{\mathsf{cp}}(a) \neq \emptyset$, $\mathsf{Con}(a) \notin \mathsf{sent}_{\mathcal{L}}$.) We consider (ii).

"$\subseteq$". We recall that $\mathsf{Def}(\mathcal{K}) = \mathsf{Def}(\mathcal{K}^{\star})$. Suppose $d \in \mathsf{Def}(\mathcal{K}) \setminus \mathsf{Cons}_{\mathcal{K}^{\star}}(\mathcal{D})$ and assume for a contradiction that $d \in \mathsf{Cons}_{\mathcal{K}}(\mathcal{D})$. Let $\mathcal{D}' = \mathcal{D} \cup \{d\}$. Since $\mathsf{Con}[\mathsf{Arg}_{\mathcal{K}}(\mathcal{D}')]$ is consistent and by (i), there is an $r \in \mathcal{R}_d$ for which $r, \neg r \in \mathsf{Con}[\mathsf{Arg}_{\mathcal{K}^{\star}}(\mathcal{D}')]$. Thus, there is a $c^{\star} = a_1^{\star}, \ldots, a_n^{\star}, b^{\star} \rightarrow \neg r \in \mathsf{Arg}_{\mathcal{K}^{\star}}(\mathcal{D}')$, where $\mathsf{Con}(a_i^{\star}) = A_i$ for each $i = 1, \ldots, n$, $\mathsf{Con}(b^{\star}) = \neg B$. Note that $r \in \mathcal{D}'$ and $\mathcal{R}_s^{\mathsf{cp}}(a_i^{\star}) = \emptyset = \mathcal{R}_s^{\mathsf{cp}}(b^{\star})$. But then, by item 2 and since $a_1^{\star}, \ldots, a_n^{\star}, b^{\star} \in \mathsf{Arg}_{\mathcal{K}^{\star}}(\mathcal{D}')$, there is a $b \in \mathsf{Arg}_{\mathcal{K}}(\mathcal{D}')$ with $\mathsf{Con}(b) = \neg B$ and there are $a_i \in \mathsf{Arg}_{\mathcal{K}}(\mathcal{D}')$ with $\mathsf{Con}(a_i) = A_i$. Thus, also $d = a_1, \ldots, a_n \Rightarrow B \in \mathsf{Arg}_{\mathcal{K}}(\mathcal{D}')$. But since $B, \neg B \in \mathrm{Con}[\mathrm{Arg}_{\mathcal{K}}(\mathcal{D}')]$ this is in contradiction to its consistency. So, $d \in \mathrm{Def}_{\mathcal{K}} \setminus \mathrm{Cons}_{\mathcal{K}}(\mathcal{D})$.

"$\supseteq$". Suppose $d \in \mathrm{Cons}_{\mathcal{K}^\star}(\mathcal{D})$. Thus, $\mathrm{Con}[\mathrm{Arg}_{\mathcal{K}^\star}(\mathcal{D} \cup \{d\})]$ is consistent and so, by item 2, is $\mathrm{Con}[\mathrm{Arg}_{\mathcal{K}}(\mathcal{D} \cup \{d\})]$. Thus, $d \in \mathrm{Cons}_{\mathcal{K}}(\mathcal{D})$. $\qquad\square$

Proof of Theorem 11.2. Let $\mathcal{D} \in \mathrm{DExt}(\mathcal{K})$. By Theorem 10.1, $\mathcal{D} = \mathrm{Cons}_{\mathcal{K}}(\mathcal{D})$. By Lemma A.6, $\mathrm{Cons}_{\mathcal{K}^\star}(\mathcal{D}) = \mathrm{Cons}_{\mathcal{K}}(\mathcal{D})$. By Theorem 10.1, $\mathcal{D} \in \mathrm{DExt}(\mathcal{K}^\star)$. The other direction is analogous. $\qquad\square$

A.3 Proofs for Section 12

Proof of Proposition 12.1

Proposition* 12.1. *Let $\mathcal{K} = \langle \mathcal{A}_s, \mathcal{R}_d, \mathcal{R}_s \rangle$ be a Reiter default theory, $\mathcal{D} \subseteq \mathcal{R}_d$, and $\mathcal{E} = \mathrm{Con}[\mathrm{Arg}_{\mathcal{K}}(\mathcal{D})]$. $\mathcal{D}$ is a Reiter D-extension of $\mathcal{K}$ iff $\mathcal{D} = \mathrm{Trig}_{\mathcal{K}}^{\top}(\mathcal{E}, \mathcal{D})$.*

Proof. ($\Rightarrow$) Let $\mathcal{D} = \langle r_1, \ldots, r_n \rangle$ be the product of $\mathtt{GreedyAccGen}(\mathcal{E}, \mathcal{D})$, $\mathcal{D}_0 = \emptyset$, and $\mathcal{D}_i = \{r_1, \ldots, r_i\}$ for $i = 1, \ldots, n$. We have to show that $\mathcal{D} = \mathrm{Trig}_{\mathcal{K}}^{\top}(\mathcal{E}, \mathcal{D})$. For ($\supseteq$) assume there is a $r \in \mathrm{Trig}_{\mathcal{K}}^{\top}(\mathcal{E}, \mathcal{D}) \setminus \mathcal{D}$. But then, r is added to $\mathcal{D}$ at line 5 and so $r \in \mathcal{D}$, which is a contradiction. For ($\subseteq$) we first observe that $\mathcal{D} \subseteq \mathrm{Trig}_{\mathcal{K}}(\mathcal{D})$ by the construction of $\mathtt{GreedyAccGen}(\mathcal{E}, \mathcal{D})$. Assume for a contradiction that $\mathcal{D} \not\subseteq \mathrm{Cons}_{\mathcal{K}}(\mathcal{E}, \mathcal{D})$. But then for some $i \in \{1, \ldots, n\}$, some $J \in \mathrm{Just}(r_i)$ is inconsistent with $\mathcal{E}$ in $\mathcal{K}$ and therefore $r_i \notin \mathrm{Cons}_{\mathcal{K}}(\mathcal{E}) \subseteq \mathrm{Trig}_{\mathcal{K}}^{\top}(\mathcal{E}, \mathcal{D}_{i-1})$, which is a contradiction. So, $\mathcal{D} \subseteq \mathrm{Cons}_{\mathcal{K}}(\mathcal{E}, \mathcal{D})$, and thus, $\mathcal{D} \subseteq \mathrm{Trig}_{\mathcal{K}}^{\top}(\mathcal{E}, \mathcal{D})$.

($\Leftarrow$) Let $\mathcal{D} = \mathrm{Trig}_{\mathcal{K}}^{\top}(\mathcal{E}, \mathcal{D})$ consist of n many rules in $\mathcal{R}_d$. It is easy to see that $\mathcal{D}$ can be enumerated by $\langle r_1, \ldots, r_n \rangle$ where $\mathcal{D}_0 = \emptyset$, $r_1 \in \mathrm{Trig}_{\mathcal{K}}(\mathcal{D}_0)$, $\mathcal{D}_1 = \{r_1\}$, and $r_{i+1} \in \mathrm{Trig}_{\mathcal{K}}(\mathcal{D}_i) \setminus \mathcal{D}_i$ and $\mathcal{D}_{i+1} = \{r_1, \ldots, r_{i+1}\}$ for every $0 \le i < n$.

Since for each $i \in \{1, \ldots, n\}$, $r_i \in \mathrm{Trig}_{\mathcal{K}}^{\top}(\mathcal{E}, \mathcal{D}_{i-1}) \setminus \mathcal{D}_{i-1}$ (note that $r_i \in \mathrm{Cons}_{\mathcal{K}}(\mathcal{E}, \mathcal{D}) = \mathrm{Cons}_{\mathcal{K}}(\mathcal{E}, \mathcal{D}_{i-1})$), there is a run of $\textsc{GreedyAccGen}(\mathcal{K}, \mathcal{D})$ in which in each round $i \in \{1, \ldots, n\}$, r_i is added to $\mathcal{D}^\star$. Note that after round n the algorithm terminates and returns $\mathcal{D}$ since $\mathrm{Trig}_{\mathcal{K}}^{\top}(\mathcal{E}, \mathcal{D}) = \mathcal{D}$ and so $\mathrm{Trig}_{\mathcal{K}}^{\top}(\mathcal{E}, \mathcal{D}) \setminus \mathcal{D} = \emptyset$. $\qquad\square$

Proof of Theorem 12.1

Theorem* 12.1. *Let $\mathcal{K} = \langle \mathcal{A}_s, \mathcal{R}_d, \mathcal{R}_s \rangle$ be a general default theory and $\mathcal{K}'$ as in Definition 12.3. Then*

1. for every Reiter P-extension $\mathcal{E}$ of $\mathcal{K}$, there is a stable A-extension $\mathcal{X}$ of $\mathcal{K}'$ for which $\mathrm{Con}[\mathcal{X}] \cap \mathrm{sent}_{\mathcal{L}} = \mathcal{E}$,

2. *for every stable A-extension $\mathcal{X}$ of $\mathcal{K}'$, $\mathrm{Con}[\mathcal{X}] \cap \mathrm{sent}_{\mathcal{L}}$ is a Reiter P-extension of $\mathcal{K}$.*

In order to prove Theorem 12.1, let $\mathcal{K} = \langle \mathcal{A}_s, \mathcal{R}_d, \mathcal{R}_s \rangle$ be a Reiter default theory and $\mathcal{K}'$ its translation as in Definition 12.3. We denote the members of $\mathcal{R}_d$ by r and their corresponding rules in $\mathcal{K}'$ by r'. In order to prove the correspondence between Reiter P-extensions of $\mathcal{K}$ and stable extensions of $\mathcal{K}'$, we show two correspondences on the level of arguments. We let $\mathrm{DExt}(\mathcal{K})$ be the set of Reiter D-extensions of $\mathcal{K}$.

Lemma A.7. *Let $\mathcal{D} \in \mathrm{DExt}(\mathcal{K})$, $\mathcal{E} = \mathrm{Con}[\mathrm{Arg}_{\mathcal{K}}(\mathcal{D})]$, $\mathcal{E}_\diamond = \{\diamond A \mid \neg A \notin \mathcal{E}\}$, and $\mathcal{X} = \mathrm{Arg}_{\mathcal{K}'}(\mathcal{E}_\diamond)$. We have:*

1. *for every $a \in \mathrm{Arg}_{\mathcal{K}}(\mathcal{D})$ there is an $a' \in \mathcal{X}$ with $\mathrm{Con}(a) = \mathrm{Con}(a')$, and*
2. *for every $a' \in \mathcal{X}$ with $\mathrm{Con}(a') \in \mathrm{sent}_{\mathcal{L}}$ there is an $a \in \mathrm{Arg}_{\mathcal{K}}(\mathcal{D})$ with $\mathrm{Con}(a) = \mathrm{Con}(a')$.*

Proof. Item 2. This is shown by an induction on the length of $a' \in \mathcal{X}$. In the base case $a' = \langle A \rangle$ for $A \in \mathcal{A}_s$ and therefore, where $a = a'$, $a \in \mathrm{Arg}_{\mathcal{K}}(\mathcal{D})$. In the inductive step a' has one of two forms, where $a'_1, \ldots, a'_n \in \mathcal{X}$ with $\mathrm{Con}(a'_1) = A_1, \ldots, \mathrm{Con}(a'_n) = A_n$:

- either $a' = a'_1, \ldots, a'_n, \langle \diamond B_1 \rangle, \ldots, \langle \diamond B_m \rangle \to C$ where
  $r = \dfrac{A_1, \ldots, A_n \quad B_1, \ldots, B_m}{C} \in \mathcal{R}_d$ and $\diamond B_1, \ldots, \diamond B_m \in \mathcal{E}_\diamond$,
- or $a' = a'_1, \ldots, a'_n \to C$ where $A_1, \ldots, A_n \to C \in \mathcal{R}_s$.

By the inductive hypothesis, there are $a_1, \ldots, a_n \in \mathrm{Arg}_{\mathcal{K}}(\mathcal{D})$ with $\mathrm{Con}(a_1) = A_1, \ldots, \mathrm{Con}(a_n) = A_n$. In the first case, $\neg B_1, \ldots, \neg B_m \notin \mathcal{E}$ and $A_1, \ldots, A_n \in \mathcal{E}$. Therefore, $r \in \mathrm{Trig}_{\mathcal{K}}^\top(\mathcal{E}, \mathcal{D})$ and so by Proposition 12.1, $r \in \mathcal{D}$. Thus, $a = a_1, \ldots, a_n \Rightarrow C \in \mathrm{Arg}_{\mathcal{K}}(\mathcal{D})$. In the second case, $a = a_1, \ldots, a_n \to C \in \mathrm{Arg}_{\mathcal{K}}(\mathcal{D})$. *Item 1* is shown analogously. $\square$

Lemma A.8. *Let $\mathcal{X} \in \mathrm{stable}(\mathcal{K}')$, $\mathcal{E} = \mathrm{Con}[\mathcal{X}] \cap \mathrm{sent}_{\mathcal{L}}$, $\mathcal{E}' = \{A \mid \diamond A \in \mathrm{Con}[\mathcal{X}]\}$, $\mathcal{D} = \{r \in \mathcal{R}_d \mid \mathrm{Just}(r) \subseteq \mathcal{E}' \text{ and } \mathrm{Body}(r) \subseteq \mathcal{E}\}$. We have:*

1. *for every $a \in \mathrm{Arg}_{\mathcal{K}}(\mathcal{D})$, there is an $a' \in \mathcal{X}$ with $\mathrm{Con}(a) = \mathrm{Con}(a')$, and*
2. *for every $a' \in \mathcal{X}$ with $\mathrm{Con}(a') \in \mathcal{E}$, there is an $a \in \mathrm{Arg}_{\mathcal{K}}(\mathcal{D})$ with $\mathrm{Con}(a) = \mathrm{Con}(a')$.*

Proof. Item 1. This is shown by an induction on the length of $a \in \mathrm{Arg}_{\mathcal{K}}(\mathcal{D})$. In the base case $a = \langle A \rangle$ where $A \in \mathcal{A}_s$. Since a has no attackers, $a \in \mathcal{X}$. For the inductive step we have two cases: either a is of the form $a_1, \ldots, a_n \to C$ or of the form $a_1, \ldots, a_n \Rightarrow C$, where $\mathrm{Con}(a_i) = A_i$ (for $i = 1, \ldots, n$) and $A_1, \ldots, A_n \rightarrow C \in \mathcal{R}_s$ resp. $\dfrac{A_1, \ldots, A_n \quad B_1, \ldots, B_m}{C} \in \mathcal{D}$ for $\Diamond B_1, \ldots, \Diamond B_m \in \mathrm{Con}[\mathcal{X}]$. By the inductive hypothesis, $a_1', \ldots, a_n' \in \mathcal{X}$. In the former case $b_1 = a_1', \ldots, a_n' \rightarrow C \in \mathcal{X}$ and in the latter case $b_2 = a_1', \ldots, a_n', \langle \Diamond B_1 \rangle, \ldots, \langle \Diamond B_m \rangle \rightarrow C \in \mathcal{X}$. The reason is that any attacker of b_1 resp. b_2 is either an attacker of some $a_i' \in \mathcal{X}$ or of some $\langle \Diamond B_i \rangle \in \mathcal{X}$. By the conflict-freeness of $\mathcal{X}$, $\mathcal{X}$ does not attack b_1 resp. b_2. By the stability of $\mathcal{X}$, $b_1 \in \mathcal{X}$ resp. $b_2 \in \mathcal{X}$. *Item 2* is shown analogously. $\qquad \square$

We are now ready to prove Theorem 12.1.

Proof of Theorem 12.1. Item 1 Let $\mathcal{D} \in \mathrm{DExt}(\mathcal{K})$. Let $\mathcal{E}, \mathcal{E}_\Diamond$, and $\mathcal{X}$ as in Lemma A.7. Then, (†) $\mathrm{Con}[\mathcal{X}] \cap \mathrm{sent}_\mathcal{L} = \mathcal{E}$. We have to show that $\mathcal{X} \in \mathrm{stable}(\mathcal{K}')$. Assume for a contradiction that there are $a', b' \in \mathcal{X}$ such that a' attacks b'. Thus, there is a B for which $\langle \Diamond B \rangle \in \mathrm{Sub}(b')$, $\Diamond B \in \mathcal{E}_\Diamond$, and $\mathrm{Con}(a') = \neg B$. By (†), $\neg B \in \mathcal{E}$ which is a contradiction to $\Diamond B \in \mathcal{E}_\Diamond$. Suppose now that $a' \in \mathrm{Arg}_{\mathcal{K}'} \setminus \mathcal{X}$. So, there is an $\langle \Diamond B \rangle \in \mathrm{Sub}(a')$ for which $\Diamond B \notin \mathcal{E}_\Diamond$. Thus, $\neg B \in \mathcal{E}$ and by (†) there is an $b' \in \mathcal{X}$ with $\mathrm{Con}(b') = \neg B$ that attacks a'. Thus, $\mathcal{X} \in \mathrm{stable}(\mathcal{K}')$.

Item 2 Suppose $\mathcal{X} \in \mathrm{stable}(\mathcal{K}')$. Let $\mathcal{E}, \mathcal{E}'$, and $\mathcal{D}$ be as in Lemma A.8. By Proposition 12.1 we have to show that (i) $\mathcal{D} = \mathrm{Trig}_\mathcal{K}^\top(\mathcal{E}, \mathcal{D})$ and (ii) $\mathcal{E} = \mathrm{Con}[\mathrm{Arg}_\mathcal{K}(\mathcal{D})]$. Item (ii) follows with Lemma A.8. Since for every $r \in \mathcal{D}$, $\mathrm{Body}(r) \subseteq \mathcal{E} = \mathrm{Con}[\mathrm{Arg}_\mathcal{K}(\mathcal{D})] \cap \mathrm{sent}_\mathcal{L}$, also $\mathcal{D} \subseteq \mathrm{Trig}_\mathcal{K}(\mathcal{D})$. Let now $B \in \mathrm{Just}(r)$ for some $r \in \mathcal{D}$. So, $\langle \Diamond B \rangle \in \mathcal{X}$ and by the conflict-freeness of $\mathcal{X}$, $\neg B \notin \mathcal{E}$. So, $\mathcal{D} \subseteq \mathrm{Trig}_\mathcal{K}^\top(\mathcal{E}, \mathcal{D})$. Consider now a $r \in \mathrm{Trig}_\mathcal{K}^\top(\mathcal{E}, \mathcal{D})$. So, $\mathrm{Body}(r) \subseteq \mathcal{E}$ and for each $B \in \mathrm{Just}(r)$, $\neg B \notin \mathcal{E}$. Thus, by the stability of $\mathcal{X}$, for each $B \in \mathrm{Just}(r)$, $\langle \Diamond B \rangle \in \mathcal{X}$ and so $B \in \mathcal{E}'$. Thus, $r \in \mathcal{D}$. $\qquad \square$

Appendix B
Proofs for Part III
B.1 Proof of Proposition 16.2

The following fact is an immediate consequence of the definitions of Π^M and $M_\Pi^\sim$.

Fact B.1. *Let $M \subseteq \mathsf{Lit}(\Pi)$ and Π be a logic program. Then,* $\mathsf{Con}[\mathsf{Arg}_{\mathcal{K}_\Pi}(M_\Pi^\sim)] \cap \mathsf{Lit}(\Pi) = \mathsf{Con}[\mathsf{Arg}_{\mathcal{K}_{\Pi^M}}]$.

Where $M \subseteq \mathsf{Lit}^\neg(\Pi)$, let $\tau(M) = \{A \in \mathsf{Atoms} \mid A \in M\} \cup \{A' \mid \neg A \in M\}$.

Lemma B.1. *Let Π be an extended logic program and $M \subseteq \mathsf{Lit}^\neg(\Pi)$ be consistent. Then, $M \in \mathsf{stable}_\top(\Pi)$ iff $M = \mathsf{Con}[\mathsf{Arg}_{\mathcal{K}_\Pi}(M_\Pi^\sim)] \cap \mathsf{Lit}^\neg(\Pi)$.*

Proof. Let $\Pi' = \tau(\Pi)^{\tau(M)}$ be the reduction model (see Definition 16.3) of the translated program $\tau(\Pi)$ modulo the translated model $\tau(M)$ and let $\mathcal{K}' = \mathcal{K}_{\Pi'}$. We have: $M \in \mathsf{stable}_\top(\Pi)$, iff $\tau(M)$ is the minimal model of Π', iff (by Fact 16.1) $\tau(M) = \mathsf{Con}[\mathsf{Arg}_{\mathcal{K}'}]$, iff (by Fact B.1)

$$\tau(M) = \mathsf{Con}[\mathsf{Arg}_{\mathcal{K}_{\tau(\Pi)}}(\tau(M)_{\tau(\Pi)}^\sim)] \cap \mathsf{Lit}(\tau(\Pi)).$$

By the 1:1 nature of τ, this is equivalent to $M = \mathsf{Con}[\mathsf{Arg}_{\mathcal{K}_\Pi}(M_\Pi^\sim)] \cap \mathsf{Lit}^\neg(\Pi)$. $\square$

Lemma B.2. *Let Π be an extended logic program, $\mathcal{X} \subseteq \mathsf{Arg}_{\mathcal{K}_\Pi}$, and $M = \mathsf{Con}[\mathcal{X}] \cap \mathsf{Lit}^\neg(\Pi)$. Then, $\mathcal{X} \in \mathsf{stable}(\mathcal{K}_\Pi)$ iff $\mathcal{X} = \mathsf{Arg}_{\mathcal{K}_\Pi}(M_\Pi^\sim)$.*

Proof. "$\Rightarrow$". Suppose $\mathcal{X} \in \mathsf{stable}(\mathcal{K}_\Pi)$. "$\supseteq$". Suppose $a \notin \mathcal{X}$. By the stability of $\mathcal{X}$ there is a $b \in \mathcal{X}$ such that $b \leadsto a$. So, there is a $\langle \sim\ell \rangle \in \mathsf{Sub}(a)$ such that $\mathsf{Con}(b) = \ell$. Since $\ell \in M$, $\sim\ell \notin M_\Pi^\sim$ and so $a \notin \mathsf{Arg}_{\mathcal{K}_\Pi}(M_\Pi^\sim)$.
    "$\subseteq$". Suppose $a \notin \mathsf{Arg}_{\mathcal{K}_\Pi}(M_\Pi^\sim)$. Thus, there is a $\langle \sim\ell \rangle \in \mathsf{Sub}(a)$ such that $\sim\ell \notin M_\Pi^\sim$. So, $\ell \in M$. Thus, there is a $b \in \mathcal{X}$ with $\mathsf{Con}(b) = \ell$ for which $b \leadsto a$. By the conflict-freeness of $\mathcal{X}$, $a \notin \mathcal{X}$.
    "$\Leftarrow$". Let $\mathcal{X} = \mathsf{Arg}_{\mathcal{K}_\Pi}(M_\Pi^\sim)$. Suppose $a \in \mathcal{X}$, $b \in \mathsf{Arg}_{\mathcal{K}_\Pi}$, and $a \leadsto b$. So, there is a $\langle \sim\ell \rangle \in \mathsf{Sub}(b)$ such that $\mathsf{Con}(a) = \ell$. So, $\ell \in M$ and so $\sim\ell \notin M_\Pi^\sim$. Thus, $b \notin \mathcal{X}$ and $\mathcal{X}$ is conflict-free. Let now $b \in \mathsf{Arg}_{\mathcal{K}_\Pi} \setminus \mathcal{X}$. So, there is a $\langle \sim\ell \rangle \in \mathsf{Sub}(b)$ for which $\sim\ell \notin M_\Pi^\sim$. Thus, $\ell \in M$ and so there is an $a \in \mathcal{X}$ with $\mathsf{Con}(a) = \ell$. Since $a \leadsto b$ we have shown that $\mathcal{X} \in \mathsf{stable}(\mathcal{K}_\Pi)$. $\square$

Theorem* 16.2. *Let Π be an extended logic program.*

1. *If* $M \in \text{stable}_\top(\Pi)$, *then* $\text{Arg}_{\mathcal{K}_\Pi}(M_{\widetilde{\Pi}}) \in \text{stable}(\mathcal{K}_\Pi)$.

2. *If* $\mathcal{E} \in \text{stable}(\mathcal{K}_\Pi)$ *and* $M = \text{Con}[\mathcal{E}] \cap \text{Lit}^\neg$, *then* $M \in \text{stable}_\top(\Pi)$.

Proof. *Ad 1* Suppose $M \in \text{stable}_\top(\Pi)$. By Lemma B.1,

$$M = \text{Con}[\text{Arg}_{\mathcal{K}_\Pi}(M_{\widetilde{\Pi}})] \cap \text{Lit}^\neg(\Pi).$$

By Lemma B.2, $\text{Arg}_{\mathcal{K}_\Pi}(M_{\widetilde{\Pi}}) \in \text{stable}(\mathcal{K}_\Pi)$.

Ad 2 Suppose $\mathcal{E} \in \text{stable}(\mathcal{K}_\Pi)$ and let $M = \text{Con}[\mathcal{E}] \cap \text{Lit}^\neg(\Pi)$. By Lemma B.2, $\mathcal{E} = \text{Arg}_{\mathcal{K}_\Pi}(M_{\widetilde{\Pi}})$. By Lemma B.1, $M \in \text{stable}_\top(\Pi)$. $\qquad\square$

References

Adams, E. W. (1975). *The logic of conditionals.* D. Reidel Publishing Co.

Antonelli, G. A. (1999). A directly cautious theory of defeasible consequence for default logic via the notion of general extension. *Artificial Intelligence, 109*(1), 71–109.

Antoniou, G., & Wang, K. (2007). Default logic. In D. Gabbay & J. Woods (Eds.), *Handbook of the history of logic* (pp. 517–556, Vol. 8). North-Holland.

Arieli, O., & Avron, A. (2000). General patterns for nonmonotonic reasoning: From basic entailments to plausible relations. *Logic Journal of the IGPL, 8*, 119–148.

Arieli, O., Borg, A., & Heyninck, J. (2019). A review of the relations between logical argumentation and reasoning with maximal consistency. *Annals of Mathematics and Artificial Intelligence, 87*(3), 187–226.

Arieli, O., Borg, A., Heyninck, J., & Straßer, C. (2021a). Logic-based approaches to formal argumentation. *Journal of Applied Logics - IfCoLog Journal, 8*(6), 1793–1898.

Arieli, O., Borg, A., & Straßer, C. (2021b). Characterizations and classifications of argumentative entailments. In M. Bienvenu, G. Lakemeyer, & E. Erdem (Eds.), *Proceedings of the 18th International Conference on Principles of Knowledge Representation and Reasoning*, 52–62. Curran Associates, Inc.

Arieli, O., Borg, A., & Straßer, C. (2023). A postulate-deriven study of logical argumentation. *Artificial Intelligence*, 103966.

Arieli, O., & Straßer, C. (2015). Sequent-based logical argumentation. *Argument and Computation, 6*(1), 73–99.

Aristotle. (1984). *The complete works of Aristotle. The revised Oxford translation. One volume digital edition.* Princeton University Press.

Asher, N., & Morreau, M. (1991). Commonsense entailment: A modal theory of nonmonotonic reasoning. In J. van Eijck (Ed.), *Logics in AI.* Lecture Notes in Computer Science, vol. 478. Springer. DOI: https://doi.org/10.1007/BFb0018430.

Asher, N., & Pelletier, F. J. (2012). More truths about generic truth. In A. Mari, C. Beyssade, & F. Del Prete (Eds.), *Genericity*, 312–333. Oxford University Press. DOI: https://doi.org/10.1093/acprof:oso/9780199691807.003.0012.

Baroni, P., D. Gabbay, & M. Giacomin (Eds.). (2018, February). *Handbook of formal argumentation.* College Publications.

Baroni, P., Giacomin, M., & Guida, G. (2001). On the notion of strength in argumentation: Overcoming the epistemic/practical dichotomy. *ECSQARU Workshop Adventures in Argumentation*, 1–8. IRIS Institutional Research Information System: OPENBS Open Archive UniBS. https://iris.unibs.it/handle/11379/159298.

Batens, D. (1986). Dialectical dynamics within formal logics. *Logique et Analyse, 114*, 161–173.

Batens, D. (2007). A universal logic approach to adaptive logics. *Logica Universalis, 1*(1), 221–242.

Batens, D. (2011). Logics for qualitative inductive generalization. *Studia Logica, 97*(1), 61–80.

Beirlaen, M., & Aliseda, A. (2014). A conditional logic for abduction. *Synthese, 191*(15), 3733–3758.

Beirlaen, M., Heyninck, J., Pardo, P., & Straßer, C. (2018). Argument strength in formal argumentation. *Journal of Applied Logics – IfCoLog Journal, 5*(3), 629–675.

Benferhat, S., Bonnefon, J. F., & da Silva Neves, R. (2005). An overview of possibilistic handling of default reasoning, with experimental studies. *Synthese, 146*(1–2), 53–70.

Benferhat, S., Cayrol, C., Dubois, D., Lang, J., & Prade, H. (1993). Inconsistency management and prioritized syntax-based entailment. *International Joint Conference on Artificial Intelligence, 93*, 640–645.

Benferhat, S., Dubois, D., & Prade, H. (1992). Representing default rules in possibilistic logic. In B. Nebel, C. Rich, & W. R. Swartout (Eds.), *Proceedings of the Third International Conference on the Principles of Knowledge Representation and Reasoning*, 673–684. Morgan Kaufmann Publishers.

Benferhat, S., Dubois, D., & Prade, H. (1997). Some syntactic approaches to the handling of inconsistent knowledge bases: A comparative study. Part 1: The flat case. *Studia Logica, 58*, 17–45.

Benferhat, S., Dubois, D., & Prade, H. (1999). Possibilistic and standard probabilistic semantics of conditional knowledge bases. *Journal of Logic and Computation, 9*(6), 873–895.

Besnard, P., & Hunter, A. (2001). A logic-based theory of deductive arguments. *Artificial Intelligence, 128*(1), 203–235.

Besold, T. R., d'Avila Garcez, A., Stenning, K., van der Torre, L., & van Lambalgen, M. (2017). Reasoning in non-probabilistic uncertainty: Logic programming and neural-symbolic computing as examples. *Minds and Machines, 27*(1), 37–77.

Bochman, A. (2005). *Explanatory nonmonotonic reasoning*. World Scientific Publishing.

Bondarenko, A., Dung, P. M., Kowalski, R. A., & Toni, F. (1997). An abstract, argumentation-theoretic approach to default reasoning. *Artificial Intelligence, 93*, 63–101.

Borg, A. (2020). Assumptive sequent-based argumentation. *Journal of Applied Logics, 2631*(3), 227–294.

Borg, A., & Straßer, C. (2018). Relevance in structured argumentation. In J. Lang (Ed.), *Proceedings of the Twenty-Seventh International Joint Conference on Artificial Intelligence*, 1753–1759.

Boutilier, C. (1994a). Conditional logics of normality: A modal approach. *Artificial Intelligence, 68*(1), 87–154.

Boutilier, C. (1994b). Unifying default reasoning and belief revision in a modal framework. *Artificial Intelligence, 68*(1), 33–85.

Brandom, R. (2009). *Articulating reasons: An introduction to inferentialism.* Harvard University Press.

Brewka, G. (1989). Preferred subtheories: An extended logical framework for default reasoning. *Proceedings of the Eleventh International Joint Conference on Artificial Intelligence (II), 89*, 1043–1048.

Brewka, G. (1991). Cumulative default logic: In defense of nonmonotonic inference rules. *Artificial Intelligence, 50*(2), 183–205.

Brown, J., & Simion, M. (2021). *Reasons, justification, and defeat.* Oxford University Press.

Byrne, R. M. (1989). Suppressing valid inferences with conditionals. *Cognition, 31*(1), 61–83.

Caminada, M., & Amgoud, L. (2007). On the evaluation of argumentation formalisms. *Artificial Intelligence, 171*, 286–310.

Caminada, M., Carnielli, W. A., & Dunne, P. E. (2012). Semi-stable semantics. *Journal of Logic and Computation, 22*(5), 1207–1254.

Caminada, M., Modgil, S., & Oren, N. (2014). Preferences and unrestricted rebut. *Computational Models of Argument: Proceedings of COMMA 2014*, 209–220.

Caminada, M., & Schulz, C. (2017). On the equivalence between assumptionbased argumentation and logic programming. *Journal of Artificial Intelligence Research, 60*, 779–825.

Cayrol, C. (1995). On the relation between argumentation and non-monotonic coherence-based entailment. *Proceedings of the Eleventh International Joint Conference on Artificial Intelligence, 95*, 1443–1448.

Chisholm, R. M. (1963). Contrary-to-duty imperatives and deontic logic. *Analysis, 24*, 33–36.

Clark, K. L. (1977). Negation as failure. In H. Gallaire, and J. Minker (Eds.), *Logic and Data Bases*, 293–322. Springer. DOI: https://doi.org/10.1007/978-1-4684-3384-5_11.

Čyras, K., & Toni, F. (2015). Non-monotonic inference properties for assumptionbased argumentation. In E. Black, S., Modgil, N., & Oren (Eds.), *Theory and Applications of Formal Argumentation*, vol. 9524, 92–111. Springer. DOI: https://doi.org/10.1007/978-3-319-28460-6_6.

Delgrande, J. P. (1987). A first-order conditional logic for prototypical properties. *Artificial Intelligence, 33*(1), 105–130.

Delgrande, J. P. (1998). On first-order conditional logics. *Artificial Intelligence, 105*(1), 105–137.

Denecker, M., Marek, V. W., & Truszczynski, M. (2011). Reiter's default logic is a logic of autoepistemic reasoning and a good one, too. *arXiv preprint arXiv:*1108.3278.

Doyle, J., & McDermott, D. (1980). Nonmonotonic logic i. *Artificial Intelligence, 13*(1), 2.

Dubois, D., & Prade, H. (1990). An introduction to possibilistic and fuzzy logics. In G. Shafer & J. Pearl (Eds.), *Readings in Uncertain Reasoning* (pp. 742–761). Morgan Kaufmann.

Dubois, D., & Prade, H. (1991). Possibilistic logic, preferential models, nonmonotonicity and related issues. *In Proceedings Twelfth International Joint Conference on Artificial Intelligence*, 419–424.

Dung, P. M. (1995). On the acceptability of arguments and its fundamental role in nonmonotonic reasoning, logic programming and n-person games. *Artifical Intelligence, 77*, 321–358.

Eagle, A. (2024). *Probability and inductive logic.* Cambridge University Press.

Eemeren, F., & Grootendorst, R. (2004). *A systematic theory of argumentation: The pragma-dialectical approach.* Cambridge University Press.

Eiter, T., Ianni, G., & Krennwallner, T. (2009). Answer set programming: A primer. *Reasoning Web International Summer School*, 40–110.

Elio, R., & Pelletier, F. J. (1994). On relevance in non-monotonic reasoning: Some empirical studies. *Relevance: American Association for Artificial Intelligence 1994 Fall Symposium Series*, 64–67.

Friedman, N., & Halpern, J. Y. (1996). Plausibility measures and default reasoning. *Journal of the ACM, 48*(4), 1297–1304.

Friedman, N., Halpern, J. Y., & Koller, D. (2000). First-order conditional logic for default reasoning revisited. *ACM Transactions on Computational Logic, 1*(2), 175–207.

Gabbay, D. M. (1985). Theoretical foundations for non-monotonic reasoning in expert systems. In K. R. Apt (ed.), *Logics and models of concurrent systems* (pp. 439–457). Springer.

Gabbay, D., M. Giacomin, S. Guillermo, & M. Thimm (Eds.). (2021). *Handbook of formal argumentation.* College Publications.

Gärdenfors, P. (1990). Belief revision and nonmonotonic logic: Two sides of the same coin? *European Workshop on Logics in Artificial Intelligence*, 52–54.

Geffner, H. (1992). High-probabilities, model-preference and default arguments. *Minds and Machines*, *2*, 51–70.

Gelfond, M., & Lifschitz, V. (1988). The stable model semantics for logic programming. *ICLP/SLP*, *88*, 1070–1080.

Gelfond, M., & Lifschitz, V. (1991). Classical negation in logic programs and disjunctive databases. *New Generation Computing*, *9*(3–4), 365–385.

Gelfond, M., Lifschitz, V., Przymusinska, H., & Truszczynski, M. (1991). Disjunctive defaults. *Proceedings of the Second International Conference on Principles of Knowledge Representation and Reasoning*, 230–237.

Gelfond, M., Przymusinska, H., & Przymusinski, T. (1989). On the relationship between circumscription and negation as failure. *Artificial Intelligence*, *38*(1), 75–94.

Giordano, L., Gliozzi, V., Olivetti, N., & Pozzato, G. L. (2009). Analytic tableaux calculi for KLM logics of nonmonotonic reasoning. *ACM Transactions on Computational Logic (TOCL)*, *10*(3), 18.

Goldszmidt, M., & Pearl, J. (1990). On the relation between rational closure and system Z. *Third International Workshop on Nonmonotonic Reasoning (South Lake Tahoe)*, 130–140.

Goldszmidt, M., & Pearl, J. (1992). Rank-based systems: A simple approach to belief revision, belief update, and reasoning about evidence and actions. *Proceedings of the Third International Conference on Knowledge Representation and Reasoning*, 661–672.

Goldszmidt, M., Morris, P., & Pearl, J. (1993). A maximum entropy approach to nonmonotonic reasoning. *IEEE Transactions on Pattern Analysis and Machine Intelligence*, *15*(3), 220–232.

Haenni, R. (2009). Probabilistic argumentation [Special issue: Combining Probability and Logic]. *Journal of Applied Logics*, *7*(2), 155–176.

Hansen, J. (2008). Prioritized conditional imperatives: Problems and a new proposal. *Autonomous Agents and Multi-Agent Systems*, *17*(1), 11–35.

Hansson, B. (1969). An analysis of some deontic logics. *Nous*, 373–398.

Hart, H. L. (1948). The ascription of responsibility and rights. *Proceedings of the Aristotelian Society*, *49*, 171–194.

Heyer, G. (1990). Semantics and knowledge representation in the analysis of generic descriptions. *Journal of Semantics*, *7*(1), 93–110.

Heyninck, J., & Arieli, O. (2019). An argumentative characterization of disjunctive logic programming. *EPIA Conference on Artificial Intelligence*, 526–538.

Heyninck, J., & Straßer, C. (2016). Relations between assumption-based approaches in nonmonotonic logic and formal argumentation. In G. Kern-Isberner & R. Wassermann (Eds.), *Proceedings of NMR2016* (pp. 65–76).

Heyninck, J., & Straßer, C. (2019). A fully rational argumentation system for preordered defeasible rules. In *Proceedings of the 18th International Conference on Autonomous Agents and Multiagent Systems* (pp. 1704–1712).

Heyninck, J., & Straßer, C. (2021a). A comparative study of assumption-based argumentative approaches to reasoning with priorities. *Journal of Applied Logics – IfCoLog Journal of Logics and Their Applications, 8*(3), 737–808.

Heyninck, J., & Straßer, C. (2021b). Rationality and maximal consistent sets for a fragment of ASPIC+ without undercut. *Argument & Computation*, (1), 3–47.

Hölldobler, S., & Kalinke, Y. (1994). Towards a new massible parallel computational model for logic programming. *Proceedings of the Workshop on Combining Symbolic and Connectionist Processing ECCAI*, 68–77.

Horty, J. F. (2002). Skepticism and floating conclusions. *Artificial Intelligence, 135*(1–2), 55–72.

Horty, J. F. (2012). *Reasons as defaults*. Oxford University Press.

Hunter, A., & Thimm, M. (2017). Probabilistic reasoning with abstract argumentation frameworks. *Journal of Artificial Intelligence Research, 59*, 565–611.

Kelly, K. T., & Lin, H. (2021). Beliefs, probabilities, and their coherent correspondence.*Lotteries, Knowledge, and Rational Belief: Essays on the Lottery Paradox*, (pp. 185–222). Cambridge University Press.

Konolige, K. (1988). On the relation between default and autoepistemic logic. *Artificial Intelligence, 35*(3), 343–382.

Koons, R. (2017). Defeasible Reasoning. In E. N. Zalta (Ed.), *The Stanford encyclopedia of philosophy* (Winter 2017). Metaphysics Research Lab, Stanford University. https://plato.stanford.edu/entries/reasoning-defeasible/.

Kraus, S., Lehman, D., & Magidor, M. (1990). Nonmonotonic reasoning, preferential models and cumulative logics. *Artificial Intelligence, 44*, 167–207.

Kyburg, H. E. (2001). Real logic is nonmonotonic. *Minds and Machines, 11*(4), 577–595.

Lehmann, D. J. (1995). Another perspective on default reasoning. *Annals of Mathematics and Artificial Intelligence, 15*(1), 61–82.

Lehmann, D. J., & Magidor, M. (1990). Preferential logics: The predicate calculus case. *Proceedings of the 3rd Conference on Theoretical Aspects of Reasoning about Knowledge*, 57–72.

Lehmann, D. J., & Magidor, M. (1992). What does a conditional knowledge base entail? *Artificial Intelligence*, *55*(1), 1–60.

Leitgeb, H. (2018). Neural network models of conditionals. In *Introduction to formal philosophy* (pp. 147–176). Springer.

Leslie, S.-J., & Lerner, A. (2022). Generic Generalizations. In E. N. Zalta & U. Nodelman (Eds.), *The Stanford encyclopedia of philosophy* (Fall 2022). Metaphysics Research Lab, Stanford University. https://plato.stanford.edu/entries/generics/.

Lewis, D. (1973). *Counterfactuals*. Harvard University Press.

Lewis, D. (1974). Semantic analyses for dyadic deontic logic. In *Logical theory and semantic analysis: Essays dedicated to Stig Kanger on his fiftieth birthday* (pp. 1–14). Springer.

Li, Z., Oren, N., & Parsons, S. (2018). On the links between argumentation-based reasoning and nonmonotonic reasoning. *Lecture Notes in Computer Science* vol. 10757 (pp. 67–85). Springer.

Liao, B., Oren, N., van der Torre, L., & Villata, S. (2016). Prioritized norms and defaults in formal argumentation. F. Cariani, D. Grossi, J. Meheus, & Xavier Parent (Eds.), *Deontic Logic and Normative Systems*. 12th International Conference, DEON 2014, Ghent, Belgium, July 12–15, 2014. Proceedings. Springer, pp. 139–154.

Liao, B., Oren, N., van der Torre, L., & Villata, S. (2018). Prioritized norms in formal argumentation. *Journal of Logic and Computation*, *29*(2), 215–240.

Lifschitz, V. (1989). Benchmark problems for formal nonmonotonic reasoning. In M. Reinfrank, J. de Kleer, M. L. Ginsberg, & E. Sandewall (Eds.), *Non-Monotonic Reasoning*, Lecture Notes in Computer Science, vol. 346. Springer, 202–219.

Lifschitz, V. (2019). *Answer set programming*. Springer.

Lin, F., & Shoham, Y. (1990). Epistemic semantics for fixed-points nonmonotonic logics. *Proceedings of the 3rd Conference on Theoretical Aspects of Reasoning about Knowledge*, 111–120.

Loui, R. P. (1995). Hart's critics on defeasible concepts and ascriptivism. *Proceedings of the 5th International Conference on Artificial Intelligence and Law*, 21–30.

Łukaszewicz, W. (1988). Considerations on default logic: An alternative approach. *Computational Intelligence*, *4*(1), 1–16.

Makinson, D. (2003). Bridges between classical and nonmonotonic logic. *Logic Journal of IGPL, 11*(1), 69–96.

Makinson, D. (2005). *Bridges from classical to nonmonotonic logic* (Vol. 5). King's College Publications.

Makinson, D., & Van Der Torre, L. (2000). Input/Output logics. *Journal of Philosophical Logic, 29*, 383–408.

Makinson, D., & Van Der Torre, L. (2001). Constraints for Input/Output logics. *Journal of Philosophical Logic, 30*(2), 155–185.

Manhaeve, R., Dumanéiæ, S., Kimmig, A., Demeester, T., & De Raedt, L. (2021). Neural probabilistic logic programming in deepproblog. *Artificial Intelligence, 298*, 103504.

McCarthy, J. (1980). Circumscription: A form of non-monotonic reasoning. *Artificial Intelligence, 13*, 27–29.

Mercier, H., & Sperber, D. (2011). Why do humans reason? Arguments for an argumentative theory. *Behavioral and Brain Sciences, 34*(2), 57–74.

Mercier, H., & Sperber, D. (2017). *The enigma of reason*. Harvard University Press.

Minker, J. (1994). Overview of disjunctive logic programming. *Annals of Mathematics and Artificial Intelligence, 12*(1), 1–24.

Modgil, S., & Prakken, H. (2013). A general account of argumentation with preferences. *Artificial Intelligence, 195*, 361–397.

Modgil, S., & Prakken, H. (2014). The ASPIC+framework for structured argumentation: *A tutorial. Argument & Computation, 5*(1), 31–62.

Moinard, Y., & Rolland, R. (1998). *Propositional circumscriptions [research report]*. INRIA-00073147. https://inria.hal.science/inria-00073147.

Moretti, L., & Piazza, T. (2017). Defeaters in current epistemology: Introduction to the special issue. *Synthese, 195*(7), 2845–2854.

Ng, R., & Subrahmanian, V. S. (1992). Probabilistic logic programming. *Information and Computation, 101*(2), 150–201.

Nogueira, M., Balduccini, M., Gelfond, M., Watson, R., & Barry, M. (2001). An a-prolog decision support system for the space shuttle. *Proceedings of the Third International Symposium on Practical Aspects of Declarative Languages*, 169–183.

Parent, X., & van der Torre, L. (2013). Input/output logic. In D. Gabbay, J. Horty, X. Parent, R. van der Meyden, & L. van der Torre (Eds.), *Handbook of deontic logic* (pp. 499–544, Vol. 1). College Publications.

Pearl, J. (1989). Probabilistic semantics for nonmonotonic reasoning: A survey. *Proceedings of the First International Conference on Principles of Knowledge Representation and Reasoning*, 505–516.

Pearl, J. (1990). System Z: A natural ordering of defaults with tractable applications to nonmonotonic reasoning. *TARK '90: Proceedings of the 3rd Conference on Theoretical Aspects of Reasoning about Knowledge*, 121–135.

Pelletier, F. J., & Elio, R. (1997). What should default reasoning be, by default? *Computational Intelligence, 13*(2), 165–187.

Perelman, C., & Olbrechts-Tyteca, L. (1969, June). *The new rhetoric: A treatise on argumentation*. University of Notre Dame Press.

Pfeifer, N., & Kleiter, G. D. (2005). Coherence and nonmonotonicity in human reasoning. *Synthese, 146*(1–2), *93*–109.

Pollock, J. (1991). A theory of defeasible reasoning. *International Journal of Intelligent Systems, 6*, 33–54.

Pollock, J. (1995). *Cognitive carpentry*. Bradford/MIT Press.

Poole, D. (1985). On the comparison of theories: Preferring the most specific explanation. *IJCAI, 85*, 144–147.

Poole, D. (1988). A logical framework for default reasoning. *Artificial Intelligence, 36*(1), 27–47.

Poole, D. (1991). The effect of knowledge on belief: Conditioning, specificity and the lottery paradox in default reasoning. *Artificial Intelligence, 49*(1–3), 281–307.

Prakken, H. (2012). Some reflections on two current trends in formal argumentation. *Logic Programs, Norms and Action*, 249–272.

Przymusinski, T. C. (1990). The well-founded semantics coincides with the three-valued stable semantics. *Fundamenta Informaticae, 13*(4), 445–463.

Reiter, R. (1980). A logic for default reasoning. *Artificial Intelligence*, 1–2(13).

Reiter, R. (1981). On closed world data bases. In *Readings in artificial intelligence* (pp. 119–140). Elsevier.

Reiter, R., & Criscuolo, G. (1981). On interacting defaults. *IJCAI, 81*, 270–276.

Rescher, N. (1976). *Plausible reasoning: An introduction to the theory and practice of plausibilistic inference*. Van Gorcum.

Rescher, N., & Manor, R. (1970). On inference from inconsistent premises. *Theory and Decision, 1*, 179–217.

Ross, W. D. (1930). *The right and the good*. Oxford University Press.

Rott, H. (2001). *Change, choice and inference: A study of belief revision and nonmonotonic reasoning*. Clarendon Press.

Saldanha, E.-A. D. (2018). From logic programming to human reasoning: How to be artificially human. *KI – Künstliche Intelligenz, 32*(4), 283–286.

Satoh, K. (1989). *A probabilistic interpretation for lazy nonmonotonic reasoning*. Institute for New Generation Computer Technology.

Schaub, T., & Wang, K. (2001). A comparative study of logic programs with preference. *IJCAI*, 597–602.

Schulz, C., & Toni, F. (2016). Justifying answer sets using argumentation. *Theory and Practice of Logic Programming*, *16*(1), 59–110.

Schurz, G. (2005). Non-monotonic reasoning from an evolution-theoretic perspective: Ontic, logical and cognitive foundations. *Synthese*, *146*(1–2), 37–51.

Sergot, M. J., Sadri, F., Kowalski, R. A., Kriwaczek, F., Hammond, P., & Cory, H. T. (1986). The British Nationality Act as a logic program. *Communications of the ACM*, *29*(5), 370–386.

Shoham, Y. (1987). A semantical approach to nonmonotonic logics. In M. L. Ginsberg (Ed.), *Readings in non-monotonic reasoning* (pp. 227–249). Morgan Kaufmann.

Spohn, W. (1988, August). Ordinal conditional functions: A dynamic theory of epistemic states. In W. L. Harper & B. Skyrms (Eds.), *Causation in decision, belief change and statistics* (pp. 105–134). Springer.

Stalnaker, R. (1994). What is a nonmonotonic consequence relation? *Fundamenta Informaticae*, *21*(1), 7–21.

Stalnaker, R. F. (1968). A theory of conditionals. In N. Reischer (Ed.), *Studies in logical theory*. Basil Blackwell.

Stenning, K., & Van Lambalgen, M. (2008). *Human reasoning and cognitive science*. MIT Press.

Straßer, C. (2009a). An adaptive logic for rational closure. *The many sides of logic*, 47–67.

Straßer, C. (2009b). The many sides of logic. In M. E. C. Walter Carnielli & I. M. L. D'Ottaviano (Eds.). College Publications.

Straßer, C. (2014). *Adaptive logic and defeasible reasoning: Applications in argumentation, normative reasoning and default reasoning*. (Trends in Logic Vol. 38). Springer.

Straßer, C., Beirlaen, M., & Van De Putte, F. (2016). Adaptive logic characterizations of input/output logic. *Studia Logica*, *104*(5), 869–916.

Straßer, C., & Michajlova, L. (2023). Evaluating and selecting arguments in the context of higher order uncertainty. *Frontiers in Artificial Intelligence*, *6*, 1133998.

Straßer, C., & Pardo, P. (2021). Prioritized defaults and formal argumentation. In F. Liu, A. Marra, P. Portner, & F. Van de Putte (Eds.), *Proceedings of DEON2020/2021* (pp. 427–446). College Publications.

Straßer, C., & Seselja, D. (2010). Towards the proof-theoretic unification of Dung's argumentation framework: An adaptive logic approach. *Journal of Logic and Computation*, *21*(2), 133–156.

Sudduth, M. (2017). Defeaters in epistemology. In F. Fieser & B. Dowden (Eds.), *Internet encyclopedia of philosophy*. https://iep.utm.edu/defeaters-in-epistemology/.

Tessler, M. H., & Goodman, N. D. (2019). The language of generalization. *Psychological Review, 126*(3), 395.

Toni, F. (2014). A tutorial on assumption-based argumentation. Argument & Computation, *5*(1), 89–117.

Toulmin, S. E. (1958). *The Uses of Argument*. Cambridge University Press.

van Berkel, K., & Straßer, C. (2022). Reasoning with and about norms in logical argumentation. In F. Toni, S. Polberg, R. Booth, M. Caminada, & H. Kido (Eds.), *Frontiers in artificial intelligence and applications: Computational models of argument, proceedings (COMMA22)* (pp. 332–343, Vol. 353). IOS Press.

Van De Putte, F. (2013). Default assumptions and selection functions: A generic framework for non-monotonic logics. In *Advances in artificial intelligence and its applications*. Lecture Notes in Computer Science, vol. 8265 (pp. 54–67). Springer.

Van De Putte, F., Beirlaen, M., & Meheus, J. (2019). Adaptive deontic logics. *Handbook of Deontic Logic and Normative Systems, 2*, 367–459. College Publications.

Van Fraassen, B. C. (1972). The logic of conditional obligation. *Journal of Philosophical Logic, 1*, 417–438.

Vesic, S. (2013). Identifying the class of maxi-consistent operators in argumentation. *Journal of Artificial Intelligence Research, 47*, 71–93.

Vreeswijk, G. A. W. (1993). *Studies in defeasible argumentation* [Doctoral dissertation, Free University Amsterdam. Department of Computer Science].

Walton, D., Reed, C., & Macagno, F. (2008). *Argumentation schemes*. Cambridge University Press.

Young, A. P., Modgil, S., & Rodrigues, O. (2016). Prioritised default logic as rational argumentation. *Proceedings of the 2016 International Conference on Autonomous Agents & Multiagent Systems*, 626–634.

Acknowledgments

I want to thank Kees van Berkel, Matthis Hesse, Jessica Krumhus, and Dunja Šešelja for their highly valuable feedback on previous drafts. I am also much obliged to Joke Meheus and Diderik Batens for introducing me to the wonderful world of NMLs. Finally, not to forget Brad and Fred: thanks to my editors, Brad Armour-Garb and Fred Kroon, for their support, trust, and good mood throughout the whole process.

For EU product safety concerns, contact us at Calle de José Abascal, 56–1°,
28003 Madrid, Spain or eugpsr@cambridge.org.